The 15-Minute Artist

DRAWING PEOPLE

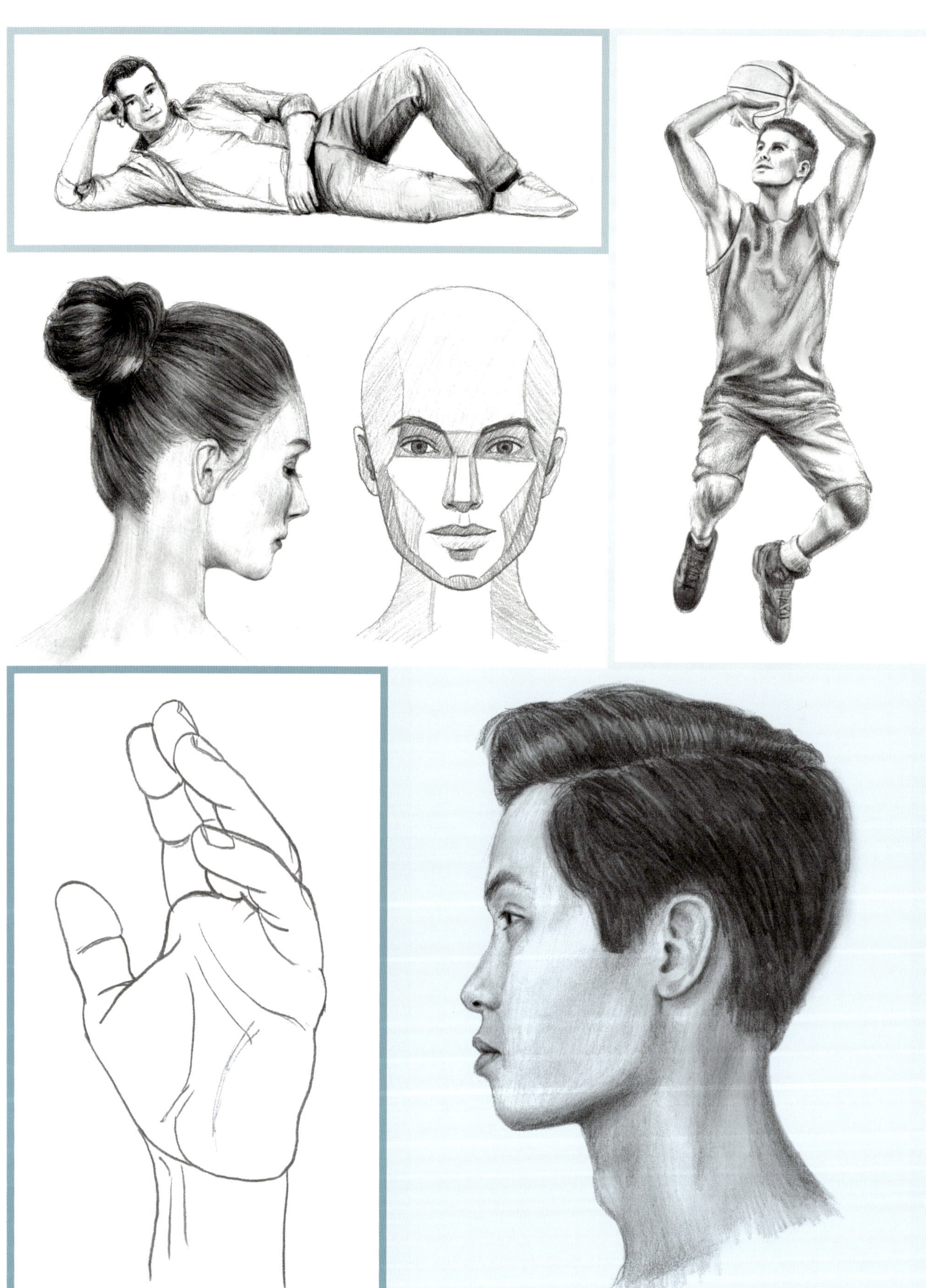

The 15-Minute Artist

DRAWING PEOPLE

The Quick and Easy Way to Draw Faces, Figures, and More

CATHERINE V. HOLMES

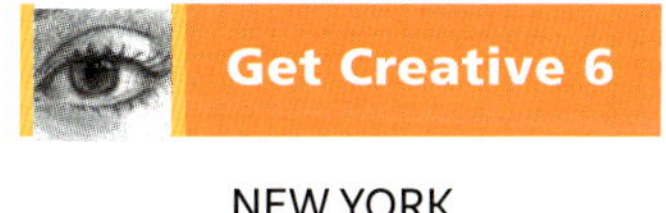

NEW YORK

**For my Charlotte
and my Taya**

Get Creative 6
An imprint of Mixed Media Resources, LLC
19 W 21st St, Suite 601, New York, NY 10010
mixedmediaresources.com

Editors
RACHEL CHLEBOWSKI
GLENI BARTELS

Creative Director
IRENE LEDWITH

Art Director
FRANCESCA PACCHINI

Chief Executive Officer
CAROLINE KILMER

President
ART JOINNIDES

Chairman
JAY STEIN

The EEA authorized representative is Authorised Rep Compliance Ltd., Ground Floor, 71 Baggot Street Lower, Dublin, D02 P593, Ireland (www.arccompliance.com).

ISBN: 978-1-68462-085-2

Library of Congress Cataloging-in-Publication Data has been applied for.

Manufactured in India

3 5 7 9 10 8 6 4 2

First Edition

Acknowledgments

Thank you to Soho Publishing for making this vision come to life! I have always believed there was a need for a book on drawing diversity and this is a great beginning. I would also like to extend my gratitude to Usher Morgan and Library Tales for providing a platform to showcase my art to the world. It is through such collaborations and partnerships that artists are able to reach a wider audience and make a meaningful impact.

I have been fortunate to have the guidance and support of my amazing family, including Virginia Thayer and Ken Holmes who have always encouraged me to create. Thank you to Rich Monsini (my reluctant muse) whose presence has been truly inspiring to me. To everyone who picks up this book, I want to extend my heartfelt gratitude. *Drawing People* has been a labor of love, a journey of self-discovery, and a testament to the power of art to connect us.

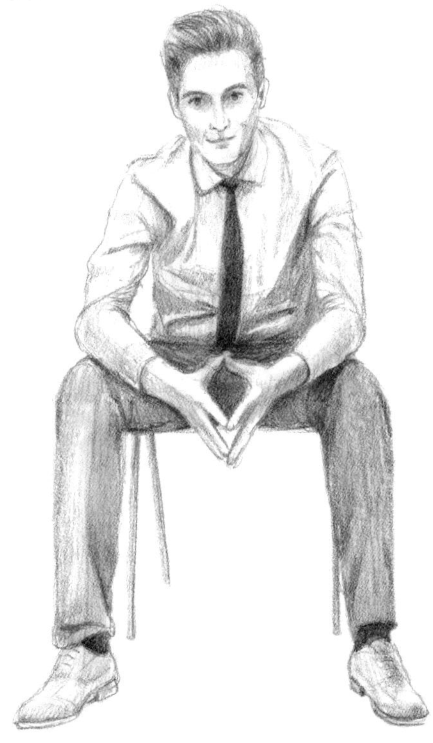

CONTENTS

Draw People, the 15-Minute Artist Way

Welcome to the newest addition to the 15-Minute Artist series! Whether you're a seasoned artist or new to the world of drawing, this book can help you create expressive, lifelike drawings of friends, family, and anyone you'd like.

Drawing people might seem complex or daunting, but fear not—this comprehensive guide will walk you through the steps, providing techniques and tips to bring your sketches to life.

Even for experienced artists, creating realistic portraits can be intimidating, but *The 15-Minute Artist: Drawing People* will demystify the creative process by transforming the human body into manageable building blocks. With easy-to-follow step-by-step illustrations for each example, you'll learn how to turn simple shapes and sketches into detailed drawings and portraits.

This book is designed for everyone, regardless of your prior experience. Whether you're familiar with the "15-Minute Method" or not, it covers all the essential skills you'll need to make drawing people accessible and enjoyable. First, we'll start with the basics of drawing. From there, we'll explore the different facets of drawing people: their bodies, faces, expressions, hairstyles, clothing, and movements.

While it's tempting to just jump right in, don't skip the rest of this section! It serves as your foundation, detailing the necessary tools and materials, drawing fundamentals, and specialized techniques specifically useful to drawing people.

Drawing, like any skill, takes practice. So don't be discouraged if it takes a couple of tries to get the results you want. Consistent practice is the key to improvement, and with each exercise, you'll notice your artistry evolving. By the book's end, my hope is that you'll not only have learned to sketch the examples in this book, but also that you'll have gained skills so that you can embark on your own people-drawing adventures.

So let's get started!

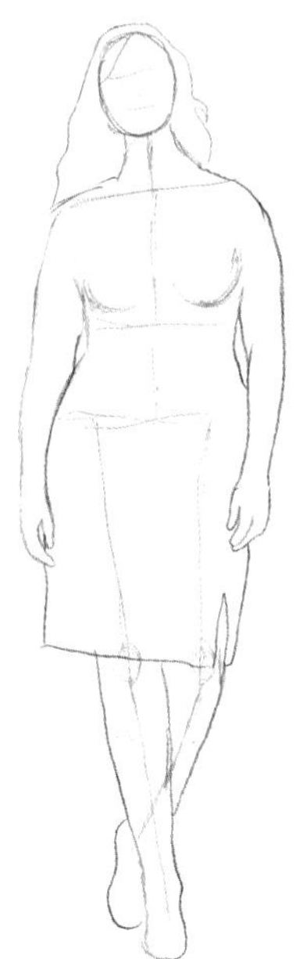 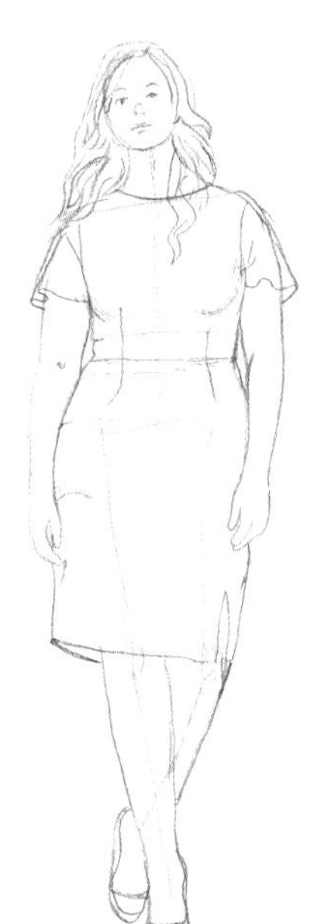 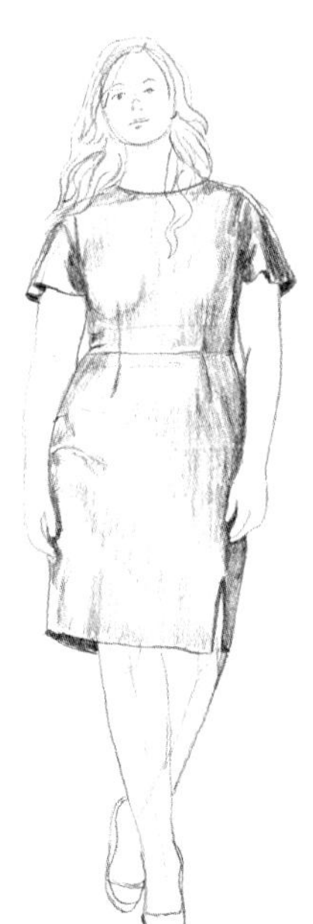 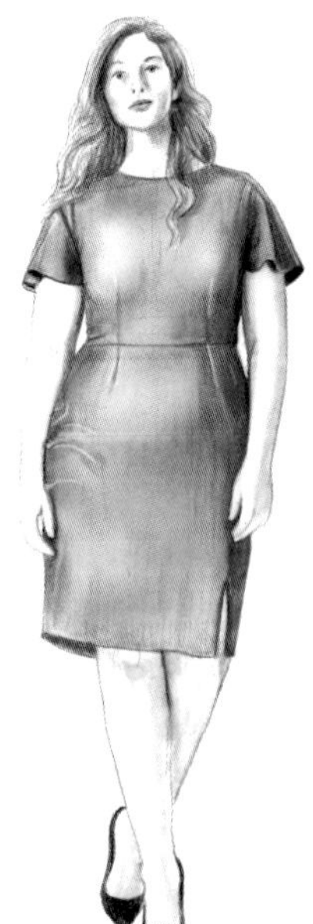

THE 15-MINUTE METHOD

This is the typical process I use with most drawings, including those I demonstrate in this book.

1. Break it down into simple shapes.
2. Connect the shapes.
3. Add details.
4. Erase the initial guidelines.
5. Shade the entire object with a medium tone.
6. Darken the darkest areas.
7. Erase areas to create highlights.

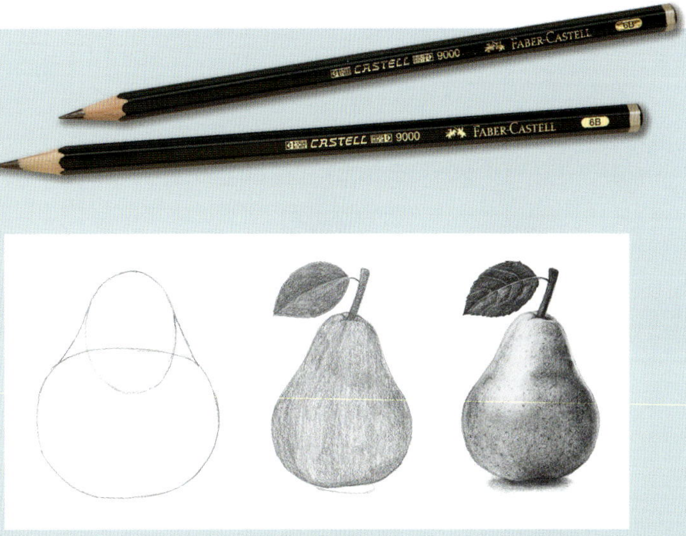

A Drawing Foundation

This section explains the techniques and vocabulary that will be used throughout the book. I suggest placing a bookmark here so you can flip back to it for reference. If you have the other books in this series, you're already one step ahead, because most of this information will be familiar.

CREATE A FRAMEWORK

The first step in the drawing process is to use simple shapes as a framework to build upon. The lines you use to draw these shapes are called "guidelines" because they guide what you draw next. Guidelines don't have to be precise. They should give you a decent idea of where to draw or mark the boundaries of a shape or its approximate center. Sketch your guidelines lightly, because they'll eventually be erased.

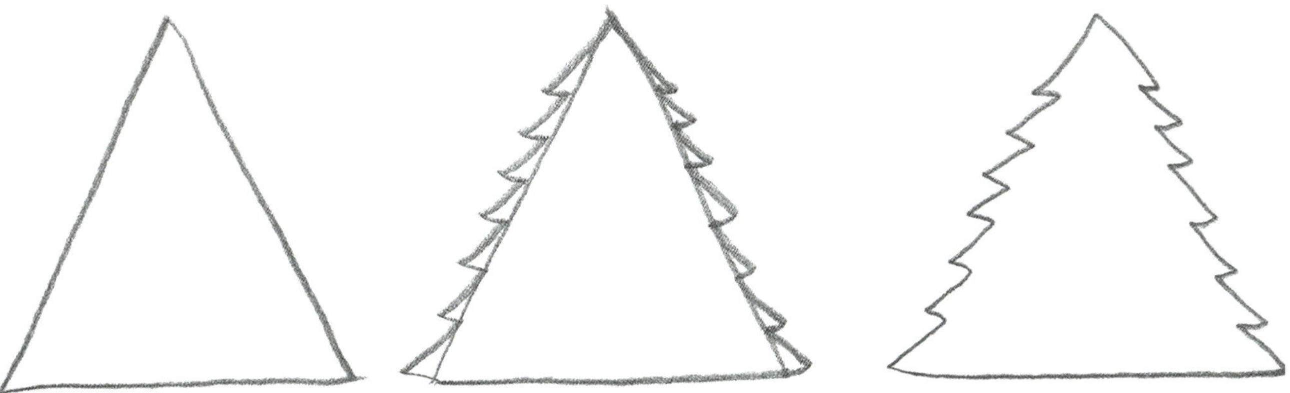

This very simplified example shows how a triangle is used as a guideline for an evergreen tree.

TONE, VALUE, AND CONTRAST

When it comes to drawing, "tone" and "value" are the terms used to describe how light or dark a color appears, especially when referring to grayscale art. When I mention adding "tone" in the steps, I'm asking you to use your pencil to introduce color, which for these tutorials, means adding different shades of gray.

The word "value" refers to how light or dark the color or tone is in an artwork. Value is created when a light source shines upon an object and forms highlights, shadows, and midtones. The difference in value between a lighter tone and a darker tone is called "contrast." The bigger the difference, the higher the contrast.

Take a look at the value scale below. It's a chart consisting of blocks of tone that starts with the lightest tone (white/highlight) on the left and gradually changes block by block into the darkest tone (black/shadow) on the right. The "midtone" is halfway between the "highlight" and the "shadow." The midtones show the real color and value of an object since highlights are brighter than the "true" color, and shadows are darker. Learning to create this scale will help you decide the appropriate type of pencil to use and the amount of pressure to apply to achieve specific tones.

So think of tones and values as the magic that brings your sketches of people to life. Together with contrast and shading (page 11), they're the secrets to making your drawings appear three-dimensional.

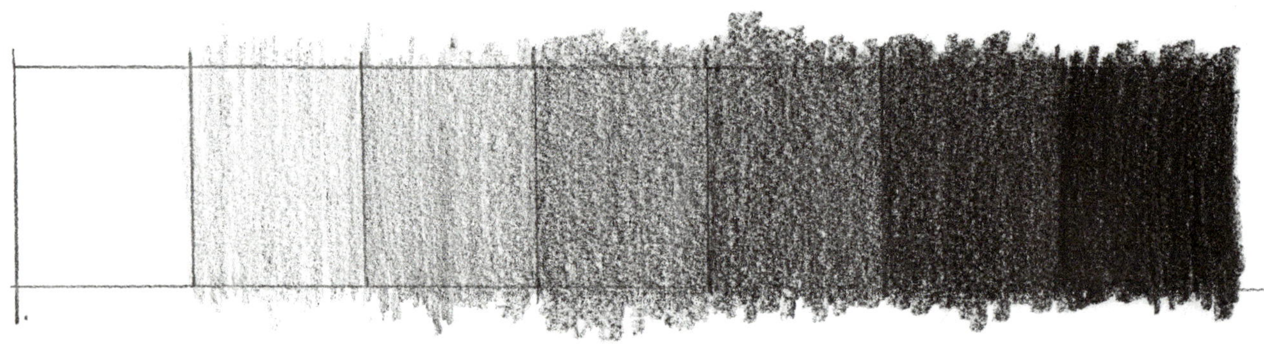

White/Highlight **Midtone** **Black/Shadow**

BUILD UP VALUE SLOWLY

When sketching people, it's important to remember not to rush into making the darkest areas too dark from the start. Begin with a lighter value and gradually build up. This allows for adjustments, since dark areas can always be intensified, but lightening them is more challenging.

TIP
Use a full range of value to create contrast and add emphasis while offering the illusion of depth.

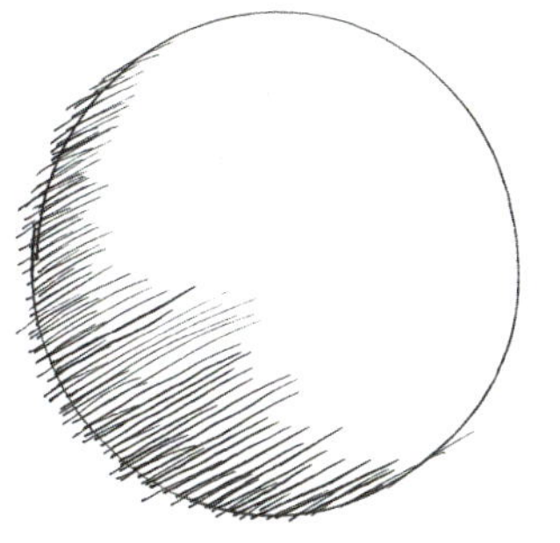

Hatching

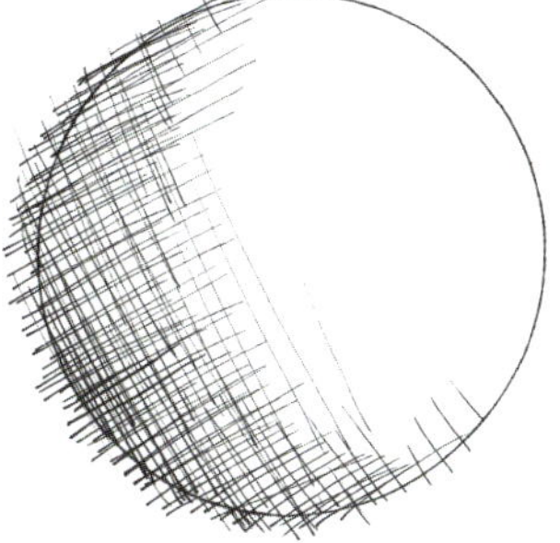

Cross-hatching

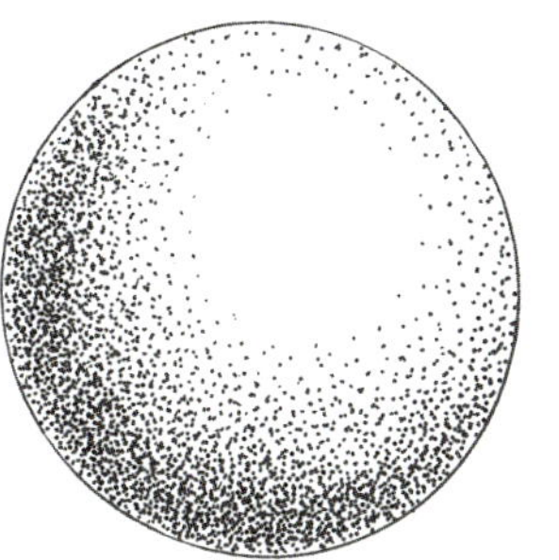

Stippling

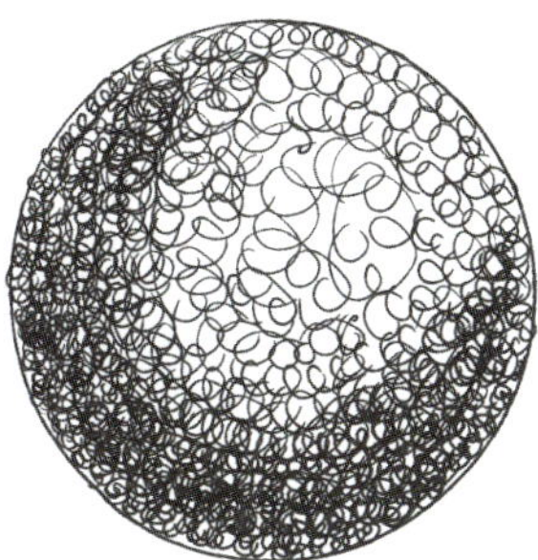

Scumbling

SHADING AND SHADOWS

Shading and shadows are two of the easiest ways to add depth, contrast, character, and movement to your drawings. Different shading techniques help convey different textures and make a drawing come convincingly to life.

Hatching uses close parallel lines. The closer together they are, the darker the shading appears. **Cross-hatching** uses two overlapping layers of hatching. **Stippling** uses lots of small dots. As with hatching, the closer together they are, the darker the shading appears. **Scumbling** uses lots of tiny, overlapping circles. Lighter pressure and larger circles result in a rougher-looking texture, while harder pressure and smaller circles look smoother. For best results, use a dull pencil so the circles are more obscured.

To understand where to place shadows, you'll need to understand light sources. A "light source" is what artists call where light is coming from, whether it's a lamp or the sun. Where and how the light hits a subject can create different kinds of shadows, as well as determine where the highlights and midtones will appear.

The area where the light source directly hits is the lightest area and is the **highlight**. The darkest shadow, or the area that receives the least amount of light, is the **core shadow**. The area with a value between the highlight and the core shadow is the **midtone**, the actual color of the subject. Finally, the **cast shadow** on the surroundings reinforces the direction of the light source and enhances the three-dimensional feel of the subject. Where the cast shadow and the subject meet is the darkest spot, called the **occlusion shadow**.

TIP

If you want to practice shading, trace or transfer your drawing to a new sheet of paper, so you can experiment.

LEARNING LIGHT SOURCES

Creating light and shadow is the most effective method of making a subject appear three-dimensional. Here are some tips to keep in mind:

- It can be helpful to lightly draw a small sun or light bulb on your drawing where the light source would be to remind you which direction it's coming from.
- Light may come from many sources and angles, which can be confusing. When starting out, try to use a single light source until you get used to how highlights and shadows behave.
- If the light source is directly above a subject, a short shadow will appear underneath. When the light source is beside a subject, this creates longer, more interesting shadows.
- When possible, keep the light source in mind as you set up your subjects for the most compelling composition. This may mean waiting for the sun to shift in the sky or moving a lamp to create the desired effect.

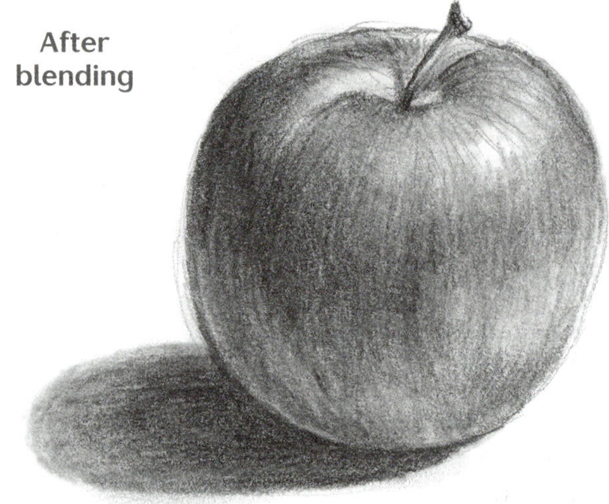

BLENDING

Blending is the technique of creating a gradual transition from one value to another. It's crucial when drawing in pencil, and we'll use it in every project in this book. Blending adds to the depth and believability of a work and can give the art a realistic appearance. I'll go into more detail about supplies on page 17, but you can use everything from specialized tools to simple household supplies for blending.

How do you blend? Gently rub the blending tool of your choice back and forth over the tones a few times to smooth them together. Don't overblend, or you'll smooth all your contrast into one gray tone. If you do, don't worry—just add another layer of graphite where the tone should be darker, and create contrast using a kneaded eraser to create highlights on over-blended areas.

UNDERSTANDING PERSPECTIVE

Understanding the principles of perspective is critical to realistically draw human figures. Artists use perspective to give two-dimensional things the illusion of three dimensions. Generally, the closer an object is to a viewer, the larger it should appear in order to look more realistic. It is also usually lower in the composition. The farther away an object is, the smaller and higher up it should appear on the drawing surface. It is also usually lighter and softer in tone and less detailed.

TIP
Whether you're doing this in color or black and white, tones should be darker the closer they are, lighter the farther away.

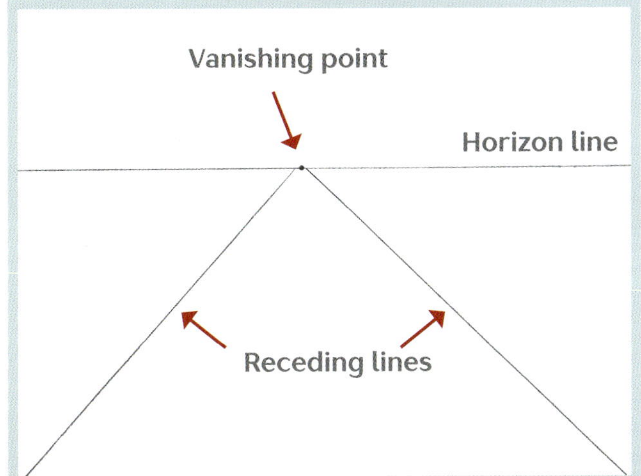

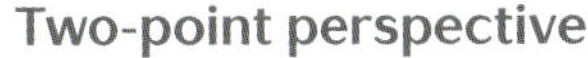

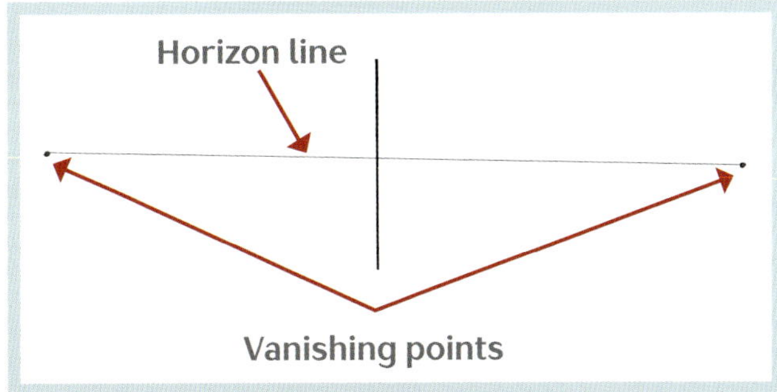

When you look down a long, straight road, the edges of the road give the illusion of meeting at a point on the horizon. This is "one-point perspective" because you have one vanishing point. "Two-point perspective" uses two vanishing points. It is often used to draw buildings and can be used with interiors as well.

CONSIDER YOUR COMPOSITION

How you frame or arrange your subject within a drawing and in relation to their surroundings can significantly change its visual impact. One of the most helpful ideas when it comes to composition is the "rule of thirds," which is really more of a guide than a rule. It involves dividing the image into thirds both vertically and horizontally and results in a grid of nine equally sized rectangles. This allows portrait photographers and artists to thoughfully consider the placement of their subjects within the frame. They can easily see if their composition is balanced and visually appealing, which will capture the viewer's attention.

For example, instead of placing the subject dead center in the frame, which can sometimes create a static and less engaging composition, the rule of thirds suggests placing the main elements of the drawing along the lines or at the intersections of the grid. For example, you might position the eyes of your subject along one of the horizontal lines, with the face occupying one of the upper or lower thirds of the frame. Placing the subject off-center within the frame adds visual interest and balance to the composition. It allows for negative space around your subject, which can draw the viewer's eye to the main focal point of the portrait.

The rule of thirds also guides the placement of elements in the background of the portrait. By positioning key background elements along the grid lines or intersections, you can enhance the overall composition and avoid distractions that may compete with your subject.

Techniques for Drawing People

There are some techniques that will come in handy when learning to draw people and portraits. This ranges from learning how to capture gestures of live subjects and conveying motion in your artwork to things to keep in mind when drawing from a reference image.

THE ART OF OBSERVATION

One of the most important skills when it comes to drawing people is learning how to observe! Whether you're drawing from a living subject or a static image, you should be looking at that reference at least 50 percent of the time. To produce a believable observational drawing, your eyes must continually move from your subject to the drawing and back again. Looking at your subject frequently will help you develop new ways of seeing. In other words, observation helps you draw what an object *actually* looks like, not *how you think* it should look. The only way to accurately capture tones, shadows, changing light conditions, various textures, proportions, and details is to look at the source of information—your subject!

GESTURE DRAWING

A "gesture drawing" is basically a quick drawing, usually completed within 30 seconds to 5 minutes, that captures the subject in its most condensed form and embodies action, movement, and expression into one connected sketch. They are great not only for warming up the fingers, hand, and arm for drawing, but they also improve your observational skills and increase your comfort level, especially when it comes to drawing people.

CONVEYING MOTION

Drawings allow an artist to capture a moment in time. The scene stands still, as it is simply an instant that is recorded. At the same time, it's possible to expand that moment with motion. From the crash of a wave on the surf

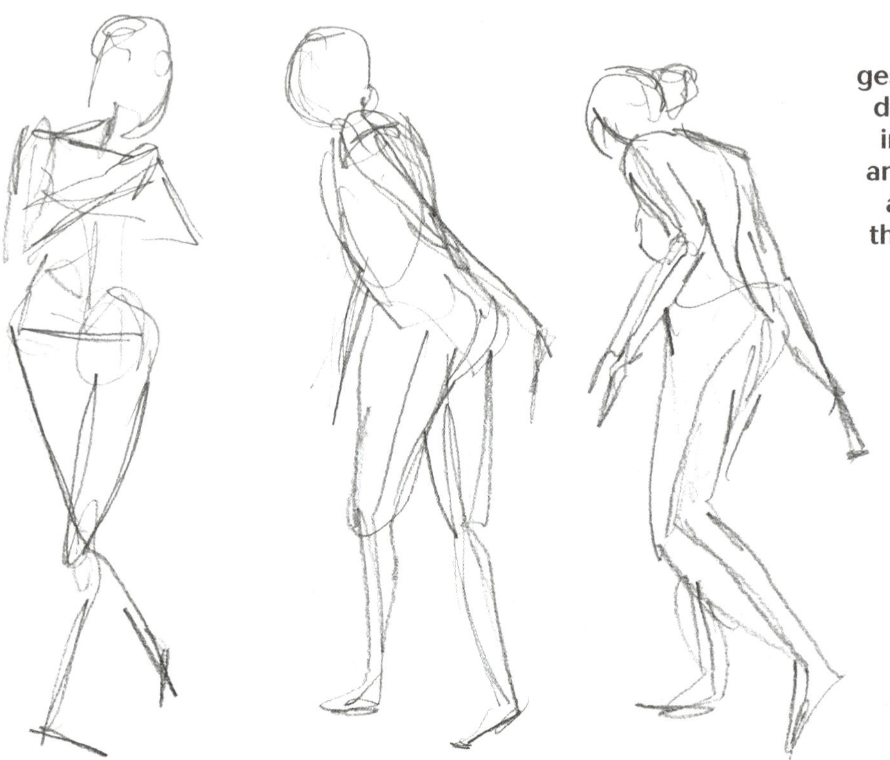

In these 30-second gestures, there is very little detail, yet there's a lot of information. The bodies are lively, showing motion and creating shapes as they contort and bend on the page.

POINTERS FOR GESTURE DRAWING

Keep these ideas in mind when you're gesture drawing. Remember that the final outcome is not meant to be a finished drawing. It's just a practice exercise!

- Sketch the main lines of your subject that indicate which way the body bends, any angles the hips or shoulders follow, leg direction, and arm direction. Use lots of curves. You are not drawing a stick figure and humans are not made of straight lines.
- Looking at the major shapes and positioning of the subject, quickly block in areas with lines and curves.
- Simplify as much as possible. There is no time to draw individual parts in any real detail.

- You should care more about how the gesture feels than how accurate it looks.
- Your hand should remain moving at all times but should be relaxed yet efficient in its movements.
- If you make a mistake, just make another line to correct it. Don't stop to erase!
- Draw lightly to begin. If time allows, you can always go over your light lines and make them more permanent.

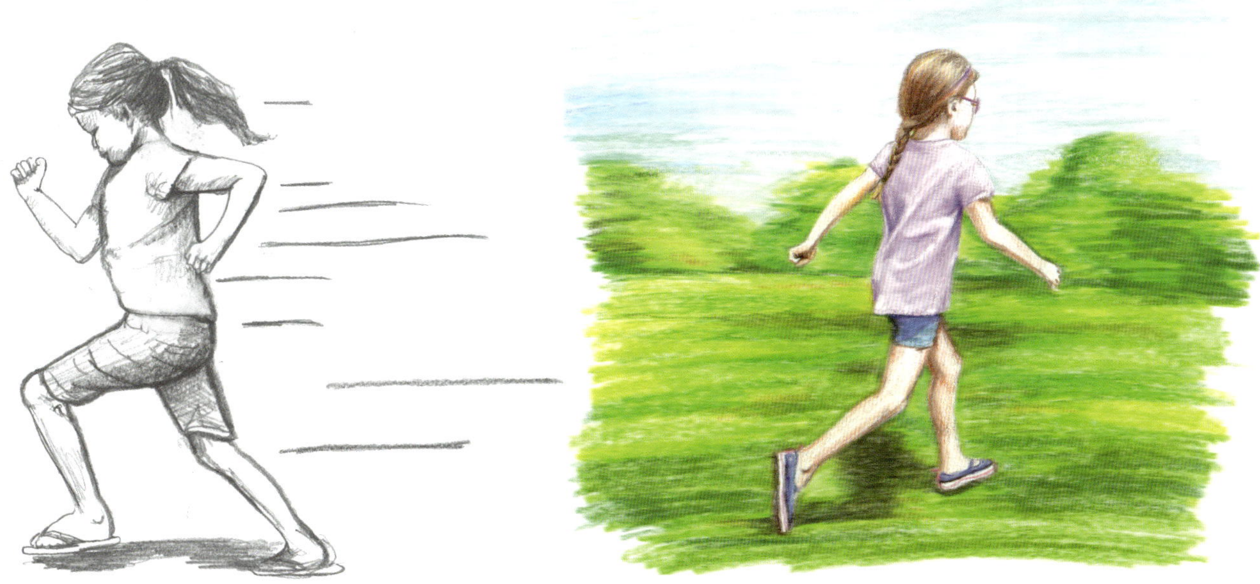

Drawing streaks to imply motion is effective but best for more cartoonish drawings.

Blurring the background is a more subtle and realistic technique.

to a running figure, there are some tricks you can use to imply motion, action, and energy. Abstract work might show turbulence or unrest via colors, placement, and choice of line/shape. More realistic works may contain gestures, diminishing sizes, distortion, or emerging forms.

- Draw or paint lines behind the object that is supposed to be moving. This straightforward technique may appear cartoonish and not realistic but it may be

the effect you want in your drawing.
- Use expressions on a subject's face to show the urgency with which they are moving.
- Draw an object about to hurtle off the edge of the paper, rather than in a relaxed position in the center.
- Capture the essence and movement of a figure with gesture drawing.
- Blur the background while keeping the main subject in focus.

USING REFERENCE IMAGES

Drawing from reference images is a valuable learning tool for artists seeking to develop their skills. Here are some things to consider when choosing a reference image:

Clarity and quality: Select a high-resolution image with clear details to ensure accuracy in your drawing.

Lighting: Opt for reference images with clear, well-defined lighting that highlights the subject's features and adds depth to your drawing. Avoid overly harsh shadows or uneven lighting that may obscure details.

Composition: Look for a reference with a balanced composition that suits your artistic vision, considering factors like lighting, background, and focal point.

Pose and expression: Choose a pose and facial expression that conveys the mood or message you want to capture in your drawing. Consider choosing reference images with dynamic poses or interesting gestures to add energy and movement to your artwork. These poses can help create a sense of narrative or emotion in your drawing.

Variety: Explore a range of reference images to find diverse subjects, poses, and angles that challenge and inspire your artistic growth.

Opt for black and white: Drawing in black and white instead of color has its advantages, which is why that's what I focus on in this book. With grayscale illustrations, you don't have to worry about color theory and instead can focus on mark-making and tones.

One trick you can use when drawing a subject from a digital image is to convert it to grayscale, or black and white. The black-and-white image makes the contrast between lights and darks more evident. By removing the color elements, you can focus on the highlights and shadows of the subject to build its three-dimensionality.

This simple trick helps identify and replicate all the values more quickly and enables you to draw more realistically.

TIP

It's okay to use another person's photographs as references for personal use, but if you're going to sell or show your artwork, you should avoid it.

TRACING A REFERENCE IMAGE

1. **Secure the reference image:** Place the reference image on a well-lit surface, ensuring it's stable and won't move while you work.
2. **Overlay with tracing paper:** Place a sheet of tracing paper over the reference image. Secure it in place with masking tape or paperweights to prevent it from shifting.
3. **Start tracing:** Using a pencil or fine-tip pen, carefully trace over the outlines and major features of the reference image. Focus on capturing the basic shapes and proportions accurately.
4. **Refine details:** Once you've traced the main outlines, you can remove the tracing paper and review your work. Use an eraser to clean up any stray lines or mistakes.
5. **Add your touch:** With the traced outline as a guide, you can now add your own artistic flair by refining details, shading, and adding texture to the drawing.
6. **Practice regularly:** Tracing can be a valuable tool for learning to draw, but it's important to balance it with freehand drawing exercises to develop your skills further.

Supplies You'll Need

The best part about drawing is that you don't need much to get started! All of the items listed here are easy to find online or in any art supply store.

THE ESSENTIALS

You'll need these drawing tools for almost every tutorial in this book (and most drawing projects you do outside of this book, as well).

Pencils: Though you can technically use a regular #2 pencil, I recommend getting a set of artist pencils, which come in "H" (hard) and "B" (soft). H has harder graphite, which leaves lighter, thinner marks and can be sharpened to a very fine tip. B has softer graphite, which leaves darker, thicker, smudgier marks. Each pencil also has a number grade. The higher the number, the lighter (for H) or darker (for B) the pencil will be. My default for these drawings is a 6B pencil.

For fine details, especially when it comes to details on clothing, I like to use a mechanical pencil, which allows for greater precision.

Paper: Cheap printer paper will make it harder to blend values and result in less attractive art (and increased frustration). You don't need to break the bank, but grab a pad of dedicated drawing paper. A medium "tooth" (roughness) works best for pencil.

Kneaded eraser: Kneaded erasers can be molded into any shape and don't leave crumbs behind like regular erasers. They're a must for the kind of precision erasing necessary for creating highlights.

Stick eraser: A stick eraser is a cylindrical eraser typically made of rubber or a similar material, with a fine tip. Its size and shape help you to precisely erase small areas without smudging or damaging the surrounding areas of the drawing, and allows for controlled erasing, making it an essential tool for adding highlights to bunched and wrinkled clothing.

Blending tools: You can use specialty tools like a blending stump, tortillon, or kneaded eraser. But you can also use household items like a tissue, cotton swab, chamois cloth, dry paintbrush, or even your finger. But you'll definitely need something to blend with.

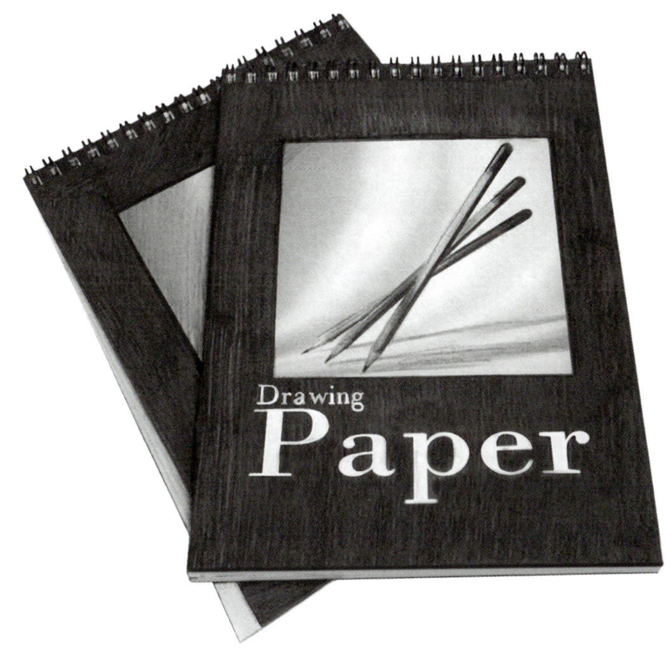

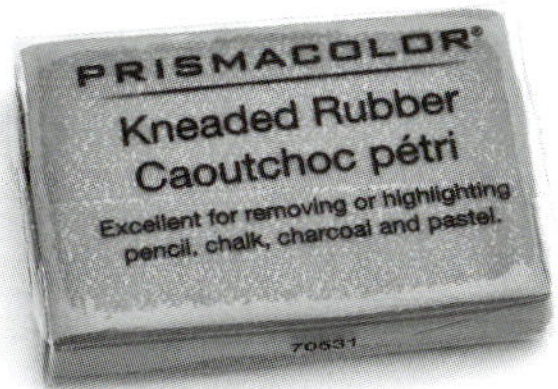

Kneaded eraser

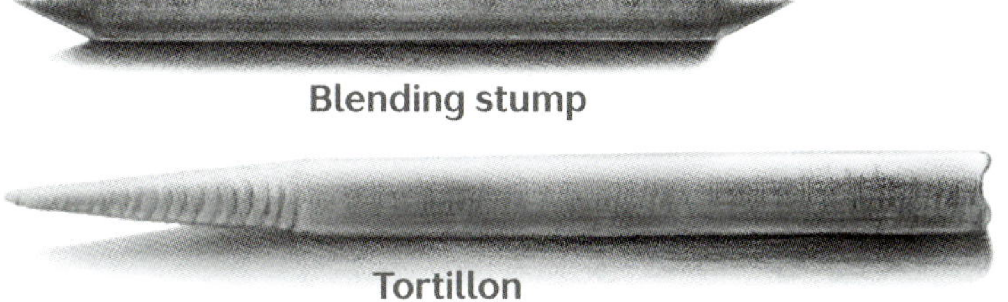

Blending stump

Tortillon

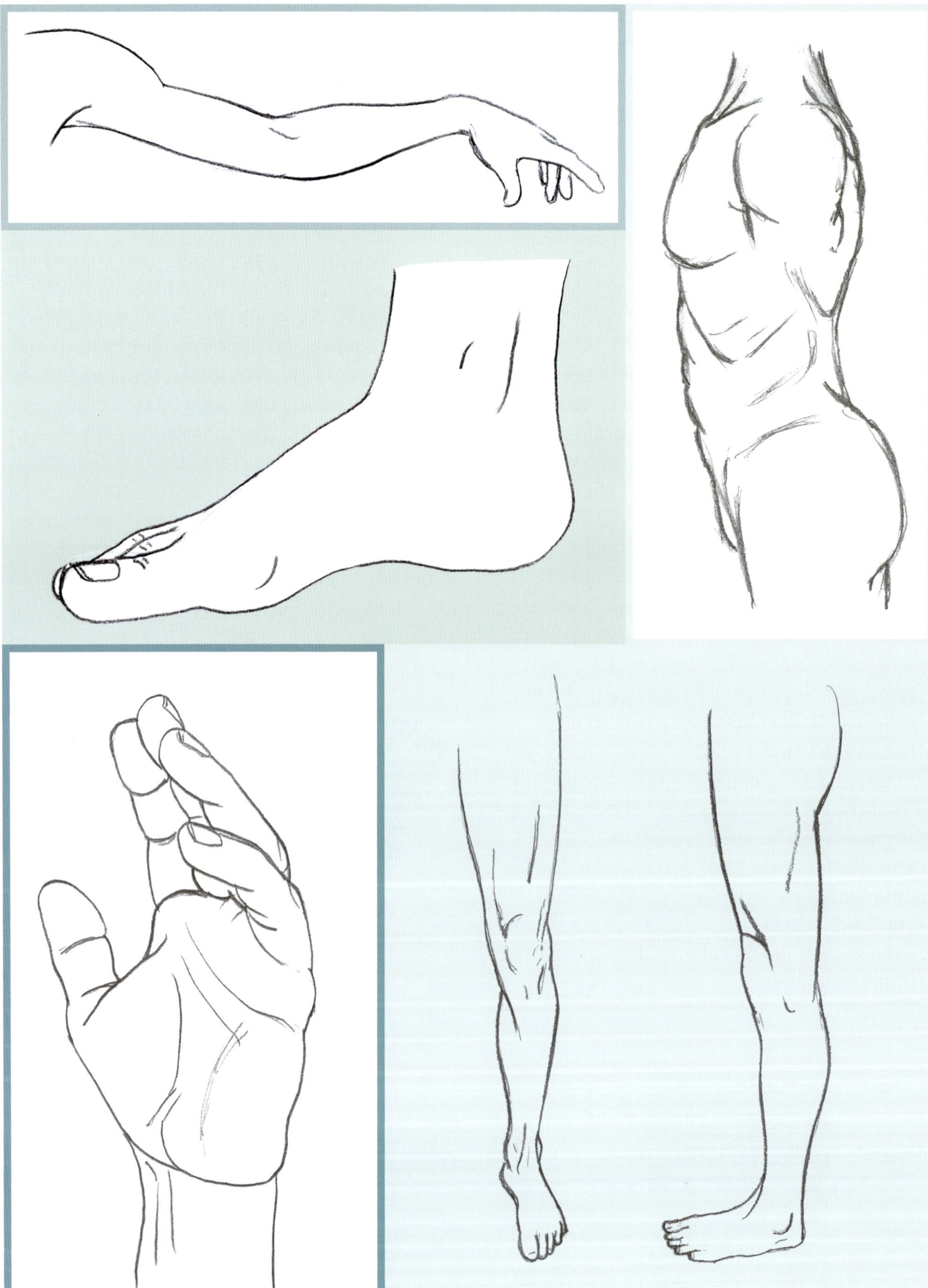

Chapter 1

BASIC BUILDING BLOCKS

We'll start our people-drawing journey by breaking down the human form into its separate building blocks. Using the 15-minute method, you'll learn how to draw everything from the head to the feet. Each demonstration is also filled with helpful tips and tricks to help you master each body part, which will be necessary for the more complicated step-by-steps in later chapters.

Drawing the Body

The human figure can be broken down into specific proportions. The generic adult measures up to be seven units (or heads) tall and two units wide. This means the average adult is as tall as seven of their heads stacked on top of each other. This will differ from person to person, so this is just a generic guideline. In this demonstration, I'll use an artist manikin to keep it as simple as possible. Then I'll show the differences in more feminine bodies as well as children's bodies.

BASIC PROPORTIONS

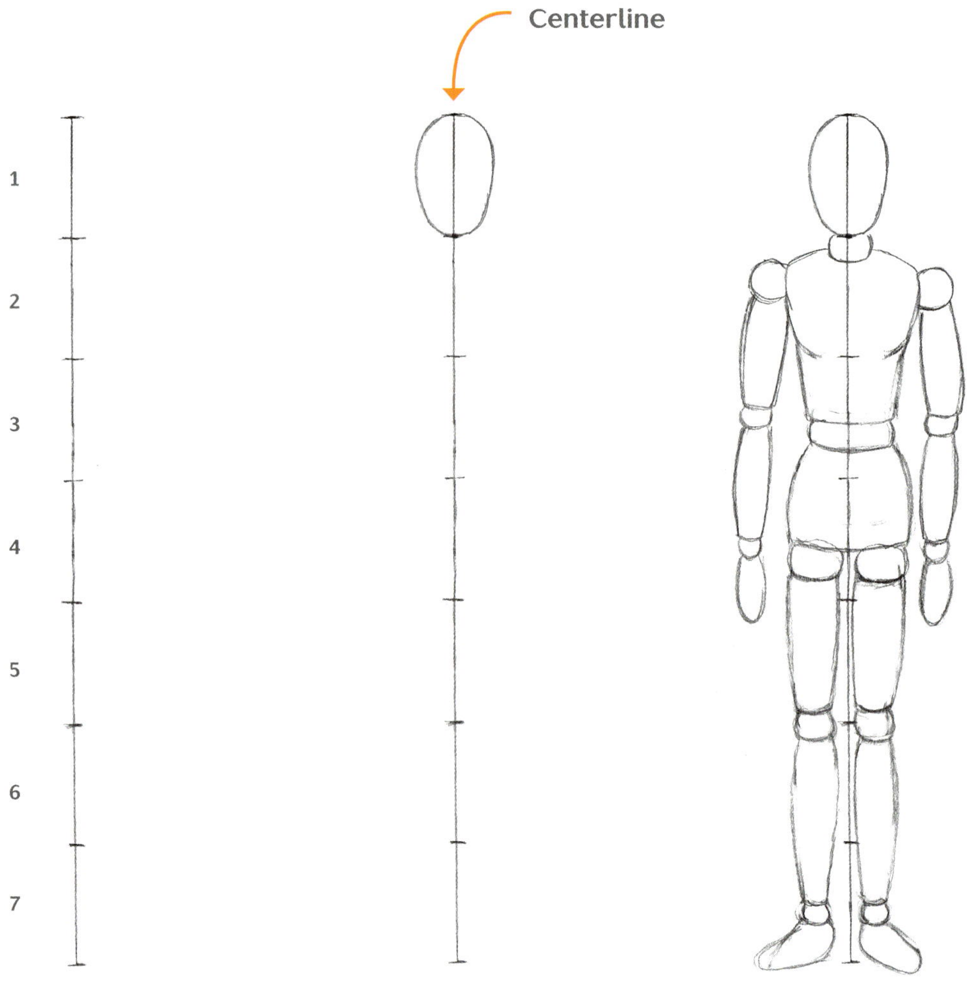

1. Draw a line the length of your subject. Then add marks that divide it into seven equal sections, or units.

2. Fill the top unit with an oval or head shape. As you'll see on the following pages, use a circle for the top of the head and add a curved shape for the jawline. The top of the head should touch the top line of the unit and the chin should touch the bottom line.

3. Use the marks that divide the body into seven sections as guidelines to fill in the torso and limbs. With these essential lines in place, you can finalize the drawing with the details that bring the figure to life. I'll show you how to draw all of those pieces in this chapter!

FRONT VIEW

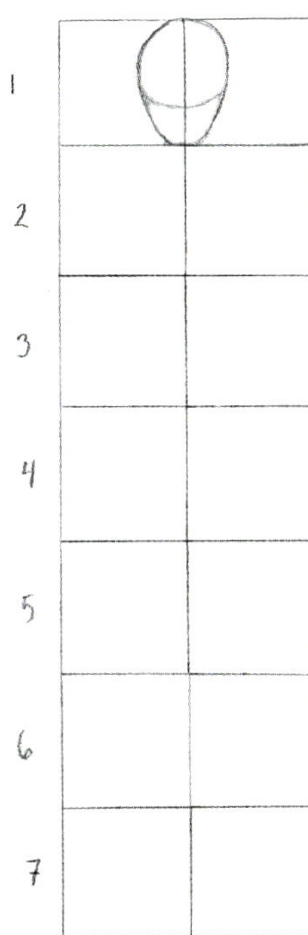

1. Draw a grid seven units high and two units wide. In unit 1, draw an oval for the head, following the directions on page 20.

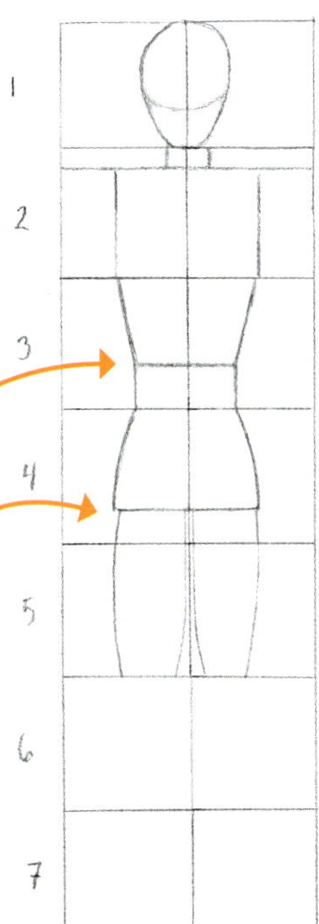

2. About one-fifth of the way down unit 2, draw a line for the shoulders. Draw the neck. From the shoulders to the bottom of the unit, start the torso. In unit 3, draw a line two-thirds down for the waist. Finish the torso with angled lines. Draw two lines from the waist to the bottom of unit 3. In unit 4, draw two curved lines flaring outward for the hips. Draw a line one-third from the bottom of the unit. Draw curved lines for the thighs in units 4 and 5.

TIP

Feminine figures tend to be shorter than masculine ones, so we'll only use 6.5 units when drawing them on pages 24–27.

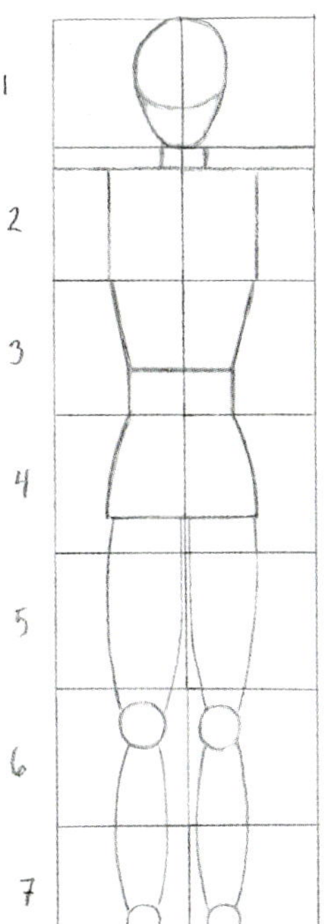

3. Add circles for the knees. Finish the thighs and use curved lines for the calves in units 6 and 7. In the bottom quarter of unit 7, draw circles for the ankles and rectangles for the feet. Connect them with angled lines.

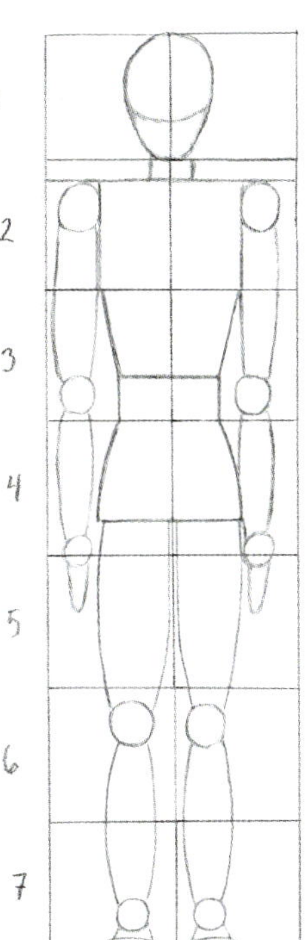

4. In unit 2, draw circles for the shoulders. Draw circles for the elbows at the bottom of unit 3 and for the wrists between units 4 and 5. Connect the circles to form the arms. Draw rounded triangles for the hands.

PROFILE VIEW

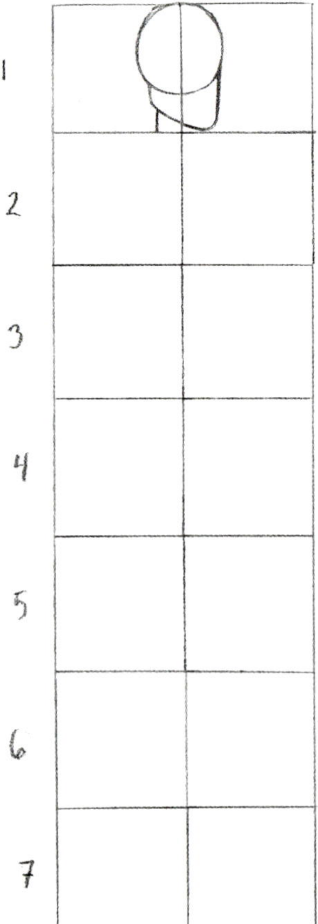

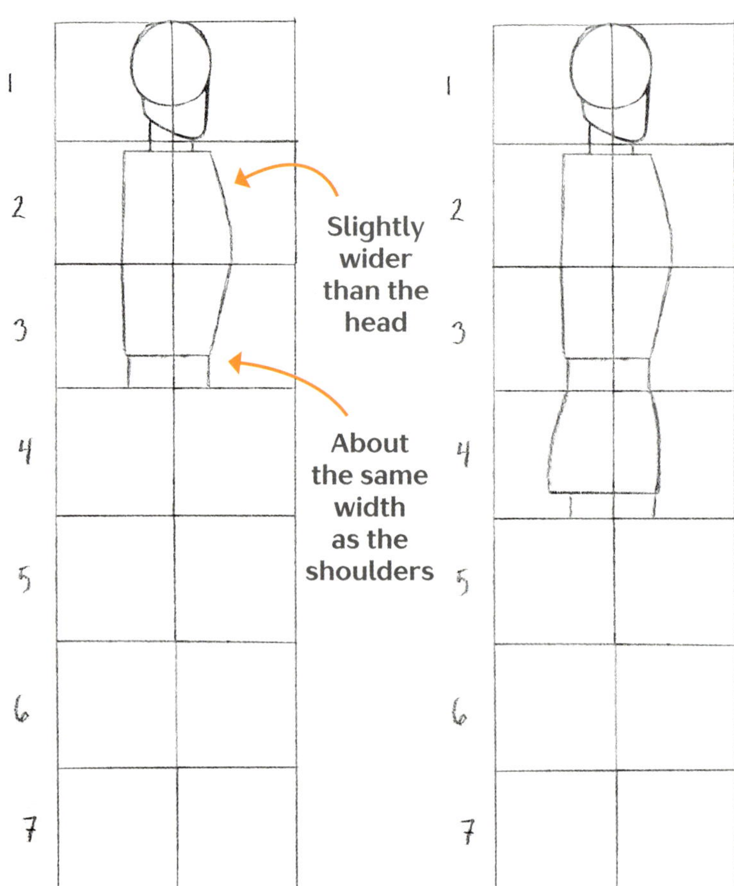

1. Draw a grid seven units high and two units wide, following the directions on page 20. In unit 1, draw a circle for the top of the head. Add a curved shape for the jawline. The top of the head should touch the top of the unit and the chin should touch the bottom.

2. About one-fifth into unit 2, draw a line for the shoulders. Draw the neck. In units 2 and 3, draw a straight line for the back and a slightly curved line for the front of the chest, stopping three-quarters down unit 3. Connect them with a line for the waist. Begin the hips with vertical lines.

3. In unit 4, draw a curved line to represent the buttocks and a straighter line for the front of the hips. Stop three-quarters down the unit, and draw a horizontal line at the bottom of the hips. Draw two vertical lines to the bottom of unit 4 to start the thigh.

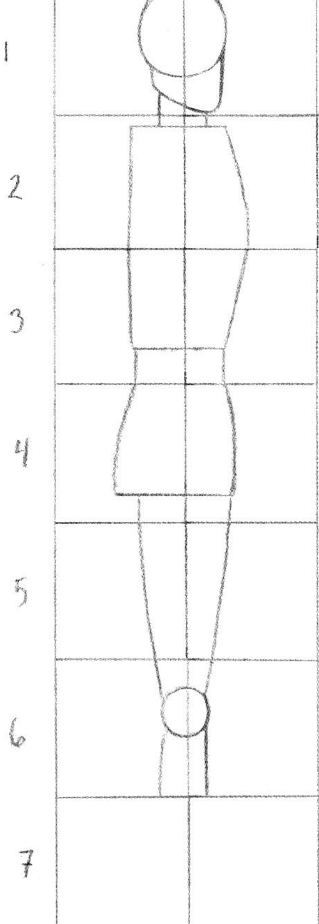

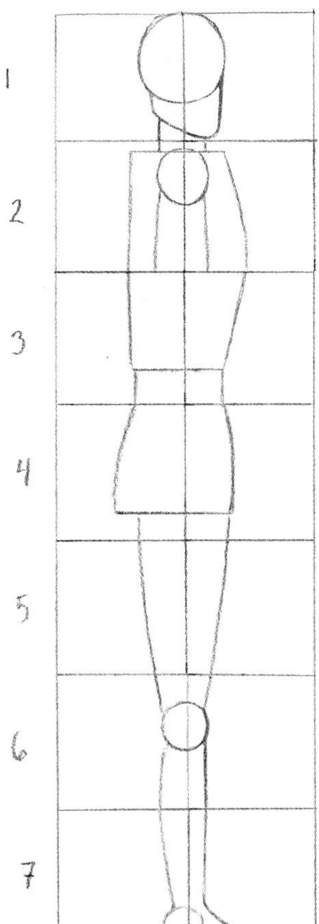

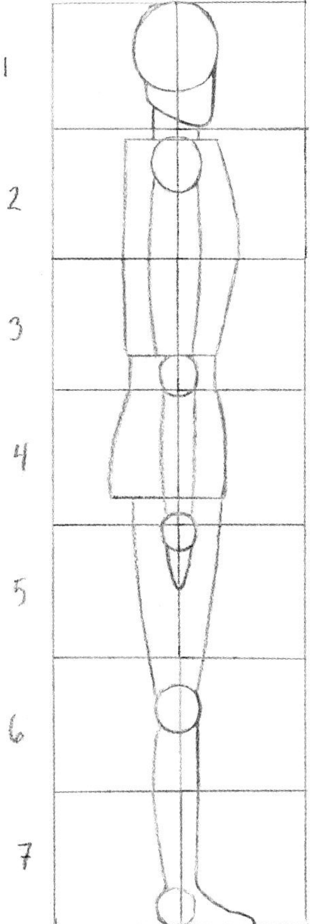

4. Draw angled lines for the legs in units 5 and 6, ending them just below the top of unit 6. Draw a circle for the knee. In the bottom half of unit 6, begin the back of the calf with a curved line and the front with a straight line.

5. Add a circle for the heel and draw the foot at the bottom of unit 7. Finish the legs by connecting the shapes. In unit 2, draw a circle for the shoulder on the centerline. Begin the upper arm from the shoulder to the bottom of unit 2.

6. Draw a circle for the elbow at the bottom of unit 3 and a circle for the wrist between units 4 and 5. Connect the circles to form the remaining upper arm and forearm. Draw a rounded triangle for the hand.

FRONT VIEW (FEMININE)

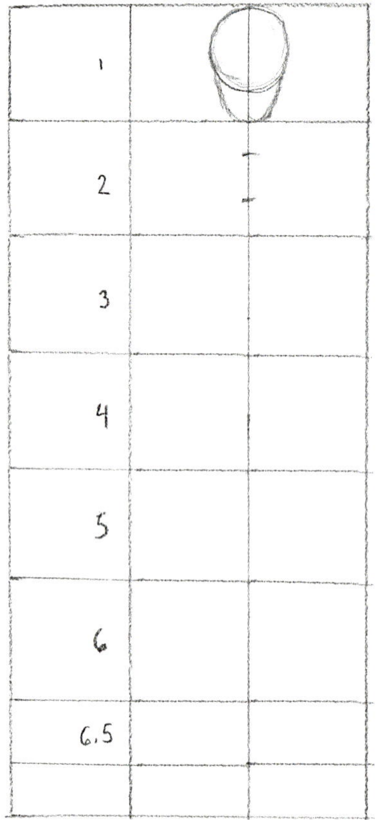

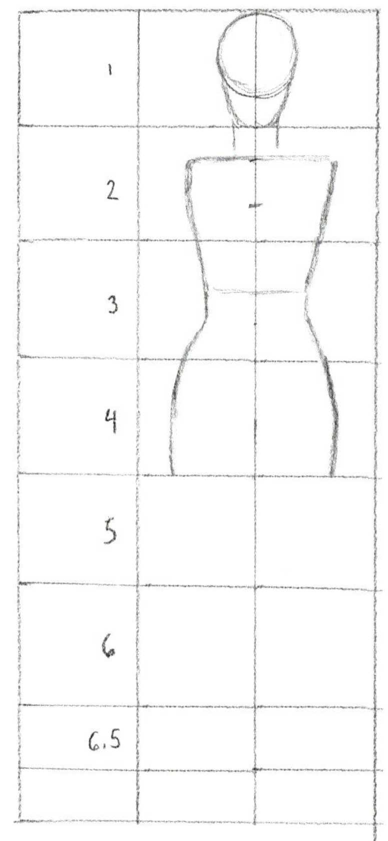

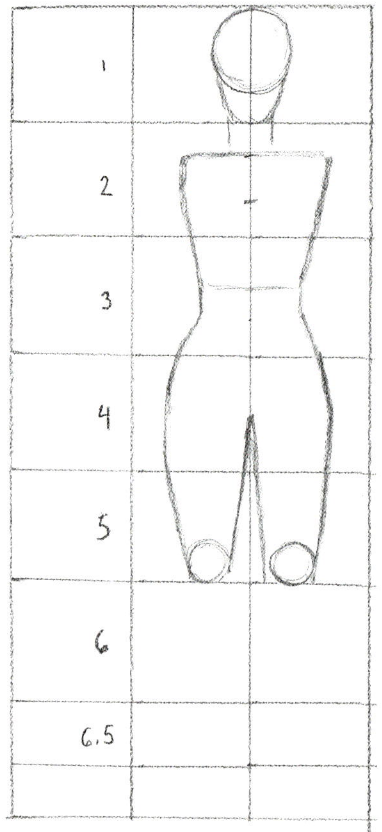

1. Draw a grid seven units high and two units wide. Divide unit 7 in half. In unit 1, draw an oval for the head, following the directions on page 20.

2. About one-fifth down unit 2, draw a line for the shoulders. Draw the neck. In units 2 and 3, draw lines angling in, stopping halfway into unit 3. Connect them with a line for the waist. Begin the hips with vertical lines, curving down into unit 4.

3. Draw two circles for the knees at the bottom of unit 5. Draw curved lines to create the thighs that connect the hips to the knees.

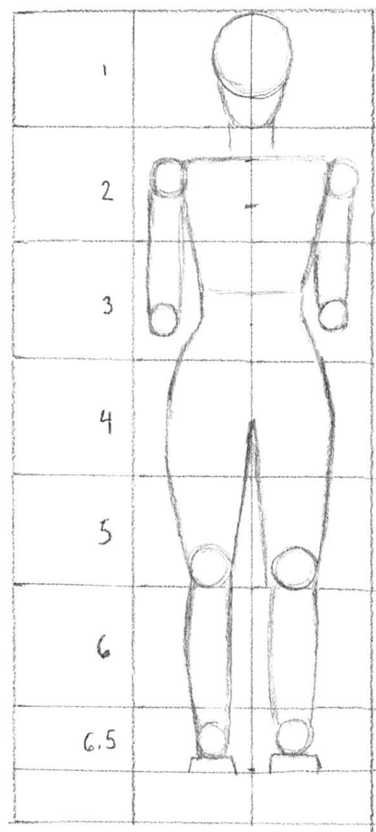

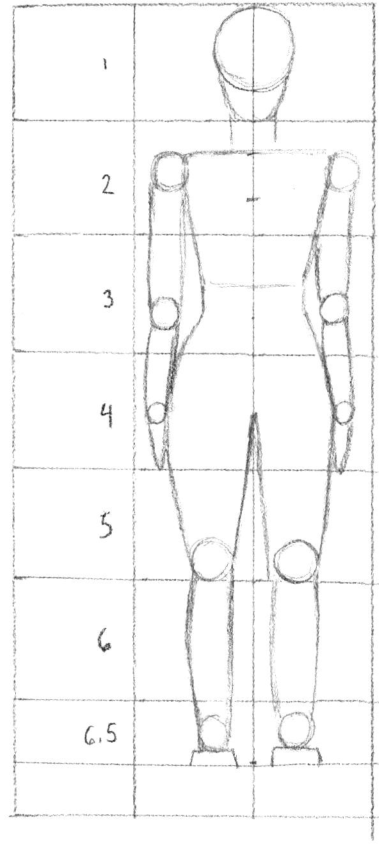

4. Add circles for the ankles about halfway down unit 6.5. Draw curved lines to form the calves in unit 6. Draw rectangles for the feet. Connect them to the calves with angled lines. In unit 2 draw circles for the shoulders, and three-quarters down unit 3 draw circles for the elbows. Connect the circles to form the upper arms.

5. Draw circles for the wrists about three-quarters down unit 4. Connect the elbow and wrist circles to form the forearms. Draw rounded triangles for the hands.

PROFILE VIEW (FEMININE)

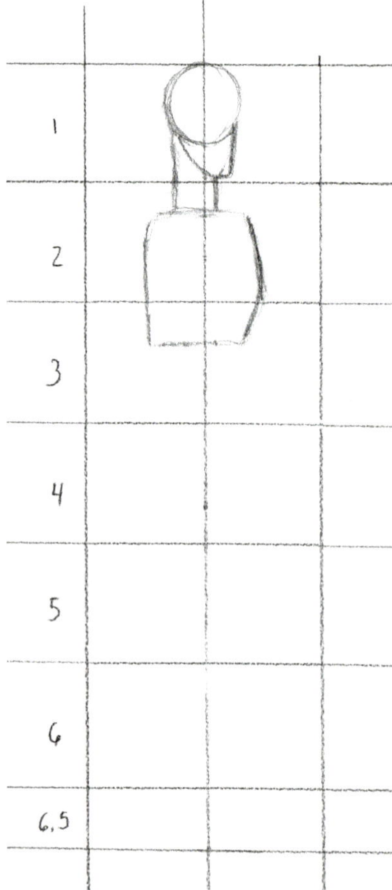 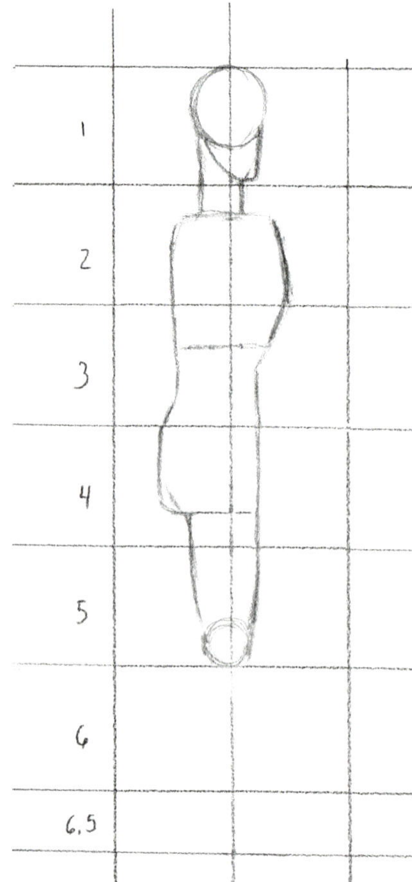 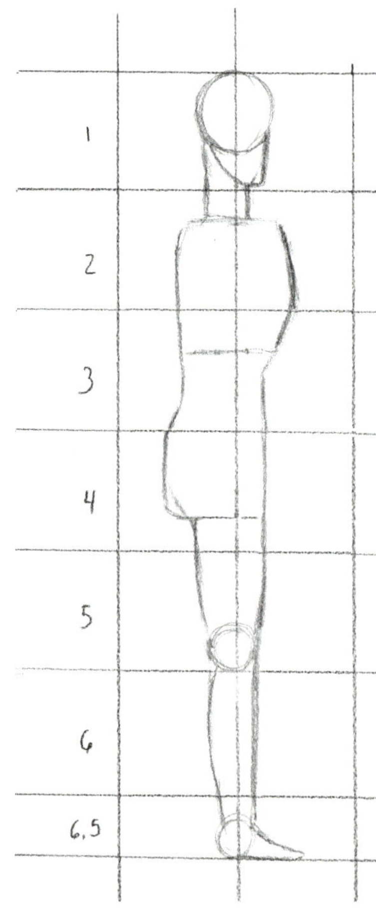

1. Draw a grid seven units high and two units wide, following the directions on page 20. Divide unit 7 in half. In unit 1, draw a circle for the top of the head. Add a curved shape for the jawline. The top of the head should touch the top of the unit and the chin should touch the bottom. About one-fifth down in unit 2, draw a line for the shoulders. Draw the neck. In units 2 and 3, draw a straight line for the back and a slightly curved line for the front of the chest, stopping a quarter of the way down unit 3. Connect them with a horizontal line for the waist.

2. Begin the hips with vertical lines. In units 3 and 4, draw a curved line to represent the buttocks and a straighter line for the front of the hips. Stop three-quarters down the unit, and draw a horizontal line at the bottom of the hips. At the bottom of unit 5, draw a circle for the knee. Draw two vertical lines to form the thigh.

3. At the bottom of unit 6.5, draw a circle for the ankle. Connect the knee and ankle with a curved line for the calf and a straight line for the shin. Draw a triangle for the foot.

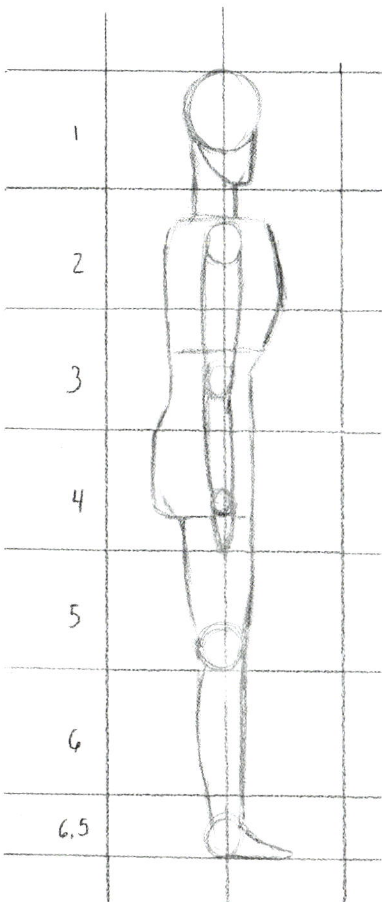

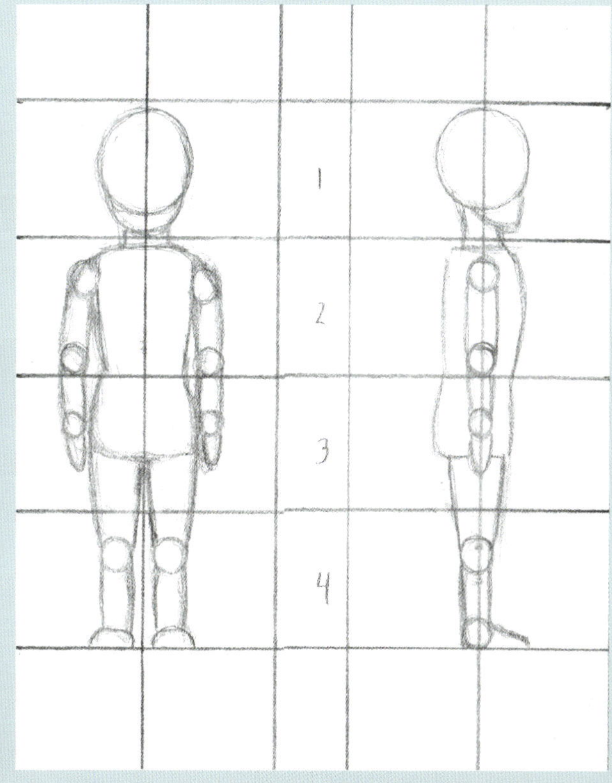

A CHILD'S BODY

For a child's body, you would create a grid that is only four units high, and adjust the proportions accordingly.

4. In unit 2, draw a circle for the shoulder on the centerline. Draw a circle for the elbow about two-thirds down unit 3. Connect the circles to form the upper arm. Draw a circle for the wrist three-quarters down unit 4. Connect the elbow and wrist circles to form the forearm. Draw a rounded triangle for the hand.

THE TORSO

As humans move, so do their muscles, skin, and bones, depending on the pose. Having some familiarity with or basic knowledge of underlying muscles can help when drawing a torso.

FRONT VIEW

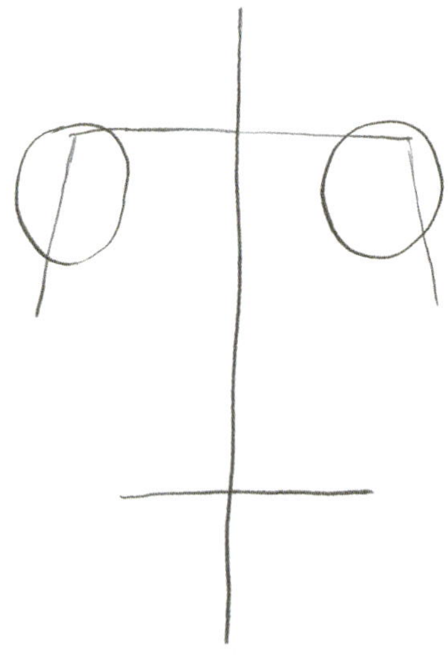

1. Draw a vertical line for the spine. Draw a horizontal line for the top of the chest and one for the pelvis. Draw two circles for the shoulders and two more lines to start the arms.

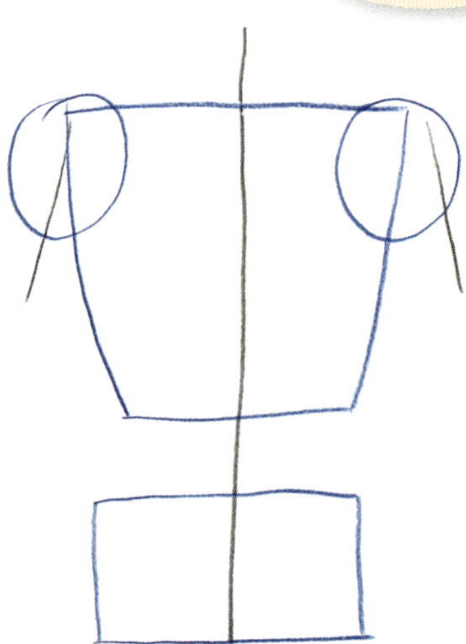

2. Draw the torso and pelvis using simple geometric shapes. Later they can be shaped and built up to be more representational.

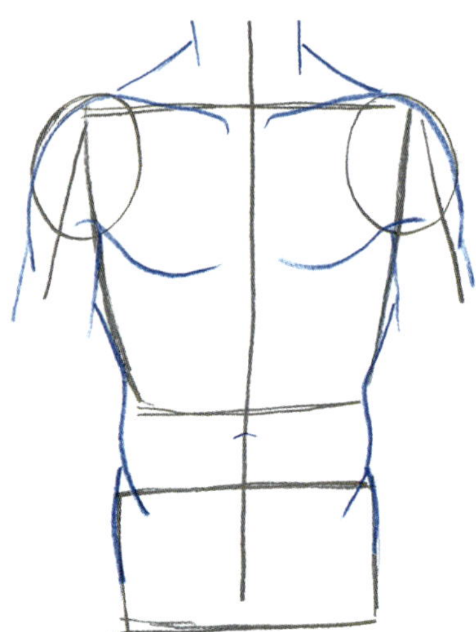

3. Draw the clavicle bones and add lines for the neck and shoulders. Add lines to connect the rib cage and hips.

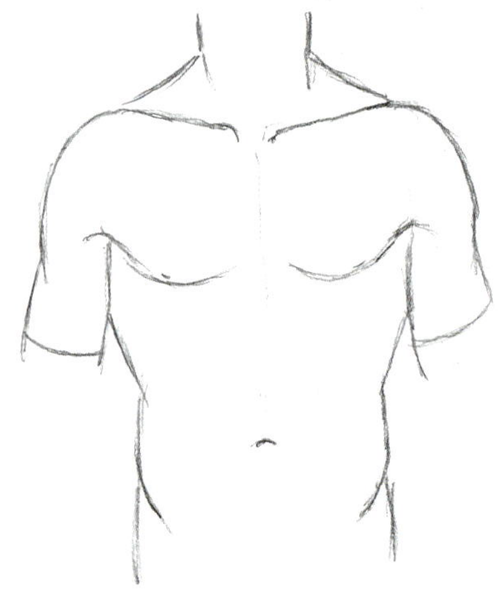

4. Erase all unnecessary guidelines.

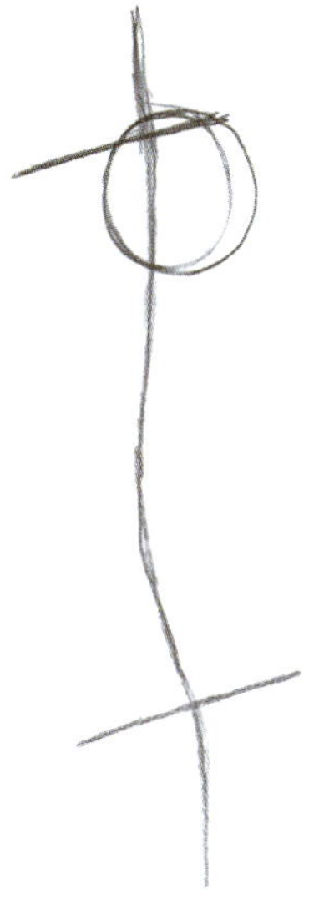

1. Draw a line for the spine that has a slight curve at the middle and toward the bottom. The top curve is for the stomach and the bottom is for the buttock. Add guidelines for the top of the shoulders and one for the hips. Draw a circle for the shoulder socket.

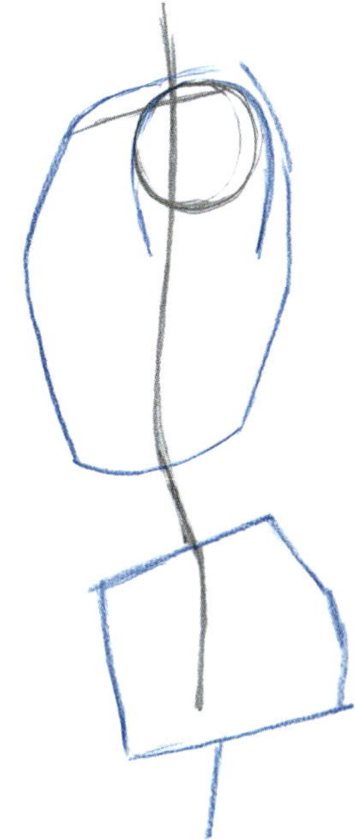

2. Draw the basic shapes. Here, I use a rounded shape for the chest and rib cage and a box for the hips. Focus not so much on the proportion but the angle. Draw guidelines for the shoulder.

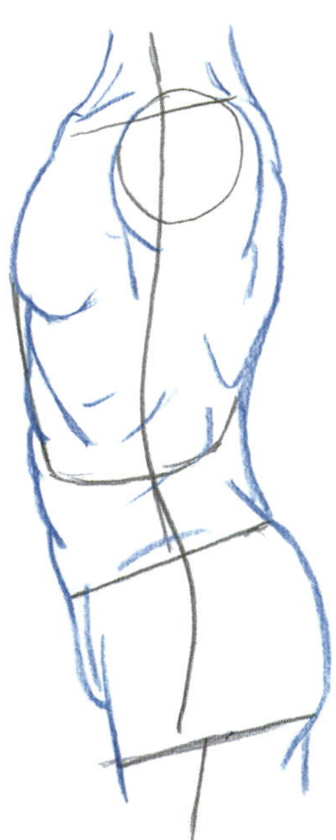

3. Connect the torso and pelvis with curved lines, adding some underlying muscle definition.

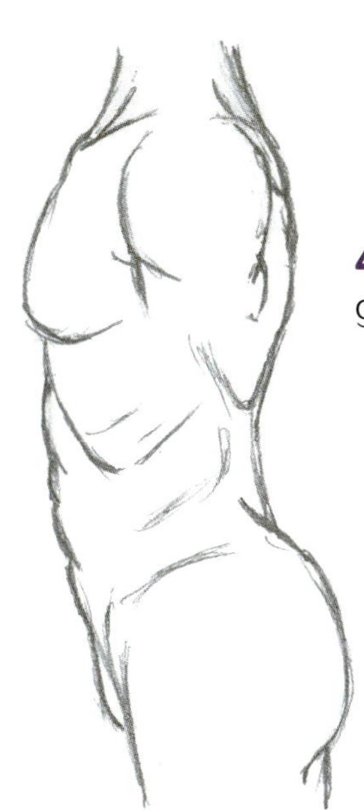

4. Erase the unnecessary guidelines.

TORSO VARIATIONS

Masculine: The shoulders are usually the widest point. There are sharp angles for the upper torso and a boxy shape for the pelvis.

Feminine: The pelvis is usually the widest point and is rounder. Feminine bodies have a narrower rib cage and waistline. The lower abdomen may protrude a bit more, and the curve of the waist is emphasized. The bone and muscle structures are finer, so they tend to be smaller. They have a higher percentage of body fat, so they should be drawn with round, smooth lines, not angles.

Child: The torso is shorter and the pelvis and shoulders are similar in width. The rib cage is about the same size as the head, and it's a small egg-like shape.

Weight: For a heavier person use soft, rounded corners. For a thinner person, show more muscle definition and use angular shapes.

THE ARM

The arm can be simplified down to circles for the shoulder, elbow, and hand, and two cylinders for the arm bones themselves.

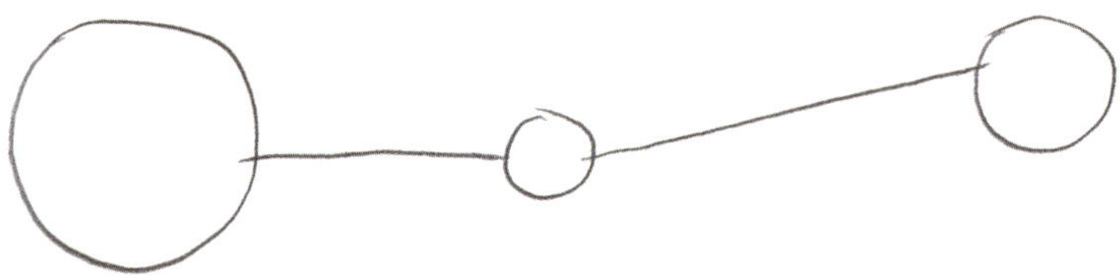

1. Draw three circles to represent the shoulder, elbow, and hand. Connect them with lines to indicate the centerline of the arm.

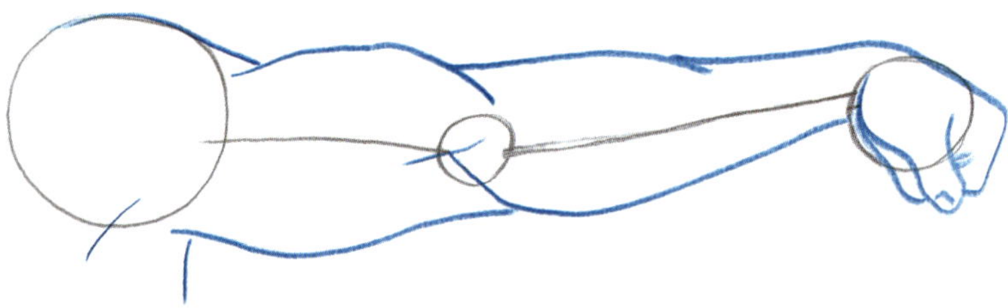

2. Draw lines connecting the circles for the upper arm and forearm. The forearm is thicker at the elbow, then tapers to the wrist. Add fingers to the hand.

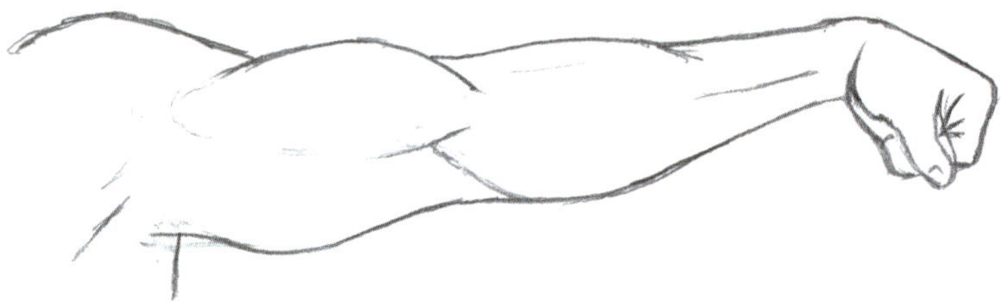

3. Erase the guidelines. Refine the shoulder muscle, which comes down into the upper arm, then runs into the tricep, which connects to the elbow.

ARM VARIATIONS

Straight: The tricep is shortened, and the bicep longer. Maintain the curvature of the arm. It's not a straight line.
Bent: The bicep is shortened and the tricep is longer.
Weight: For more muscular arms, add curves and lines for definition. If the arm is heavier, the curves will be elongated and softer. Flesh might also bunch around joints.

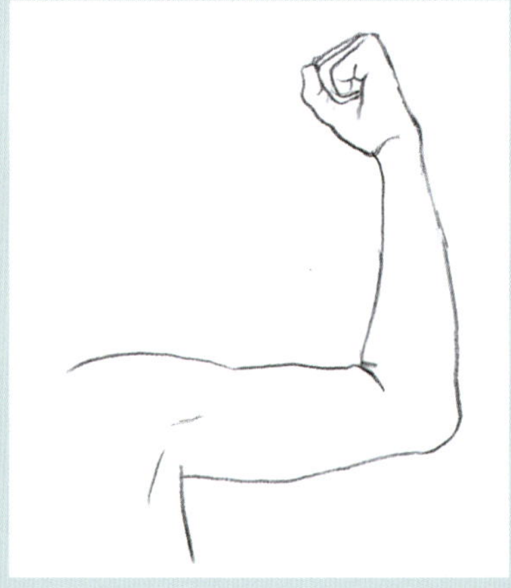

TIP
The arm can be difficult to draw due to all its movement options—vertical, horizontal, and other rotations—so observation is crucial for realistic representation.

THE HAND

Hands can seem difficult to draw, but at their most basic forms, they are simply circles and lines.

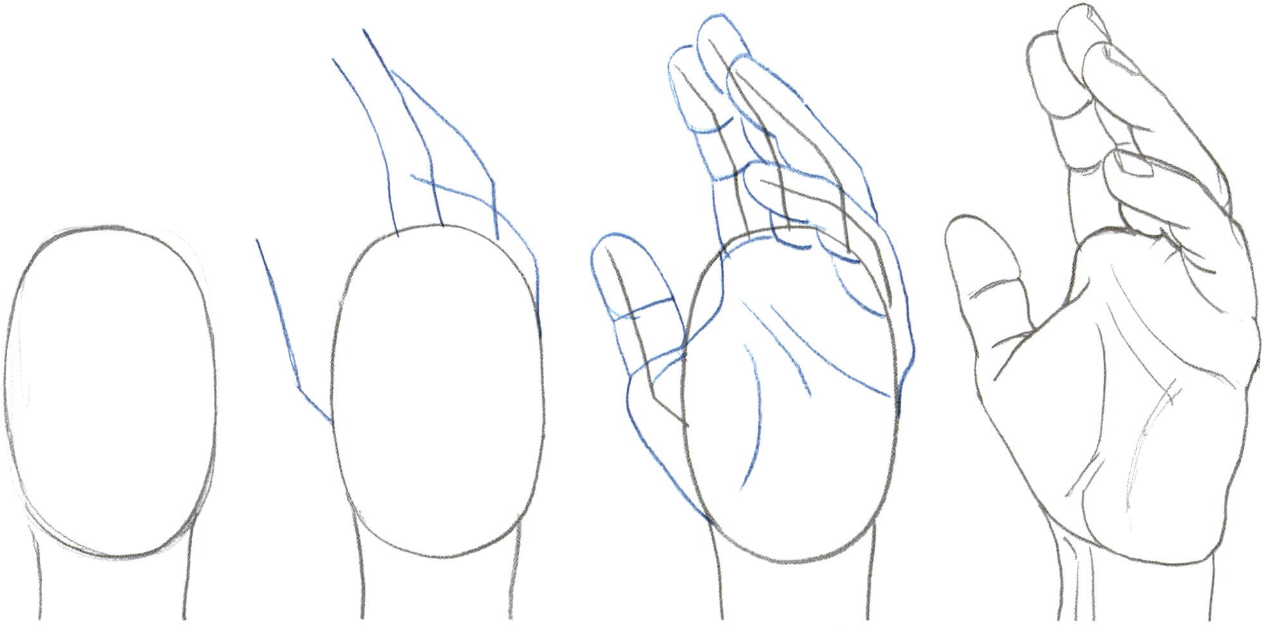

1. Draw an oval for the palm and curved lines for the wrist.

2. Draw five lines for the fingers. They can be curved or straight, depending on your preference. If they are bent, they will overlap, as shown.

3. Add thickness to fingers. Refine the shape of the palm, and add lines for joints and where the hand is bent.

4. Erase all unnecessary guidelines. Add the nails and additional lines for wrinkles as needed.

HAND VARIATIONS

Masculine: A masculine hand, compared to a feminine one, has sharper angles and the planes are more accentuated. The hands are thicker, and the fingers more rounded.

Feminine: Feminine hands usually have a finer, more delicate bone structure and are smaller in size. The fingers are longer and thinner and taper toward the nails. The wrists can be slender.

Child: The fingers are shorter, fleshier, and stubbier than adults'. There is only a slight difference between the width of the palm and the wrist.

Age: Older skin has defined folds, noticeable veins, and accentuated joints. There will be more and deeper wrinkles and crevices.

Weight: Larger hands have less bone projections and dimpling at the knuckles and joints.

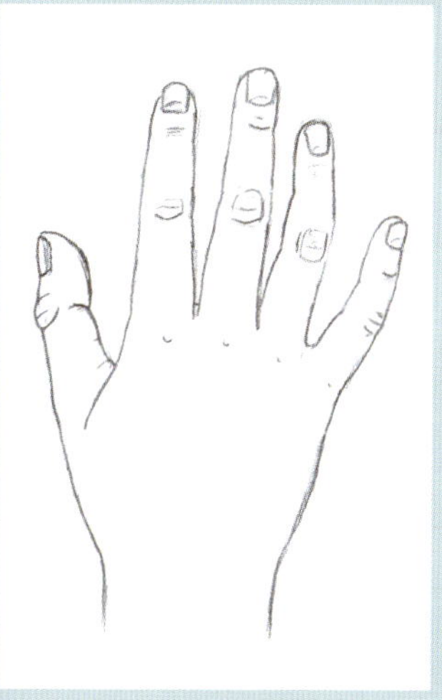

THE LEG

Legs are just circles and ovals connected by organic lines. The size and shape of the legs will depend on an individual's weight and height.

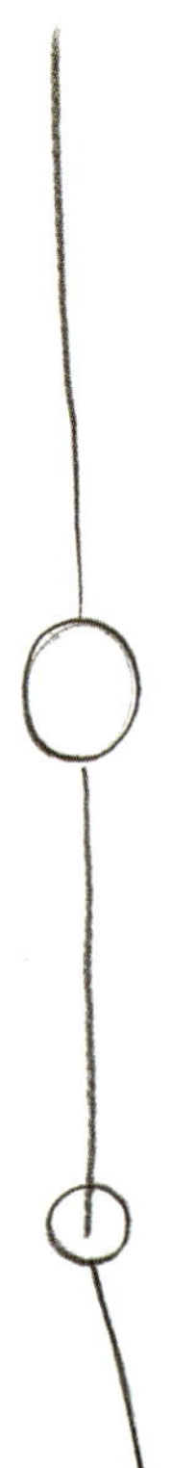 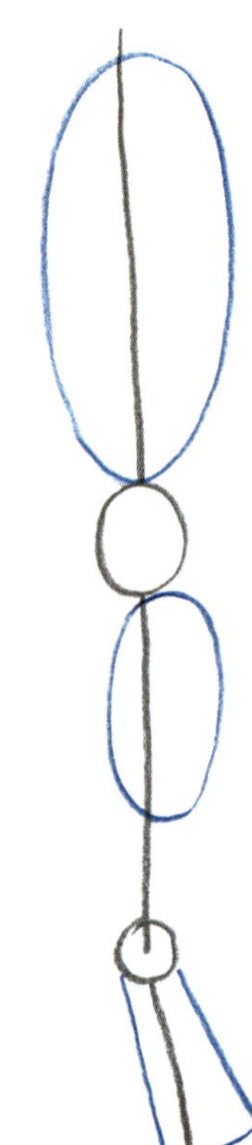 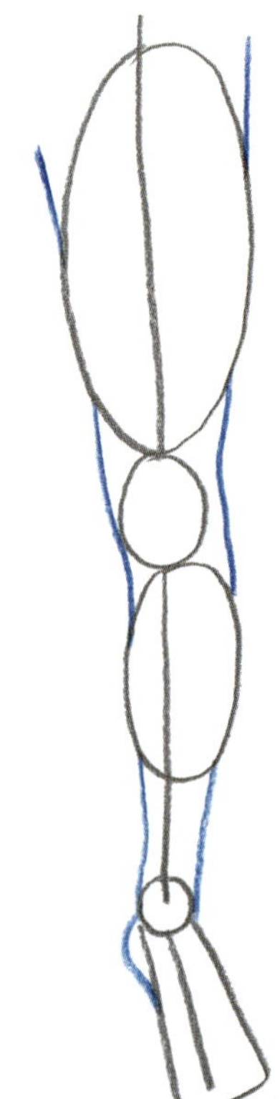 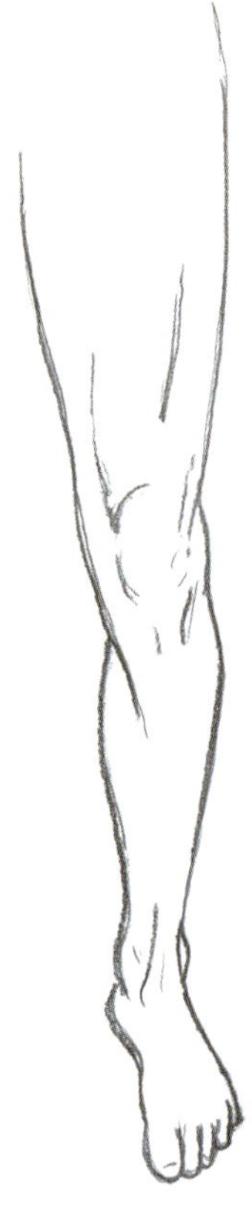

1. Draw a line for the thigh, then draw a circle for the knee. Draw another line for the calf and a smaller circle for the ankle. The second line should be about two-thirds of the length of the first. Draw an even shorter line for the foot.

2. Draw an oval around the top line for the thigh. Draw a smaller oval around two-thirds of the second line for the calf. For this example, this line is a bit off center. Draw a boxy shape for the foot.

3. Connect the leg shapes using curved lines. Add a heel to the foot shape.

4. Draw the toes. Add definition for the knee, thigh muscles, and feet. Erase the guidelines.

SIDE VIEW

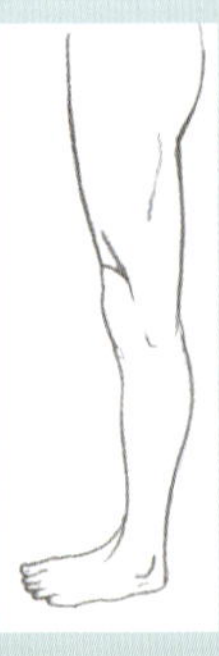

In all ages and genders, calves are more visible from the side, so your oval should be more off center than with a front view.

THE FOOT

A foot can be simplified into three circles, which are then connected with lines. Think of a separated snowman on its side when drawing the basic shapes for the foot.

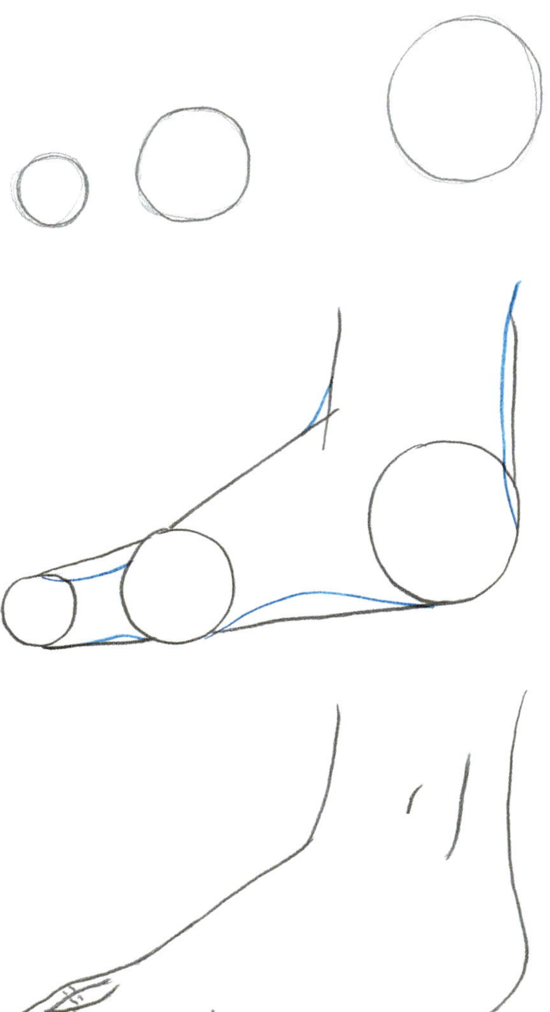

1. Draw three circles for the heel, ball of the foot, and toes. The circles become smaller and smaller as they move toward the toe.

2. Using the circles as a guide, draw the outline of the foot and the ankle. Create a guideline for the big toe. Draw the arch of the foot.

3. Add the toenail and draw in the other toes behind the big toe. Add definition to the foot and the ankle. Erase the guidelines.

LEG & FEET VARIATIONS

Feminine: From the top of the hips to the bottom of the glutes, a rounded or circular shape works best since the buttock is usually curvier. The legs are more rounded, regardless of weight or muscularity. They have more curves, whereas masculine legs are typically more angular.

Child: Children's limbs appear proportionately thicker than adults'. The shorter legs make them look plump. Their toes are short and round, and their feet are rounded, with a lack of definition in the ankles.

Weight: In larger bodies, the thickest point of the leg is still the thighs, but overall the legs are rounded, and there's less definition in the ankles. Flesh can fold and dimple around joints.

Drawing the Head & the Face

While every face is different, the proportions of the head and the face are relatively uniform within age groups, whether a baby, a teen, or an adult. These proportions will affect where the features are placed on the face, so practicing the basics before moving on to more complicated drawings will set a good foundation.

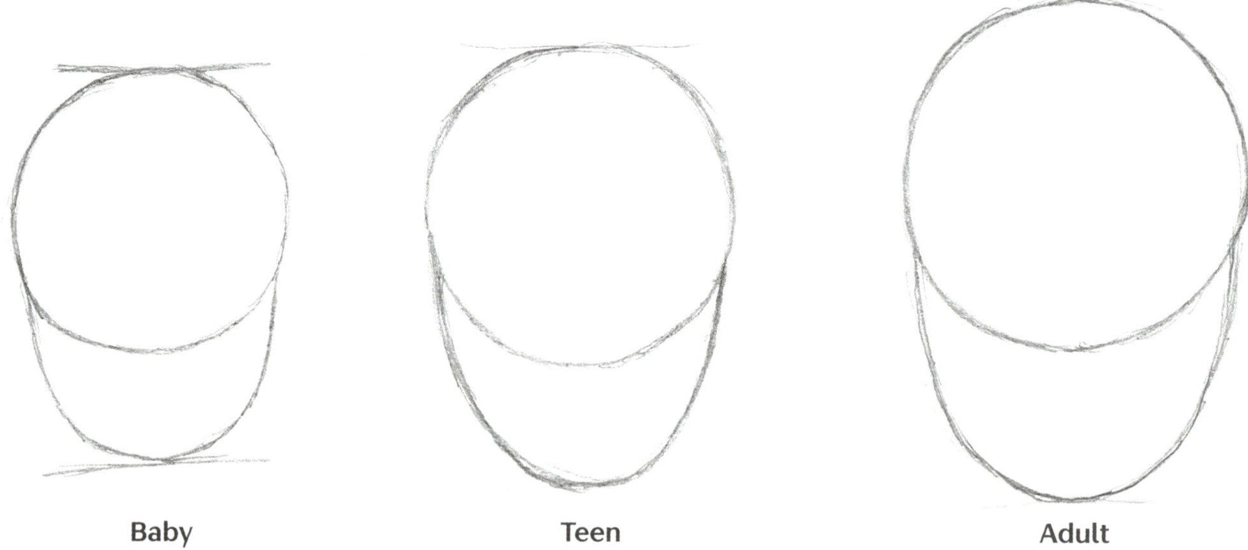

BABY PROPORTIONS

A baby's head is a "U" shape attached to a ball. The bone structure is not yet completely developed, so the jawbone, cheekbones, and the bridge of the nose are relatively small. This makes the baby's face smaller in proportion to its skull. The face, from the brows down, only occupies about half of the whole area of the head. Distances between the nose, lips, and chin are shorter, making the features appear larger. The ears measure from the eyes to the mouth.

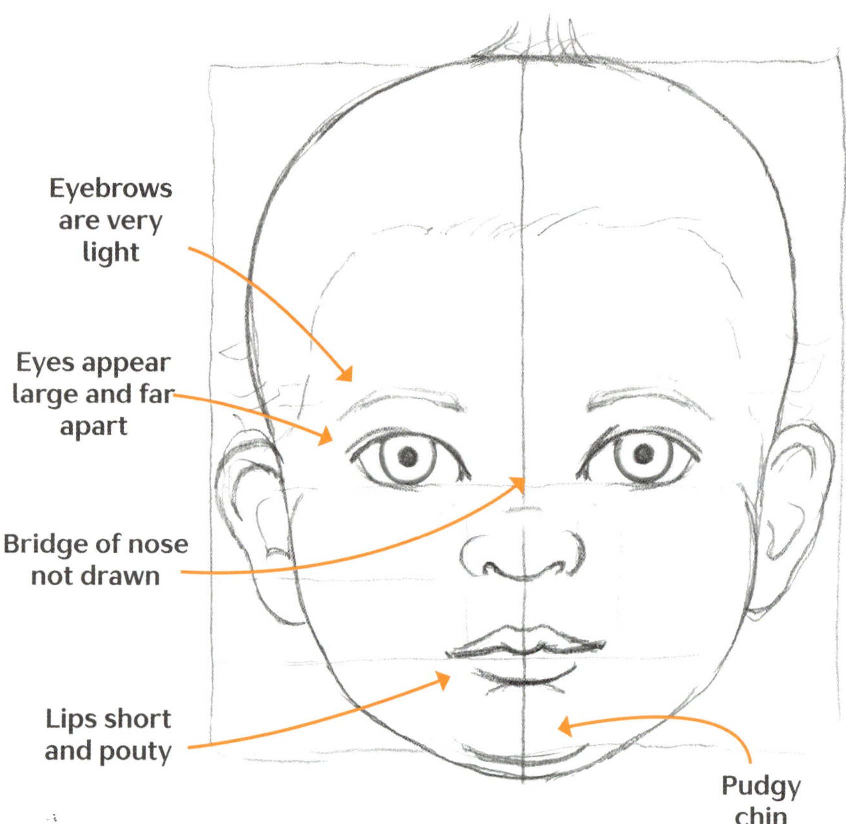

TEEN OR CHILD PROPORTIONS

For a young teen or child, the head shape is larger, and the "U" shape is longer and leaner. The eyes take up less space, and the eyelid is more visible. The lips are relaxed, but the upper lip is still thinner than the lower lip. The chin is now part of the jaw, not a separate curved shape. The ears are smaller relative to the size of the head.

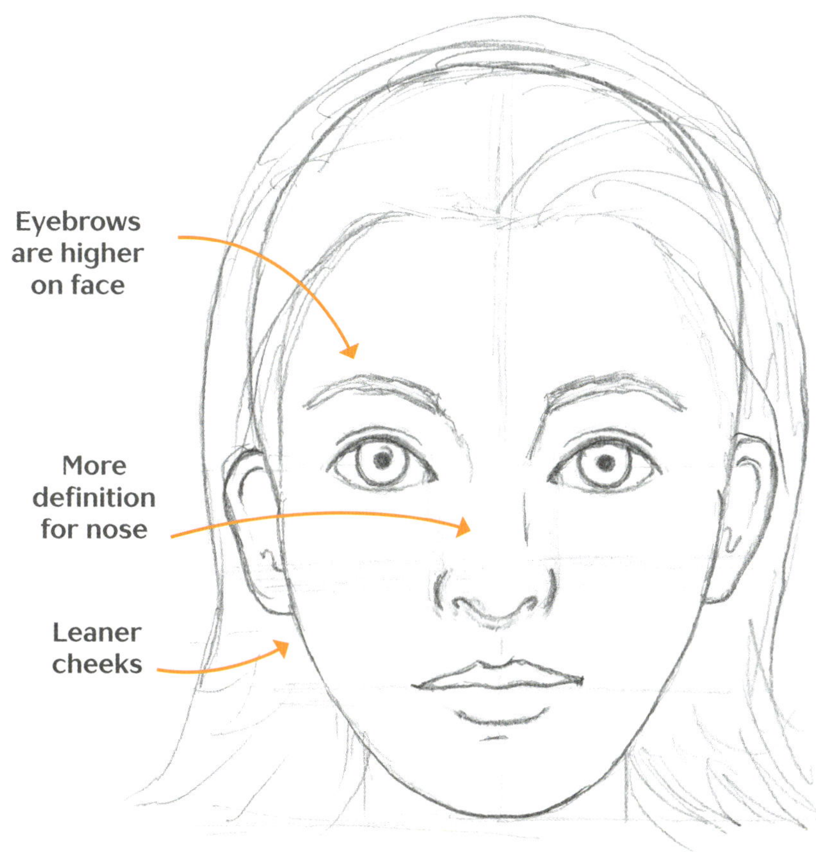

ADULT PROPORTIONS

An adult face shows proportions that have changed with age, but the differences can be subtle. The eyes have more lines to define them, including lines at the corners of the eyes. The ears are located in the same spot as on a teen, but they are slightly bigger. The hairline is slightly higher, and the chin is more defined, with the shape of the jaw more delineated.

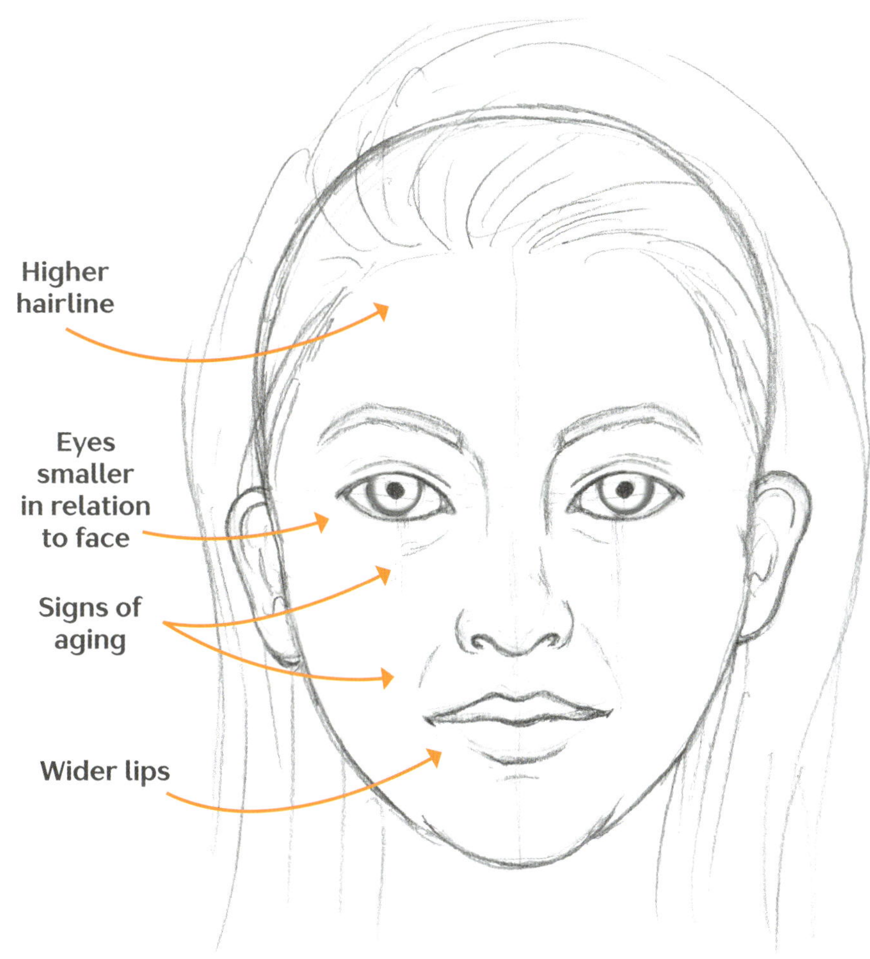

AVOID PERFECT SYMMETRY

"Symmetry" is a fundamental part of geometry, nature, and shapes. Simply put, it means an artwork is the same on both sides. Whether we are conscious of it or not, our brains seek out symmetry because it's pleasing to us.

However, perfect symmetry in nature is very rare. Almost every natural object has some degree of "asymmetry," meaning that both sides are not exactly the same. Some cases of asymmetry are more noticeable than others, such as in the case of fiddler crabs, animals with antlers, or flounder (which only has eyes on one side of its face!). But human faces are not perfectly symmetrical, either, and making them so makes them seem off-kilter and unnatural. Take the faces shown here for example.

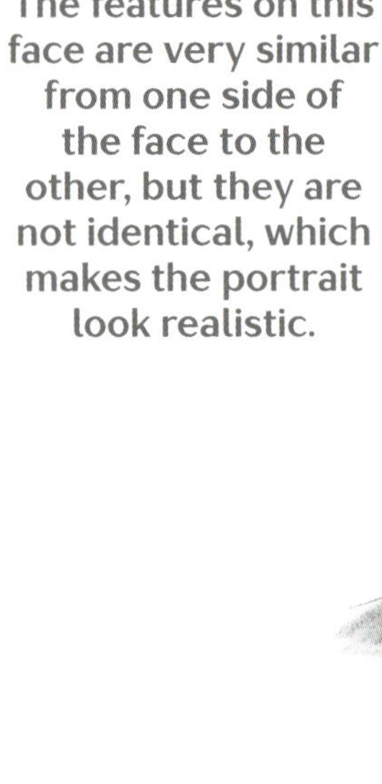

The features on this face are very similar from one side of the face to the other, but they are not identical, which makes the portrait look realistic.

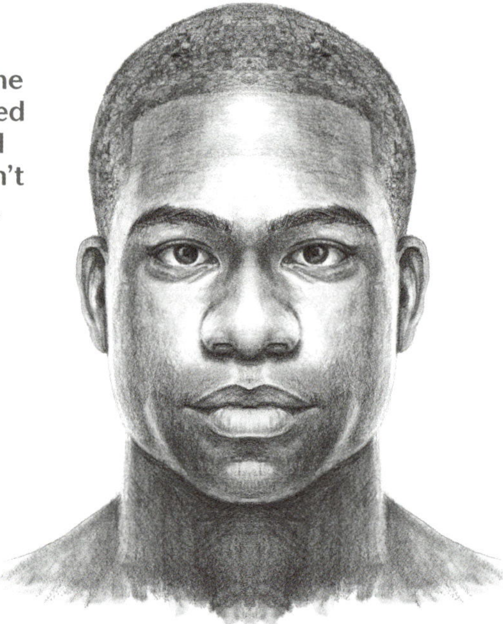

In this example, the left side is mirrored on the right, and the portrait doesn't look quite right.

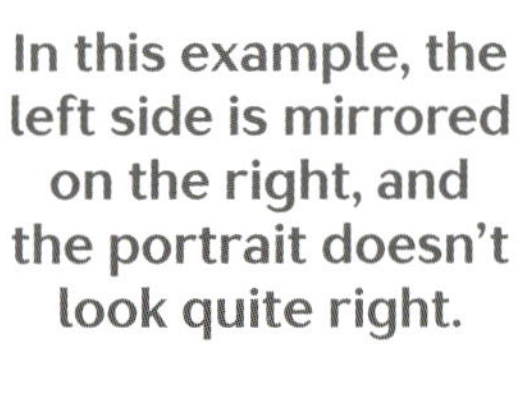

When the right side of the face is mirrored, the result is also somewhat odd, and the subject looks like a completely different person.

THE PLANES OF THE FACE

The human head is a 3D object, but it is often rendered to look like a flat surface. If you look closely at a face, you'll notice that individual areas protrude or recede. These areas are called "planes," and they help create dimension. Learning the planes of the face and noting where areas of the head go in and out will help you shade realistically and aid in drawing features.

How planes and features are shaded depends on where the light source is coming from. In this example the light is shining from above, which makes the planes that recede inward appear darkest.

Nose: The nose has four major planes: the center front, the sides of the nose, and the bottom. The bottom of the nose is almost always in shadow.

Lips: The upper lip is a downward-facing plane (receding) while the bottom lip is actually an upward-facing plane (protruding). The upper lip usually appears darker than the lower.

Eyes: The brow bone extends past the eyes, causing a shadow to appear on this downward-facing plane. This area has been simplified and made all one tone of a dark value, but the eyes protrude a bit, so some light will hit them.

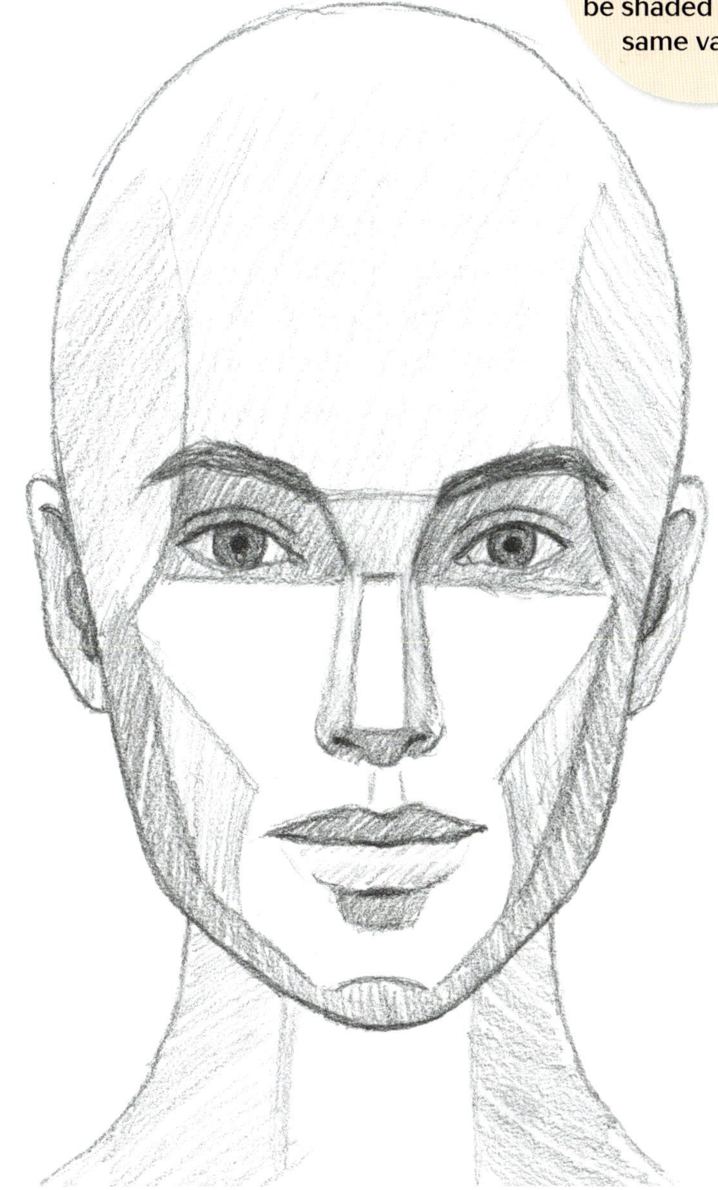

This is a very simplified guide to the planes of the face that indicates the general location of the main planes. The planes can easily become more complicated, as every curve and turn of the face can be broken down into much more than what is shown here.

Sides of the head: The face drastically changes direction at the sides of the skull. These planes have been established with curves on the sides of the head.

Jaw: The area under the cheek and jawline connects the side of the head with the front plane, shown as a receding plane.

THE HEAD & THE FACE

The placement of the eyes, nose, mouth, and other features is almost the same for everyone, whether you're drawing a front-facing, 3/4, or profile view. Slight changes in the shape and size of each feature make us look unique, but it's helpful to understand how to draw a basic face before we move on to more complicated drawings.

FRONT VIEW

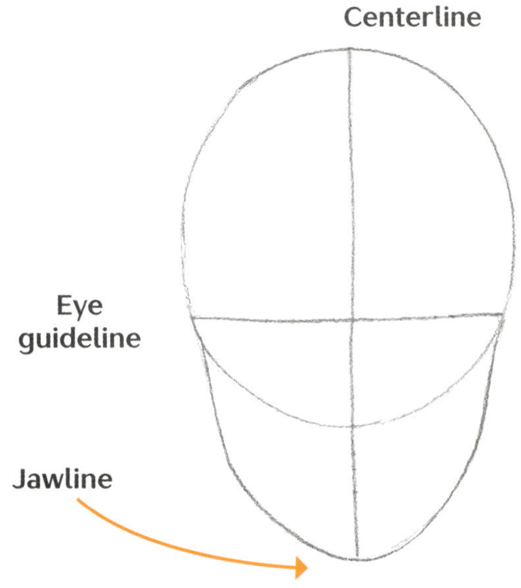

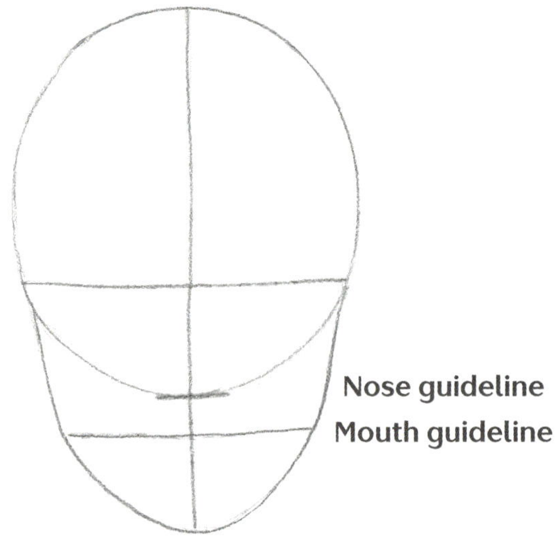

1. Draw a circle. Then draw a vertical line to mark the center of the face. It should extend down to where the chin will end. Then draw a horizontal line about three quarters down the circle for the eyes. Draw a "U" shape for the jawline, making sure to touch the end of the centerline to complete the shape of the face.

2. Draw a small horizontal line at the bottom of the circle. This will be the bottom of the nose. Then draw a horizontal line as the mouth guideline a quarter of the way between the nose and the chin.

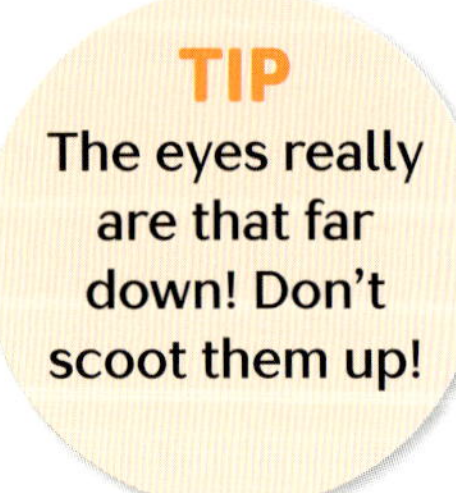

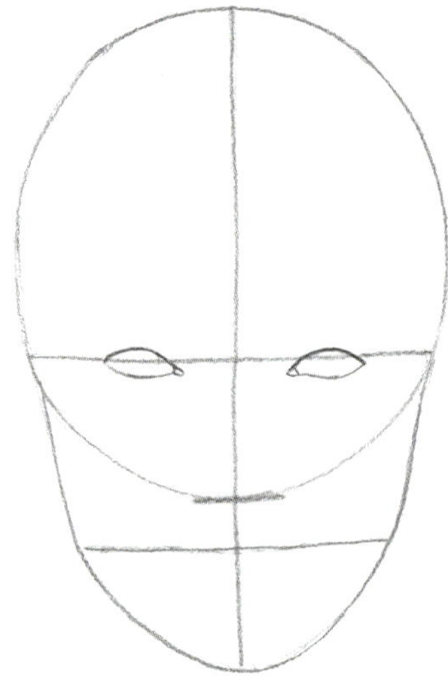

3. On the eye guideline, draw two rounded football shapes for the eyes. The space between your eyes is exactly the length of one eye, and the head is five eyes wide.

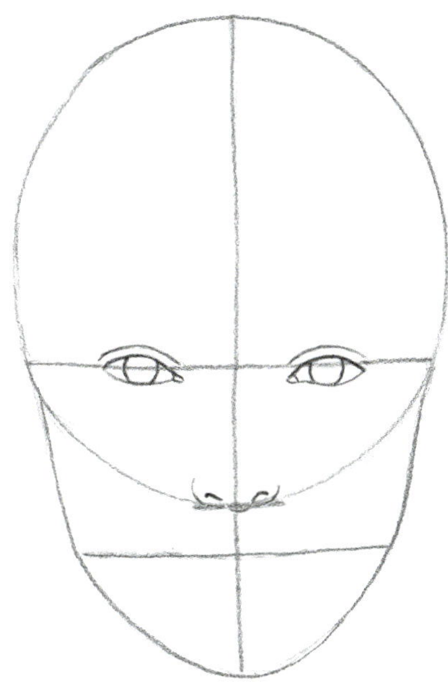

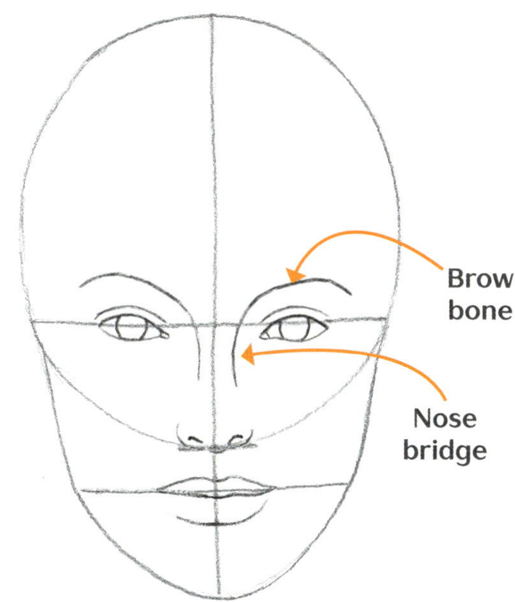

4. Draw the bottom of the nose on the nose guideline. It's a half-circle with smaller half-circles for the nostrils. Draw circles for the irises. Add curved lines that follow the contour of the tops of the eyeballs for the eyelids.

5. Above each eyelid, draw curved lines for the brow bones and the bridge of the nose. Draw the upper and lower lips around the mouth guideline. The lower lip is usually fuller than the upper lip.

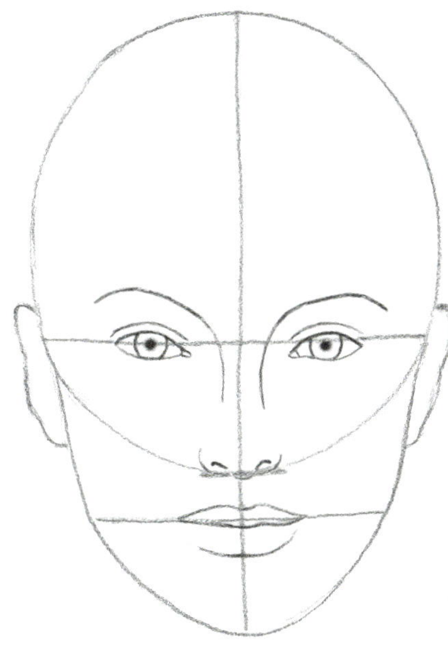

6. Draw small black circles for the pupils. For the ears, draw a curved shape that is close to the head. Ears should span from just above the eye guideline to the nose guideline.

7. Erase the guidelines and refine the features: thicken the eyebrows, color the lips, add definition to the ears, and add the philtrum (the groove that runs from the top of the lip to the nose).

PROFILE VIEW

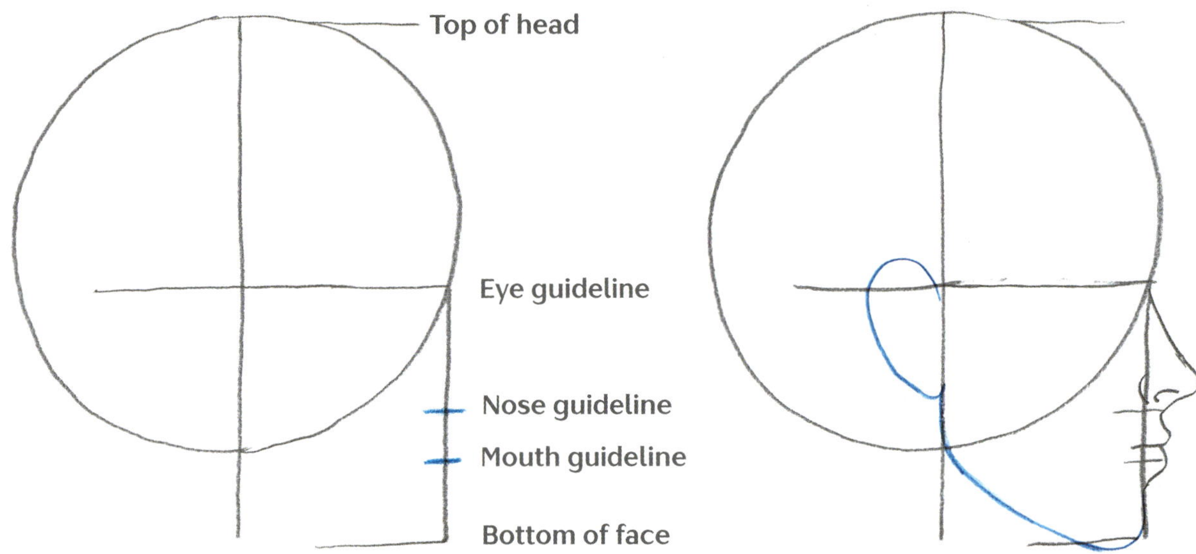

1. Draw a circle for the head. Divide the circle in half with a vertical line. Add guidelines for the top of the head and the bottom of the face. Add a guideline for the eyes about two-thirds down the centerline. Connect the eye guideline and the bottom of the face with a vertical line. Make a guideline for the nose halfway down. Just below that, make a guideline for the mouth.

2. Draw the outline of the nose, top and bottom lips, chin, and jawline. The jawline starts at about the nose guideline. The nose should start near the eye guideline and end at the nose guideline. The mouth guideline should cut the lower lip in half. Draw the ear at the top of the jawline. Use curved lines for the nostril and side of the nose.

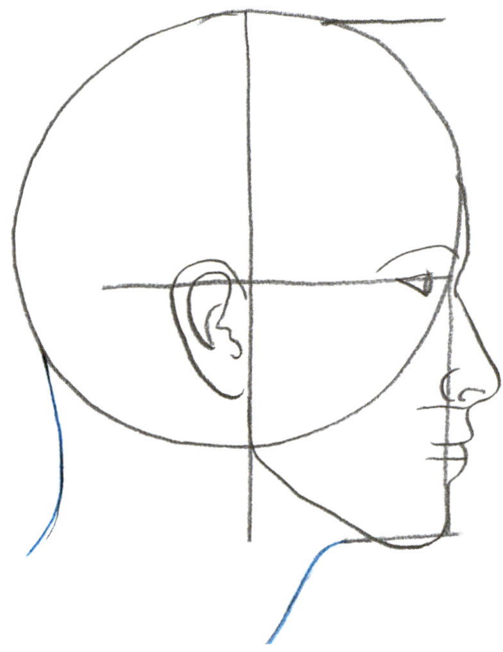

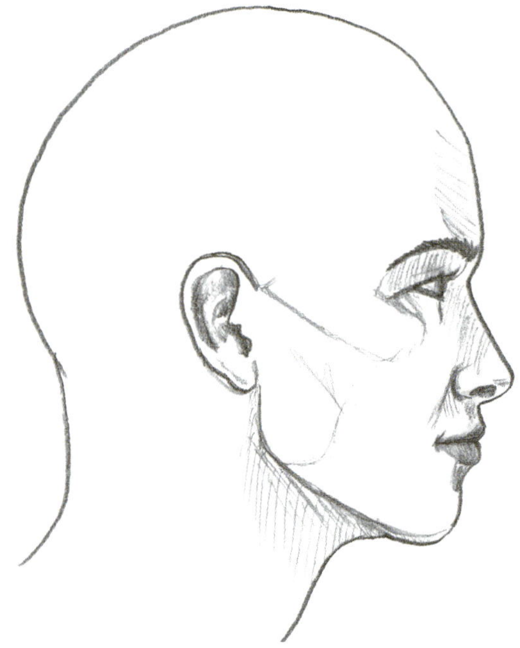

3. In a profile view, the eye is a triangle. Draw that and a curved line for the brow bone. Refine the shape of the forehead and add the ear details. Add curved lines for the neck.

4. Erase the guidelines and refine the features: thicken the eyebrows, add value to the lips, nose, cheekbone, ear, and neck.

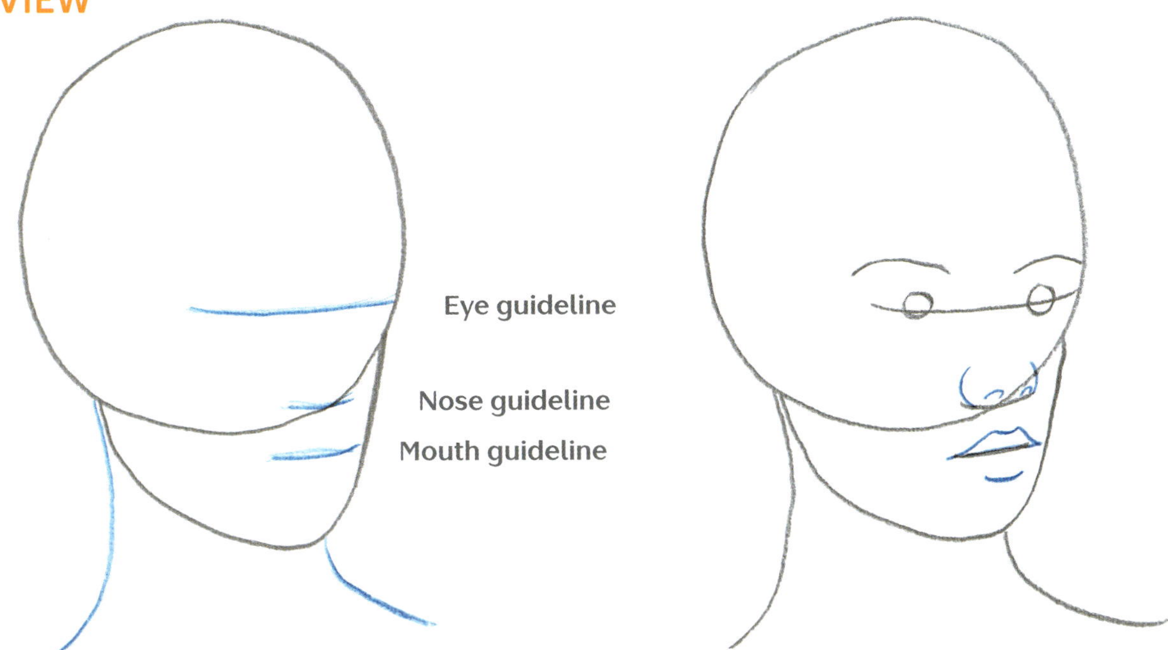

1. Draw a circle for the head and a "U" shape for the jaw. Draw a guideline at the lower third of the circle for the eyes, one at the bottom of the circle for the nose, and one about a third down the jaw for the mouth. Draw curved lines for the neck and shoulders.

2. Add two circles for irises and slightly curved lines for the eyebrows. Using a variety of small curved lines, draw the bottom of the nose, the nostrils, and the upper and lower lips. The upper lip is usually smaller than the lower lip.

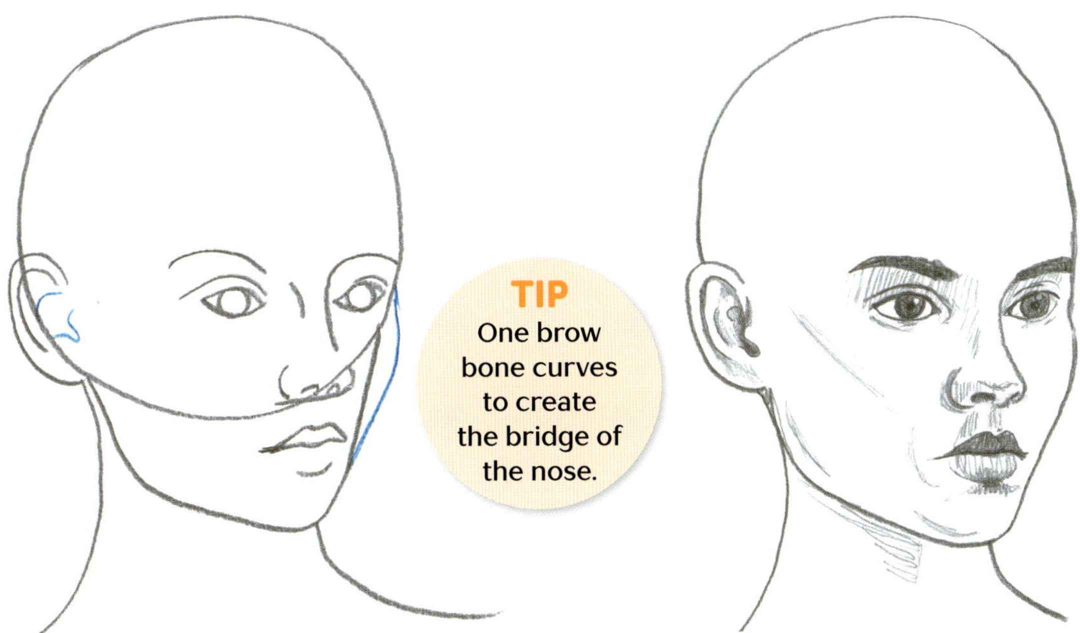

3. Add two rounded football shapes for the eyes around the irises. Draw the ear, which should span from the eye guideline to where the circle and jawline meet. Draw a set of curved lines above the eyes for the eyelids and a set for the brow bones. Refine the shape of the face.

4. Erase the guidelines and refine the features: thicken the eyebrows and add value to the lips, nose, cheekbone, ear, and neck.

THE EYE

Most artists are fascinated with drawing eyes, and for good reason! No other small subject contains so much beautiful detail.

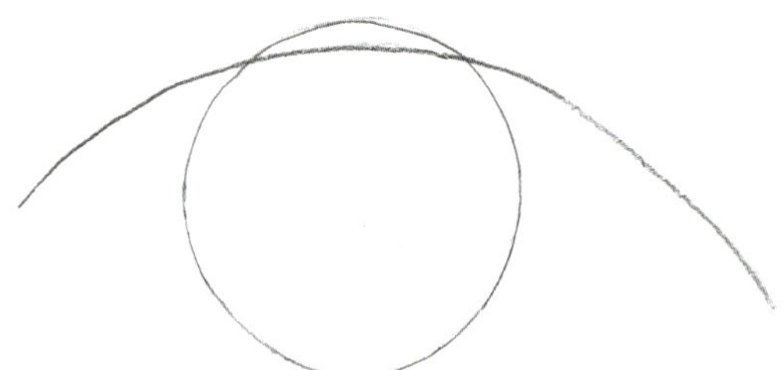

1. Draw a circle for the iris. Then draw an arch cutting through the very top of the circle for the top of the eyelid.

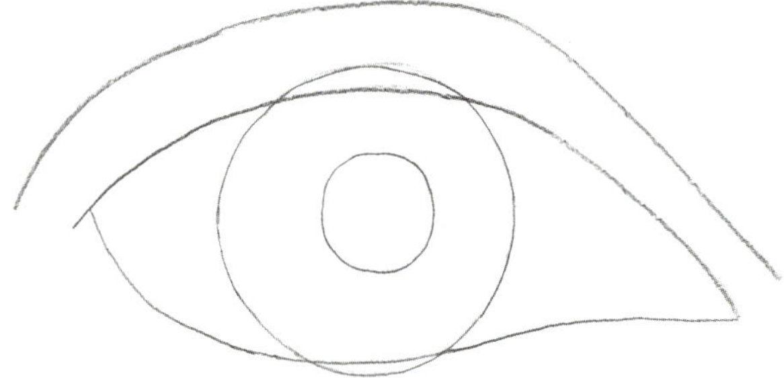

2. Above the top eyelid curve, draw a curved line that follows it to create the eyelid. Finish the football shape of the eye with a curved line that cuts through the very base of the iris. Draw a circle in the center of the iris for the pupil.

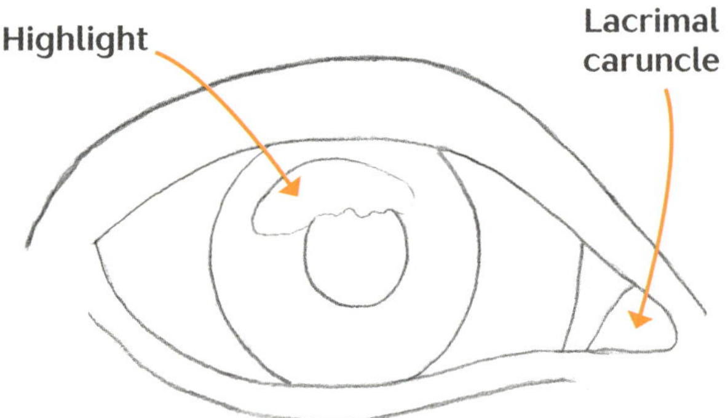

3. Draw a kidney-shaped highlight in the eye, a curved line for the lower lid, and curved lines for the lacrimal caruncle (the meaty part of the eye that is near the bridge of the nose).

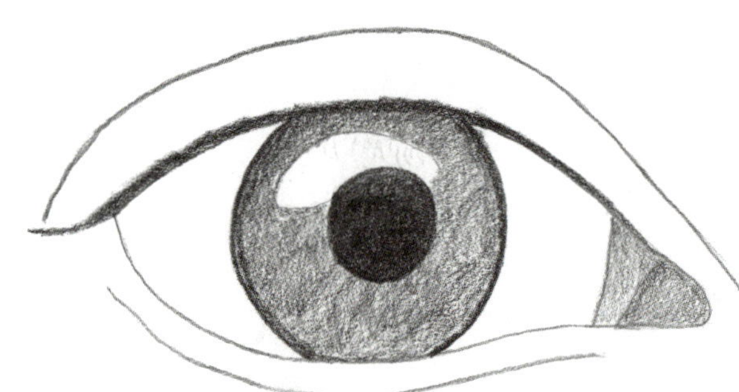

4. Begin to add tone. The iris should have a light layer of tone while the pupil should be darker. Darken the upper lid and the lacrimal caruncle.

TIPS FOR EYE-CATCHING EYES

Follow these tips to make your eyes more lifelike.

- The pupil should be black and the iris lighter.
- Make the pupils and the eyebrows the darkest areas on the face. There are exceptions, but this applies for most faces.
- Draw "spokes" radiating from the pupil for detail.
- Leave a white highlight somewhere in the iris.
- Make the upper lash line darker than the lower one.
- Draw the lashes shorter as they grow toward the center of the face. They should curve and fan outward as you move to the outer edge.
- Eyelashes are darker where they meet the eyelids.

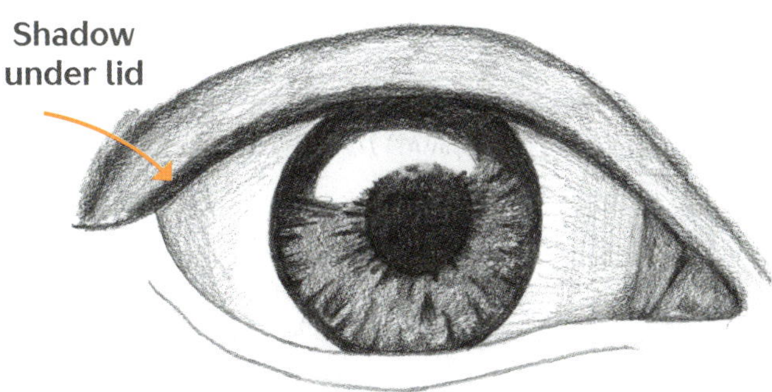

5. Add spokes and dark lines radiating from the pupil. Darken the edge around the iris and add a very light layer of tone to the lid, the white of the eye, and the lacrimal caruncle.

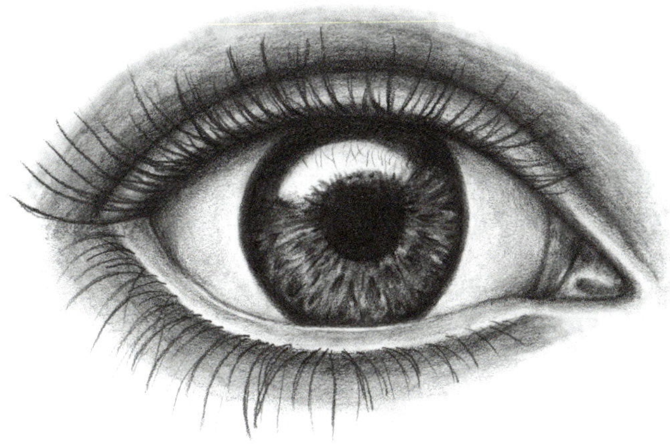

6. Draw a light layer of lashes. Continue to refine the details of the eye with shading.

DRAW REALISTIC EYEBROWS

Every eyebrow is different, but they all share similar traits. These tips can help you draw eyebrows that look natural.

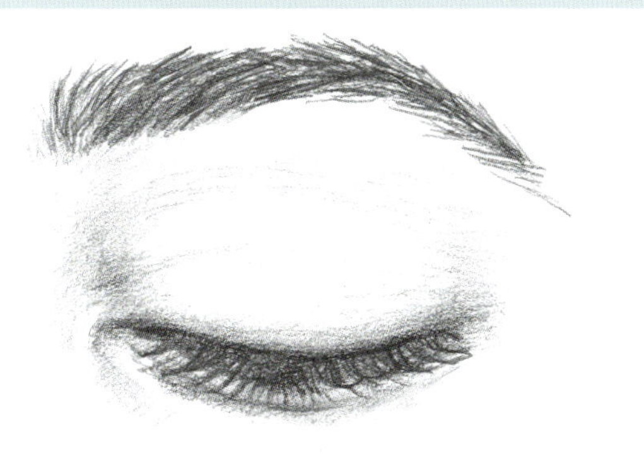

- The length of a brow is slightly longer than the width of the eye.
- Don't outline the eyebrow. It will be difficult to erase and look unnatural.
- Keep strokes thin. Parts of the brow may knit together and appear blended, but there are a lot of areas where individual hairs stand out.
- Eyebrow strokes are not a predictable pattern. They can grow up, down, and from the sides.
- Draw the eyebrows thinner toward the ears. Hairs near the center are darker and overlap more. Some hairs overlap at the ends, too.

These are three examples of eyebrows that do not look natural.

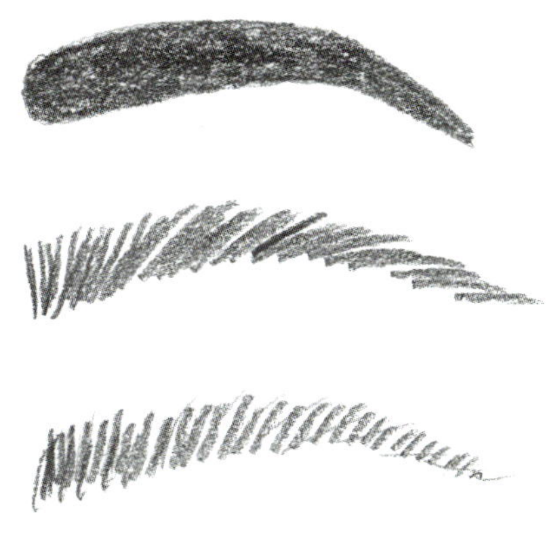

THE EAR

The curving contours of the inner ear are fun to draw! Spend some time studying photographs to learn the right way to draw them.

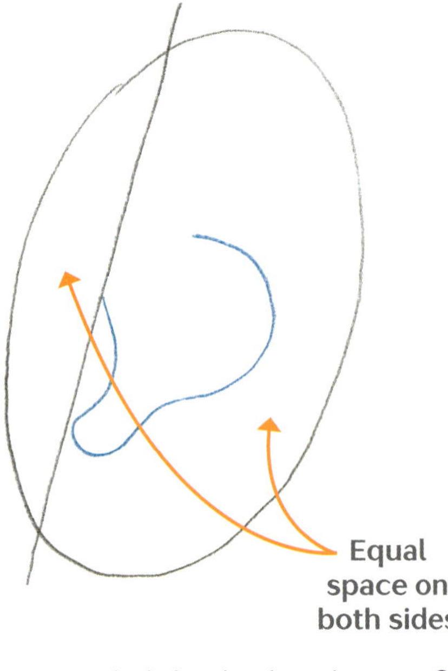

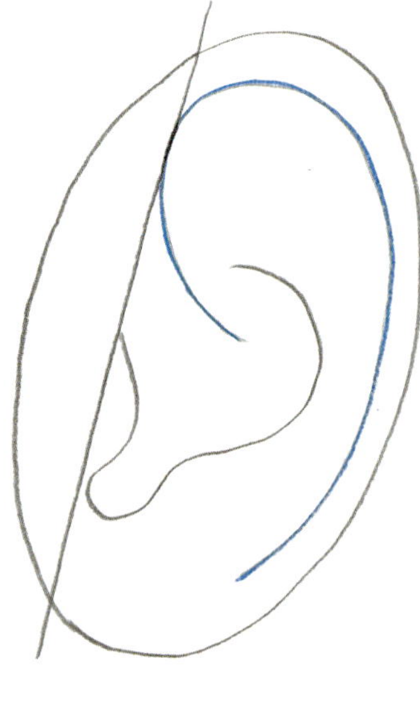

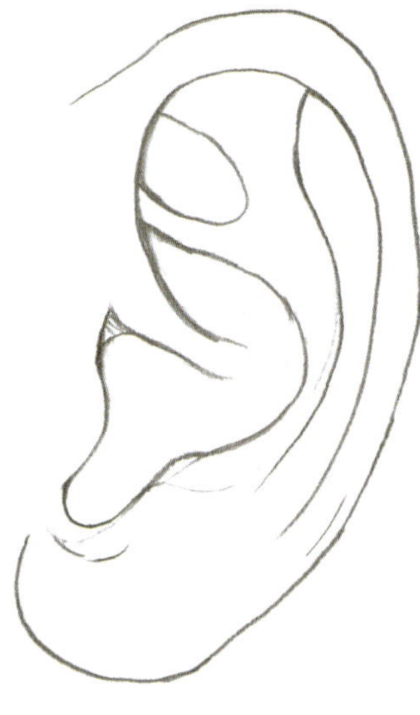

1. Draw a slightly tilted oval. Ears are not perfectly vertical. They angle away from the face at the top. Draw a diagonal line to mark where the ear attaches to the head. The line should be about one-fifth inside the oval. Starting about halfway down the line, draw a curved "question mark" shape for the inner ear.

2. Starting from inside the previous shape, draw a curved line that touches the diagonal line, then follows the curve of the oval to create a contour for the ridge on the outer ear.

3. Add more curves to create the "Y" shape inside the ear. Add a curve to the bottom of the ear for the earlobe and further refine the contours of the inner ear. Erase the guidelines.

PLACING THE EARS

When drawing a portrait, placing the ears correctly is crucial for achieving a realistic likeness. A simple guideline to follow is to start the ears around the same level as the eyes and align the top with the eyebrows. The bottom of the ears should align with the base of the nose. Remember that ears come in various shapes and sizes, so observe reference images or your own ears for guidance. Practice drawing ears from different angles to improve your understanding of their structure and placement. With time and practice, you'll develop a better eye for positioning ears accurately in your portraits.

THE NOSE

The nose might look complicated, but it's really just a few basic shapes that can be tweaked to show all the different, unique noses there are.

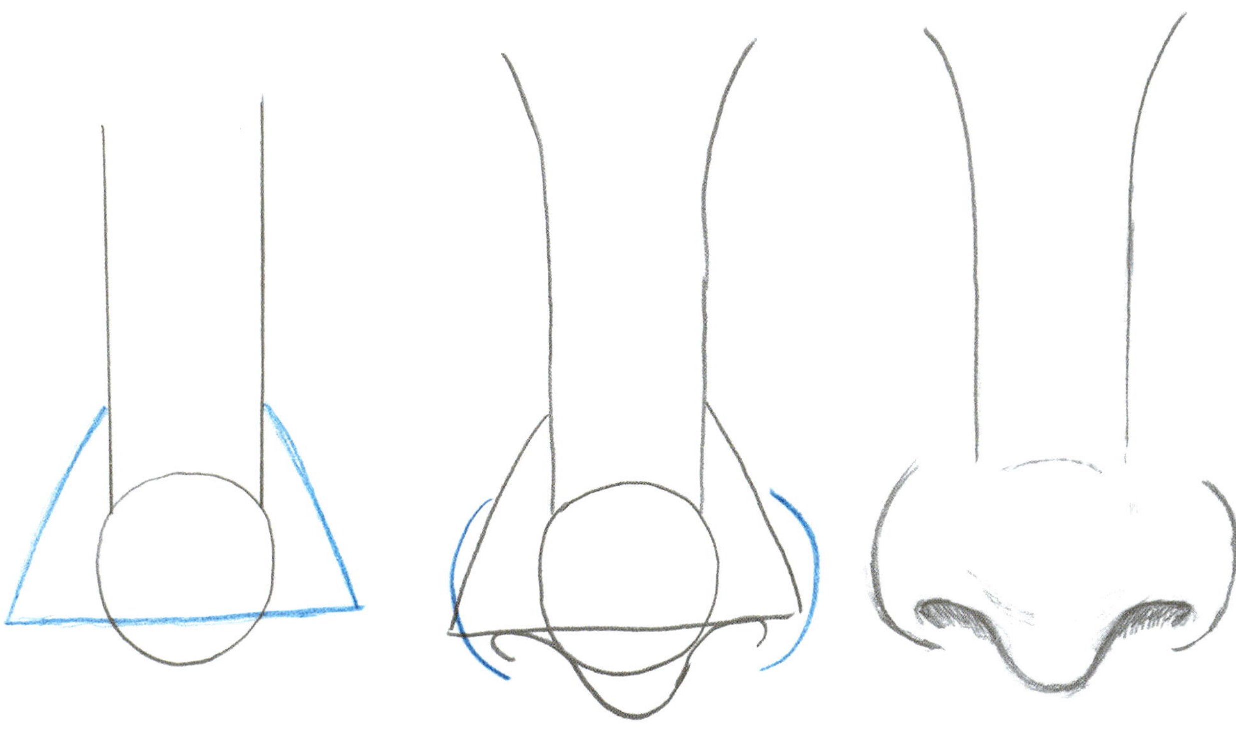

1. Draw a circle for the ball of the nose and two vertical lines on each side for the bridge of the nose. Draw a horizontal line about a quarter of the way up from the bottom of the circle. Then draw two angled lines on either side to form the nostrils, making a triangle.

2. Add curved lines that flare outward to the top of the bridge of the nose. These will lead into the brow bones. Add curved lines at the points of the triangle to refine the shape of the nose. Add a "U" shape under the circle for the tip of the nose, and draw curved lines on either side for the nostrils.

3. Erase the guidelines. Most of the shape of the nose will be formed by shading, which helps it look more realistic compared to the hard lines of the initial sketch.

THE MOUTH

A mouth can show so much personality, but before we move on to expressions (page 69), you'll want to master the basics.

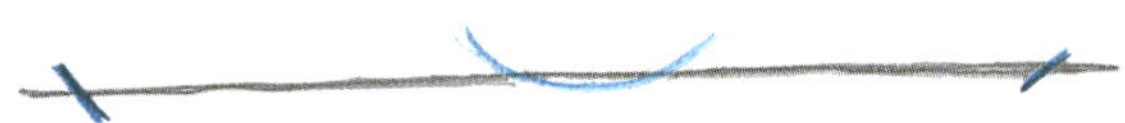

1. Draw a horizontal guideline. Add two short diagonal lines on either side for the corners of the mouth. In the center, draw a wide "U" shape.

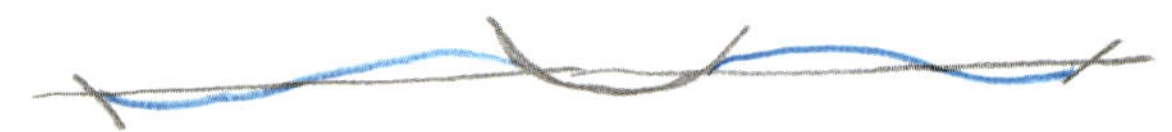

2. Draw curved lines from each side of the "U" that connect to the corners of the mouth. They should curve above the guideline, then dip below it where they touch the corners of the mouth. This is where the lips meet.

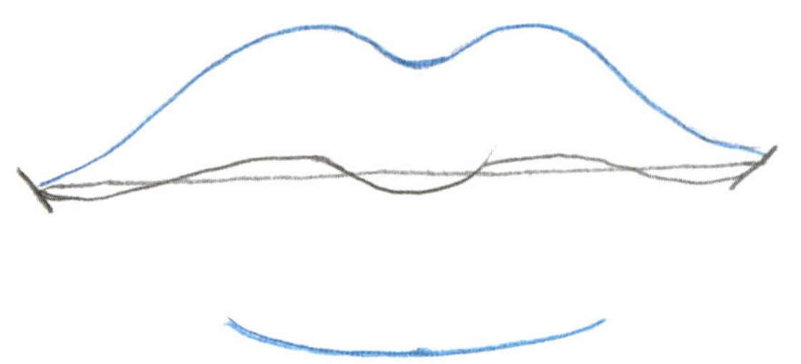

3. Draw another "U" shape above the first one. Then, connect the "U" to the corners of the mouth with curved lines. Draw a hint of a curved line underneath to indicate the bottom lip. The lower lip is usually fuller than the upper lip and is not usually connected with a solid line.

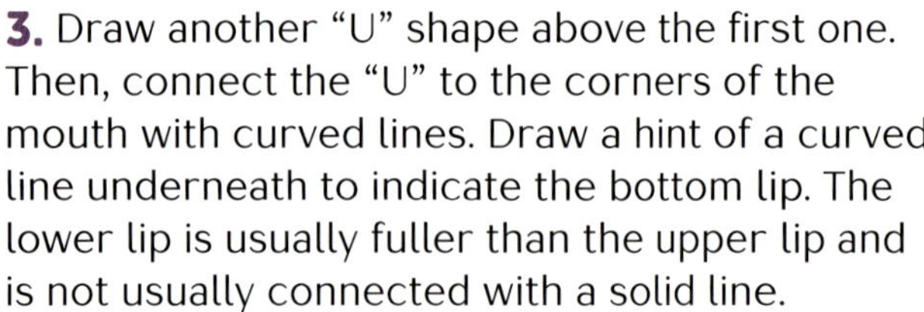

TIP
For fuller lips, draw the "U" higher, or for leaner lips, bring it closer to the first "U."

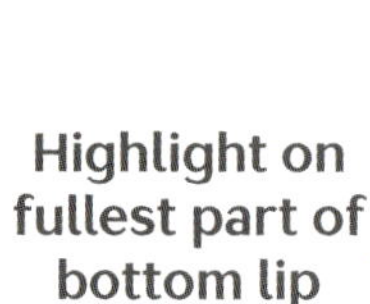

Highlight on fullest part of bottom lip

4. Thicken the line between the lips and the curve that forms the bottom lip. This shows where the lip recedes toward the face and indicates fullness. Refine the lips by adding texture and shading.

THE TEETH

Human teeth are an important part of any portrait that features a smile, but they can be intimidating to draw realistically. Shapes, sizes, and angles of teeth can vary greatly from person to person or even tooth to tooth, so it is important to observe when you're drawing.

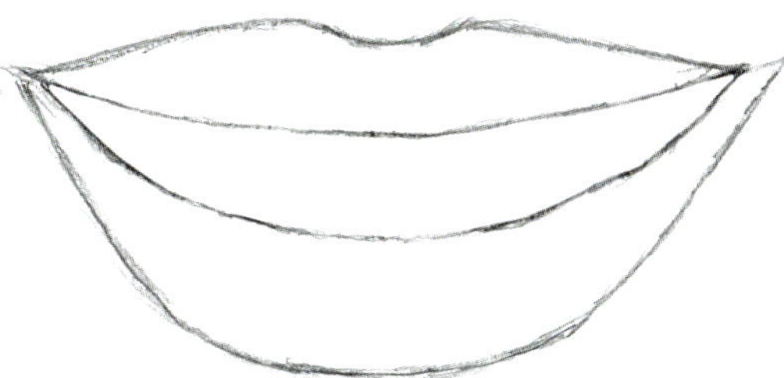

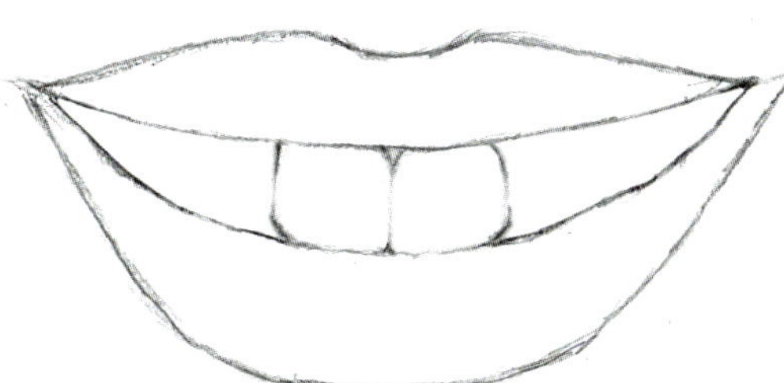

1. Draw a basic outline sketch of the mouth, as shown on the previous page. Create a half-moon shape in the middle where the teeth will go.

2. Draw the two center teeth, taking care to include the gumline curve above each tooth. On some people, the gumline is covered, and on others, it is clearly visible.

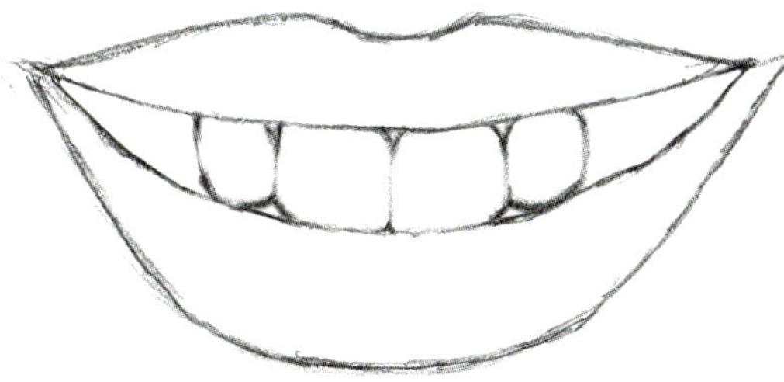

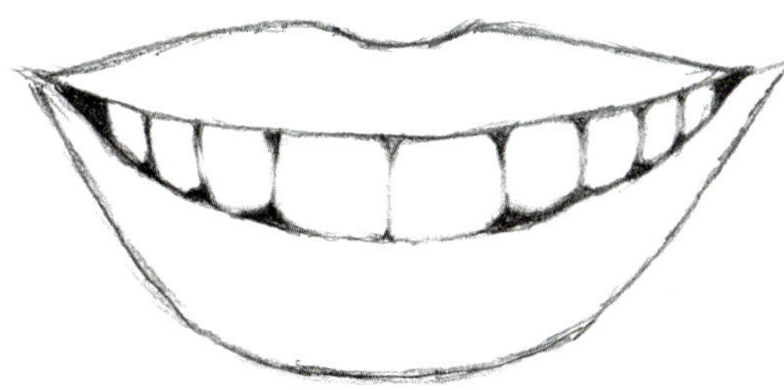

3. Draw the teeth on either side of the front teeth, using lighter lines to separate them. Avoid drawing them as mirror images. Notice the size difference and placement.

4. Draw the rest of the teeth. Find the areas that have the darkest shadows, usually between the teeth near the top and bottom, and fill them in with tone.

THE RIGHT WAY & THE WRONG WAY

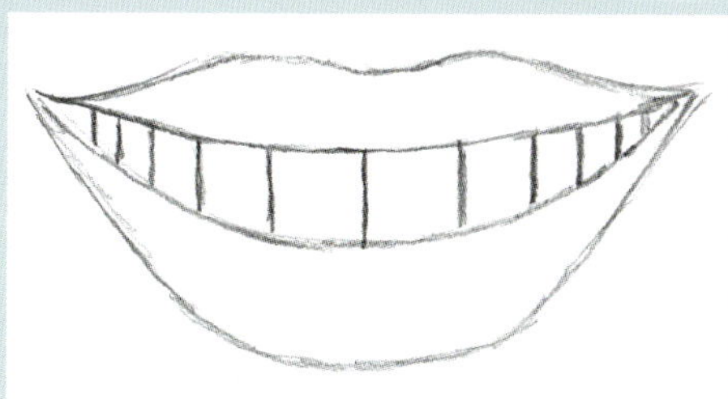

Wrong! Teeth are drawn as perfect rectangles.

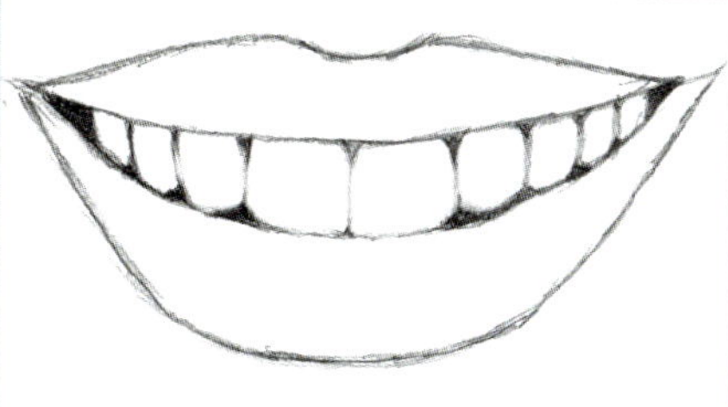

Right! Teeth are slightly rounded and not perfectly parallel.

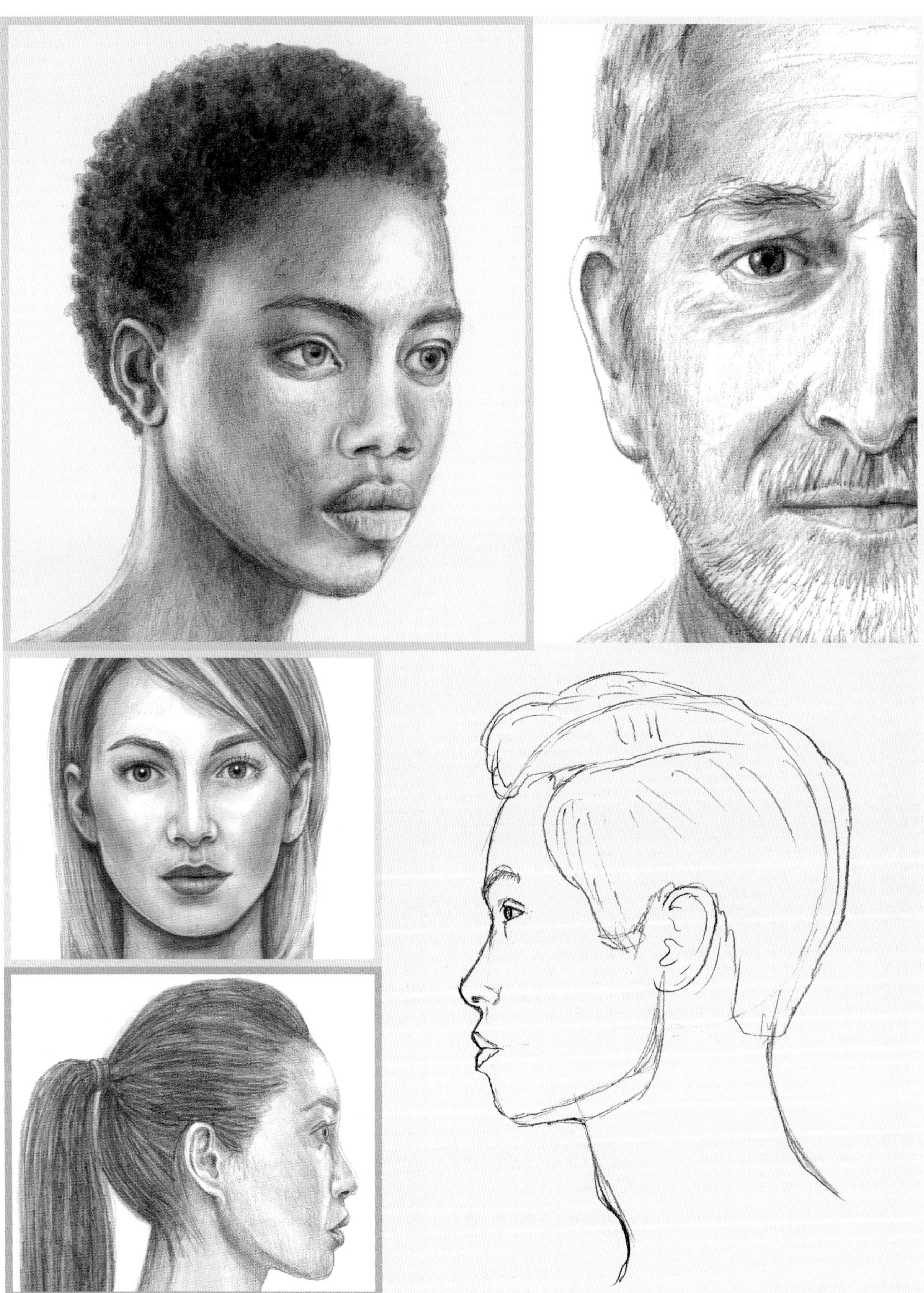

Chapter 2

DRAWING
FACES

Even though they are all made up of the same features—the eyes, nose, and mouth—everyone's face is unique to them, due to genetics and personal preferences.

In this chapter, we'll practice putting the basic features together to draw different faces in a variety of views. While we will draw the hair in these portraits, our primary focus is on the facial features. (We'll go more in-depth about drawing hairstyles in Chapter 4.)

MASCULINE FACE

FRONT VIEW

In more masculine faces, the neck is usually shorter, thicker, and features an Adam's apple. The jawline and chin are prominent, and the eyebrows are thick with rough edges.

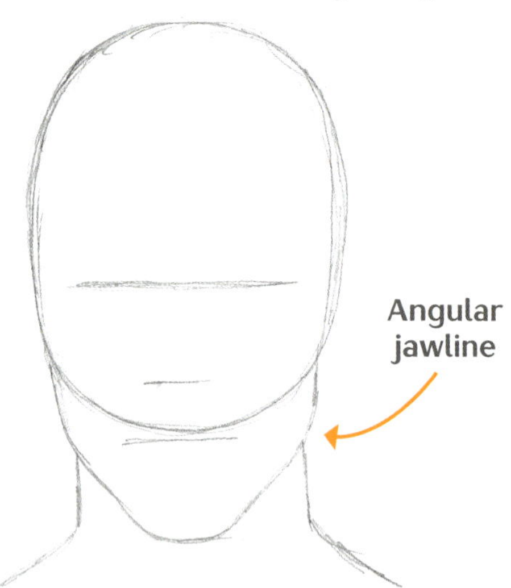

Draw the Basics

1. Draw a head following the steps on page 38. Include all necessary guidelines for the eyes, mouth, and nose. For a masculine face, the chin and jawline should be angular. Sketch the neck and the tops of the shoulders.

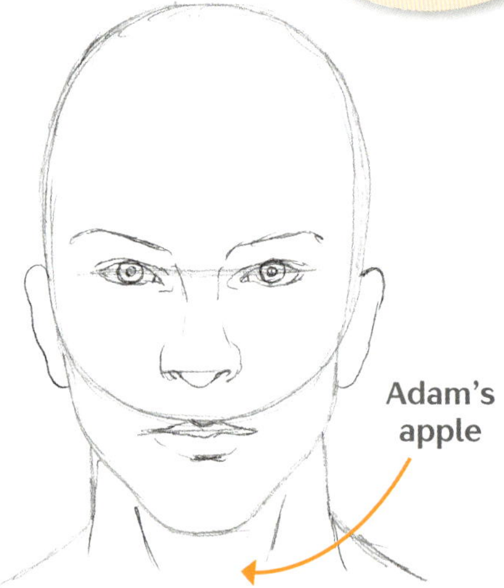

2. Using the guidelines, draw the eyeballs, including the irises and pupils. Draw a guideline for the eyebrows. Sketch the nose, nostrils, and mouth. Draw the ears. Begin to refine all the features: add eyelids and the Adam's apple.

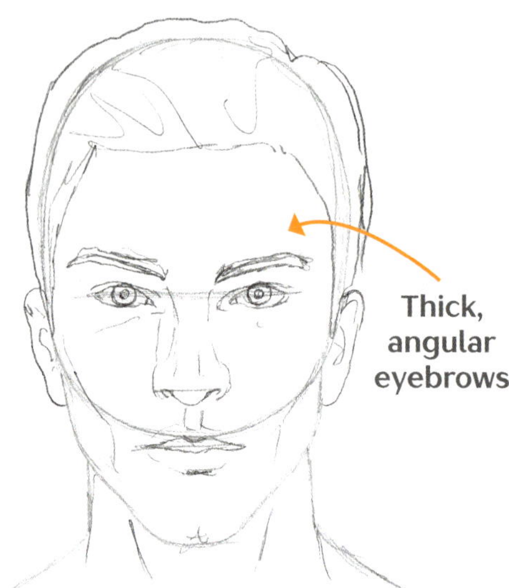

Add Details

3. Add more details to the features. Thicken the eyebrows. Add contours to the ears, cheeks, nose, and chin.

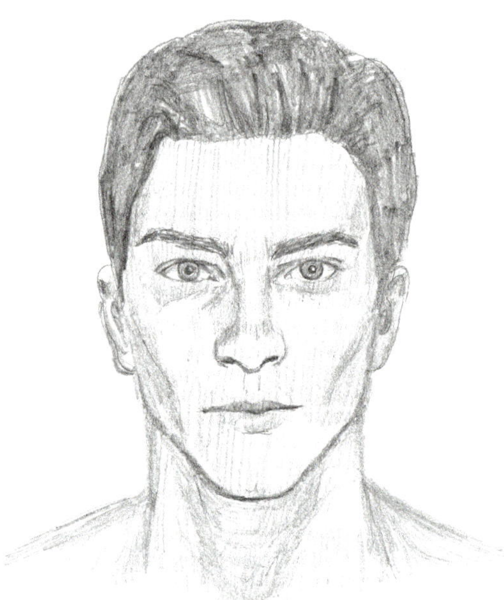

4. Erase the guidelines. Add a light layer of tone to the face. Define the cheekbones, neck, ears, and eye area with shadows. The hair, eyebrows, irises, pupils, upper lip, and nostrils should be the darkest tones.

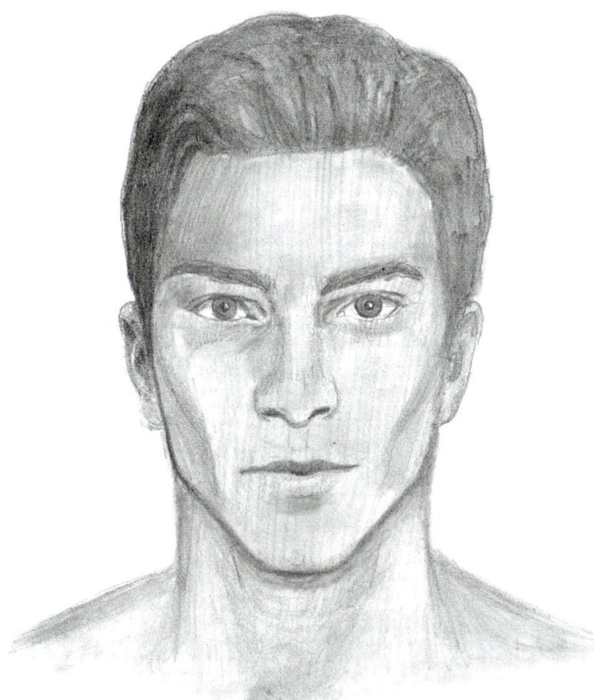

5. Smooth the tones using a tissue on larger areas and a blending tool on the smaller areas.

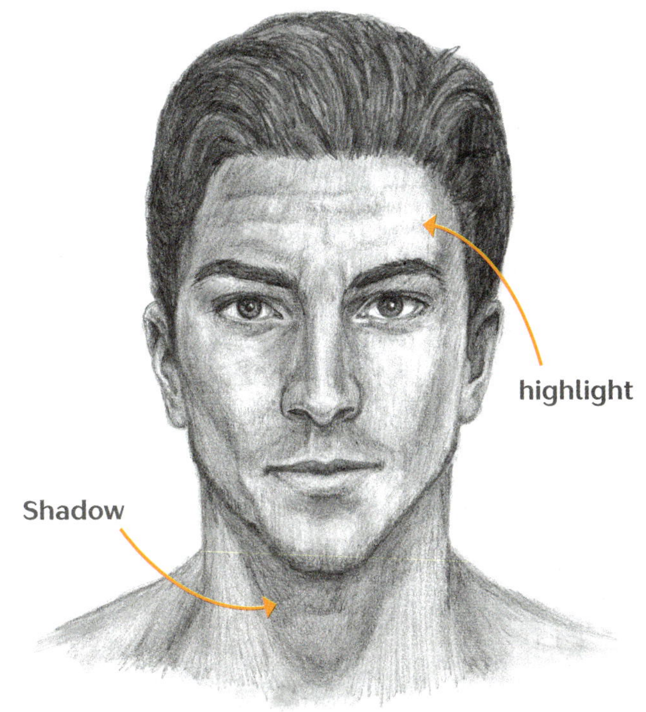

Build Contrast

6. Add another layer of tone, concentrating on contrast. Deepen shading and lines on the face, giving each shadow sharp, angular edges. Pay attention to where there should be highlights and keep those areas light. Use short strokes to define the hair and eyebrows. Keep the eyelashes very short.

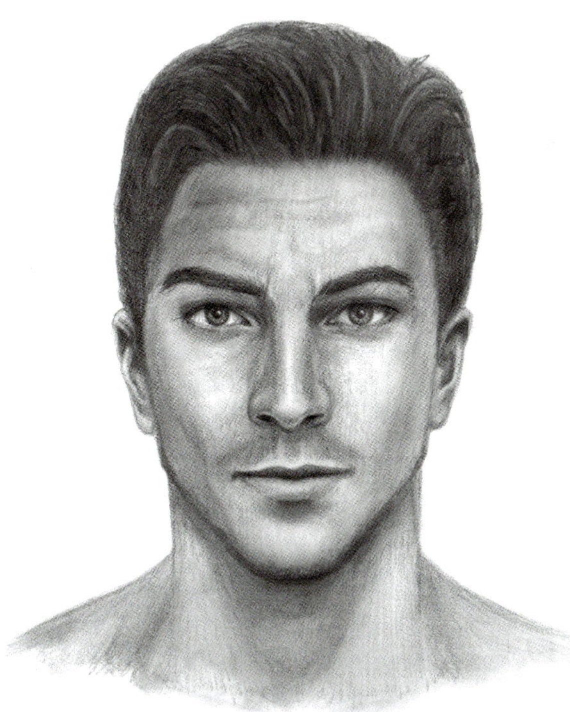

7. Smooth and blend tones further. Use a kneaded eraser to accentuate the highlighted areas.

PLACING THE HAIRLINE

No two hairlines are alike! They'll vary in shape and position, depending on your subject, so observe reference images or your own hairline for guidance. Practice sketching different hairlines from various angles to develop a better understanding of their positioning in relation to the rest of the face.

PROFILE VIEW

A masculine profile is typically angular and chiseled, but it's important to note that since there is a plethora of variations in facial features, every profile will be unique!

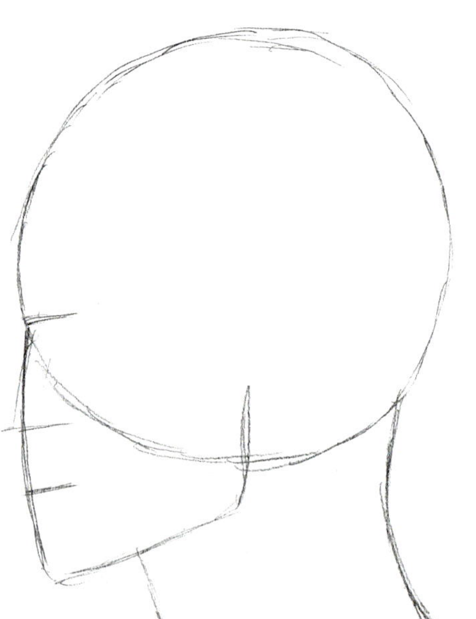

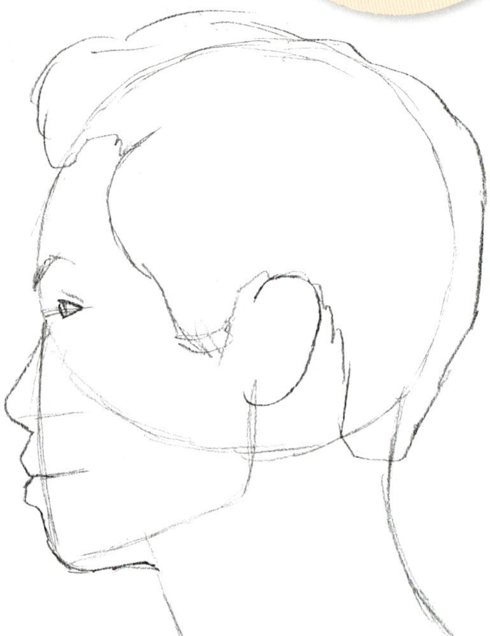

Draw the Basics

1. Draw a head following the steps on page 40. Include all necessary guidelines for the eyes, mouth, and nose. For a masculine face, the chin and jawline should be angular. Sketch the neck.

2. Draw a sideways triangle for the eye and add a narrow oval for the pupil. Using the guidelines, sketch the outline of the nose, lips, and chin. Add the eyebrow and the ear. Sketch in the shape of the hair.

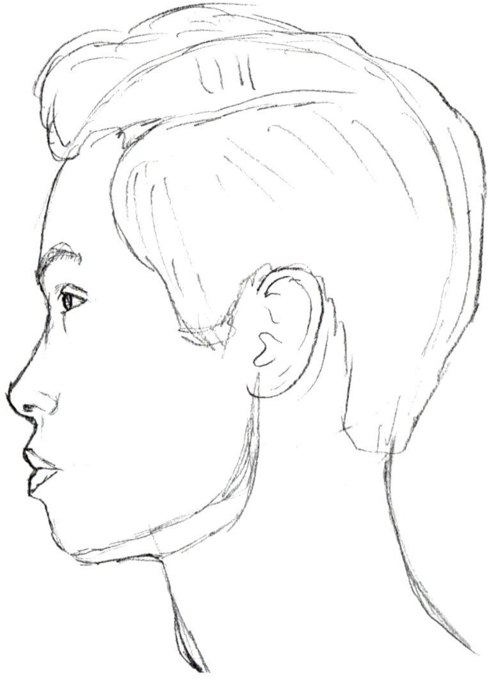

Add Details

3. Erase the guidelines no longer needed. Refine the features, including the shape of the forehead, lips, jawline, and neck. Thicken the eyebrows. Add details to the ears, eye area, nose, and hair. Delineate a shadowed area under the chin, which should follow the jawline up to the ear.

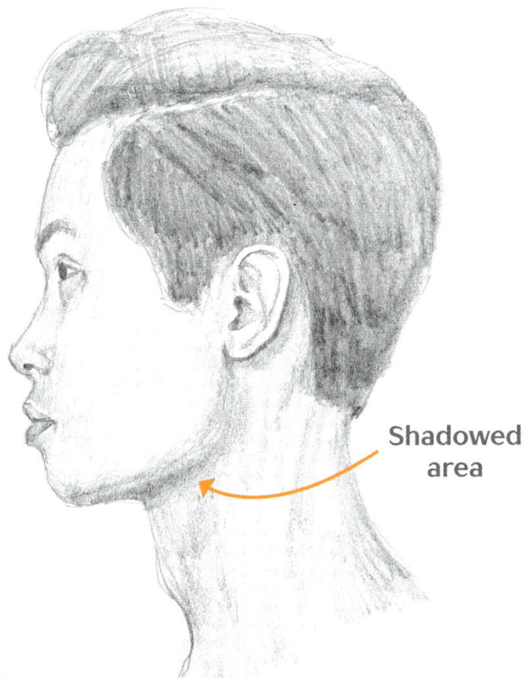

Add Tone

4. Erase the remaining guidelines. Add a light layer of tone to the face. Define the area under the chin, around the eye, inside the ear, the nose, and the lips with shading. Darken the hair, eyebrow, and pupil.

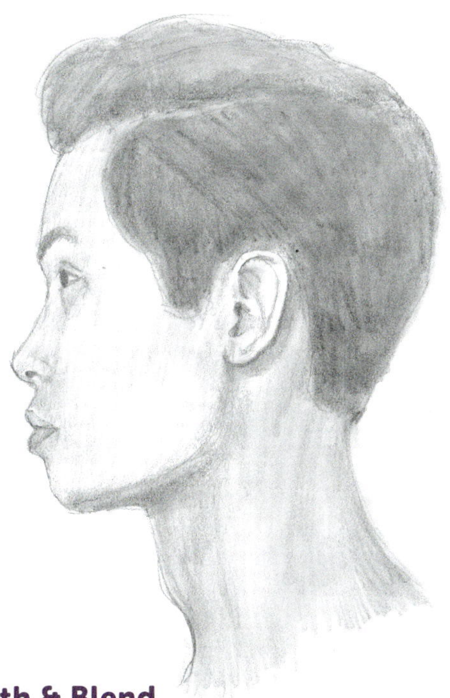

Smooth & Blend

5. Smooth tones using a tissue on larger areas and a blending tool on the smaller areas.

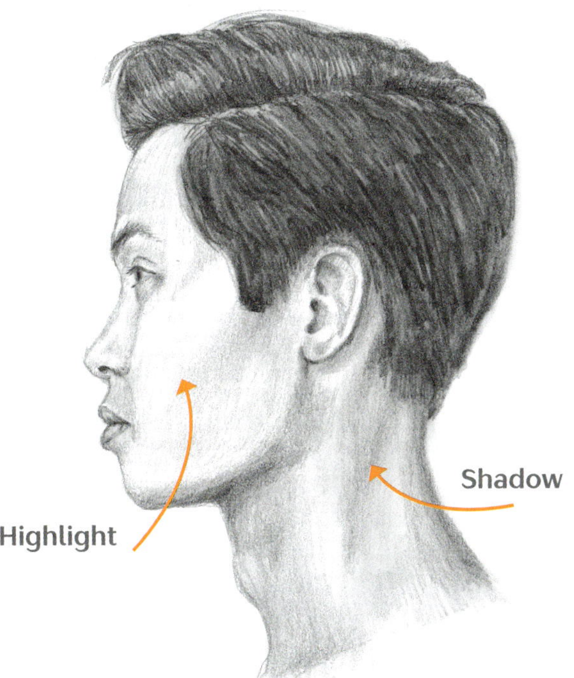

6. Add another layer of tone, concentrating on dark and light contrast. Deepen shading and lines on the face, giving each shadow sharp, angular edges. Pay attention to where there should be highlights and keep those areas light. Use short strokes to define the hair and eyebrows. Keep the eyelashes very short.

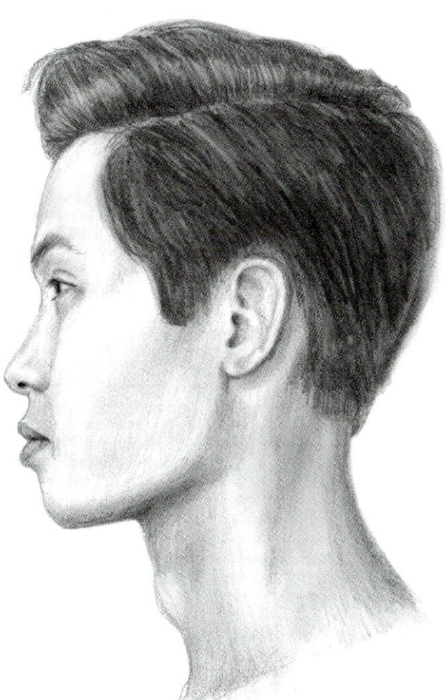

Accentuate Highlights

7. Smooth and blend tones further. Use a kneaded eraser to accentuate the highlighted areas.

3/4 VIEW

The highlights and shadows in this drawing are the result of light coming from the upper left, which illuminates the cheekbone and nose.

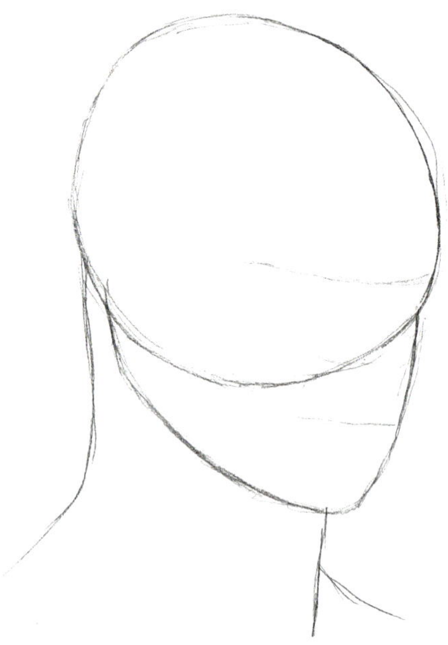

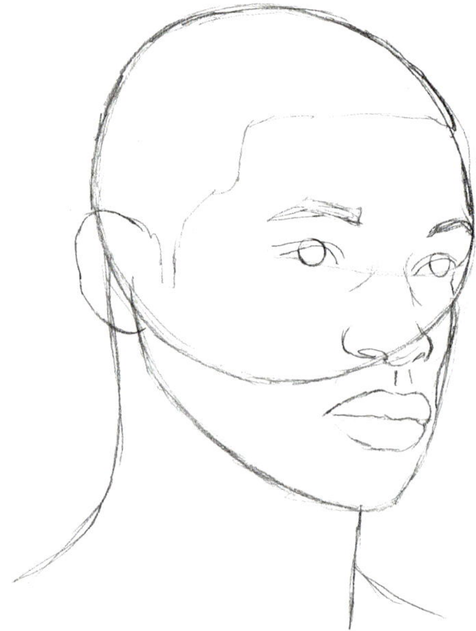

Draw the Basics

1. Draw a head following the steps on page 41. Include all necessary guidelines for the eyes, mouth, and nose. For a masculine face, the chin and jawline should be angular. Sketch the neck and shoulders.

2. Using the guidelines, draw two rounded football shapes for the eyes. Draw circles for the pupils. Sketch the eyebrows. Draw in the hairline. Sketch the nose, including the bridge and the nostrils. Sketch the mouth. Draw the ears. Begin to refine all the features: add eyelids and adjust the shape of the face.

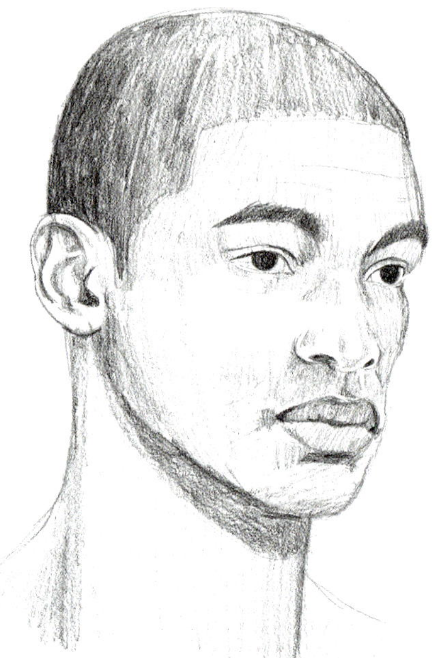

TIP
Remember that hair is not plastered to the head even with the shortest of haircuts.

Add Details

3. Erase any unneeded guidelines. Draw the ear details and lower eyelid. Add lines to the forehead. Add a light layer of tone, concentrating in the areas that will be darkest, like under the chin, inside the ear, the pupils, and any hair.

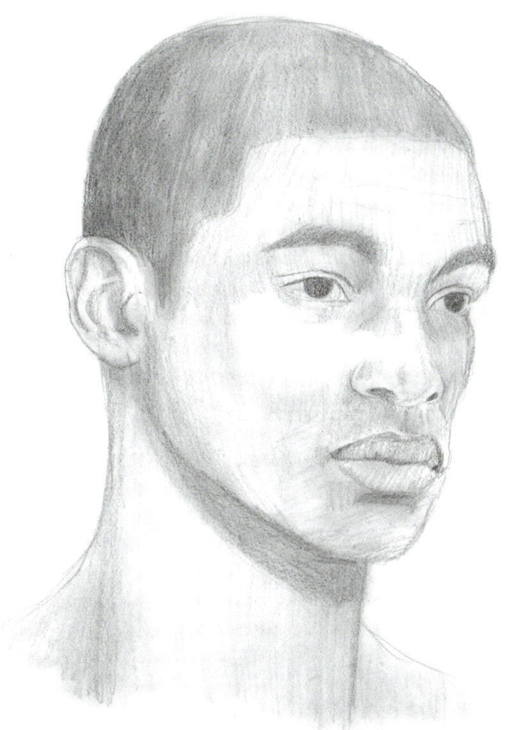

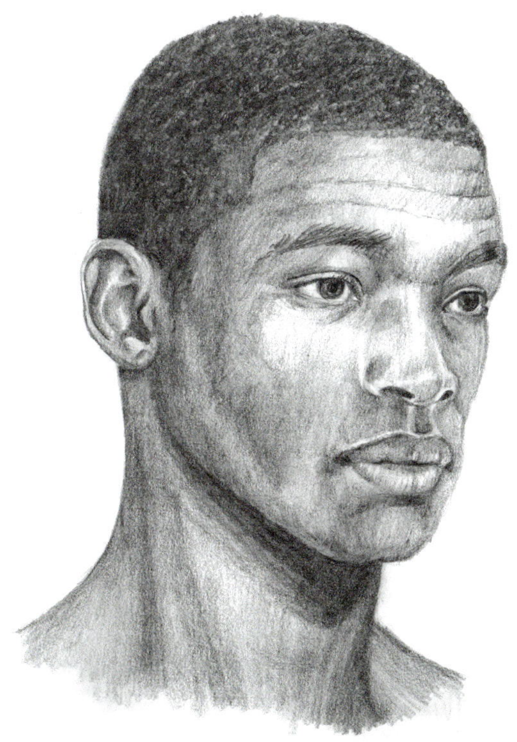

Smooth & Blend

4. Smooth tones using a tissue on larger areas and a blending tool on the smaller areas.

5. Add another layer of tone, concentrating on contrast. Deepen shading and lines on the face. Pay attention to where there should be highlights and keep those areas light. Use short strokes to define eyebrows and scumbling to create the texture of the hair. Keep the eyelashes very short.

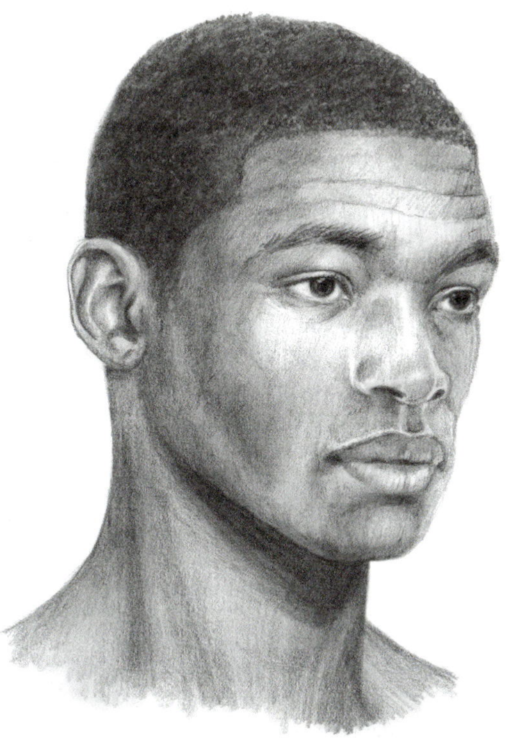

TIP

The far eye may appear slightly smaller than the closer one as it is farther from the front. Notice how close the lips are to the far side of the cheek and how much of the cheek is visible—not much in this case.

Accentuate Highlights

6. Smooth and blend tones further. Use a kneaded eraser to accentuate the highlighted areas.

FEMININE FACE

FRONT VIEW

Focus on the placement and proportions of the facial features in this drawing. Notice that they are a bit softer than in the drawings of a more masculine face.

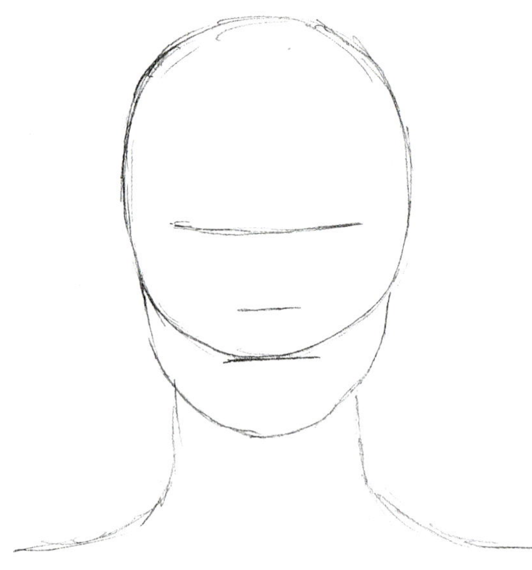

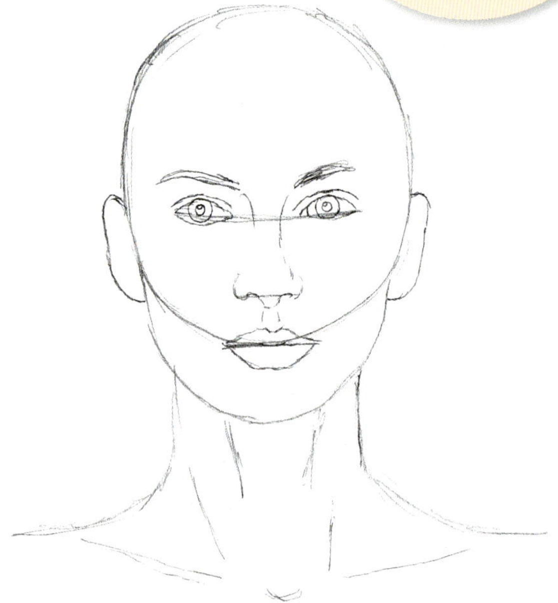

Draw the Basics

1. Draw a head following the steps on page 38. Include all necessary guidelines for the eyes, mouth, and nose. For a feminine face, the chin and jawline should be softer and more rounded. Sketch the neck and shoulders.

2. Using the guidelines, draw two rounded football shapes for the eyes. Draw circles for the irises and pupils. Sketch the eyebrows and nose. Sketch the mouth. Draw the ears. Then begin to refine all the features: add eyelids, thicken the eyebrows, and refine the nose and mouth area. Add definition to the neck and clavicle.

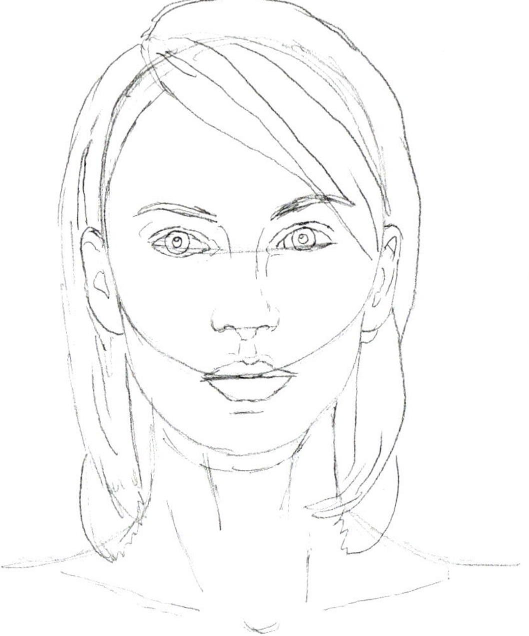

3. Draw the outline of the hair, rounding the hairline to reduce the appearance of the forehead. Begin filling in the hair with lines. Add details to the ears.

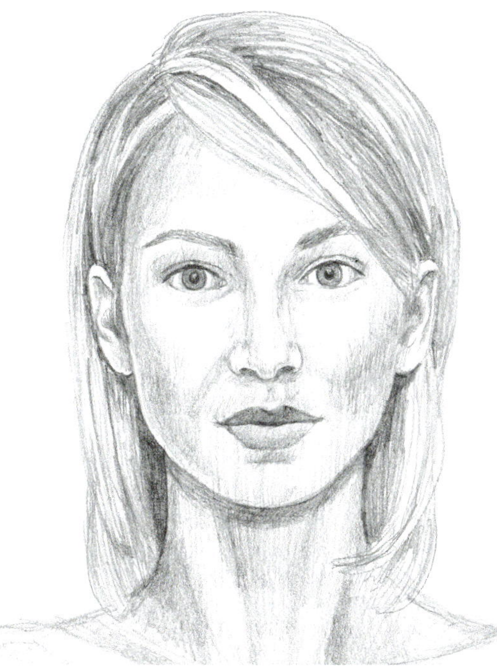 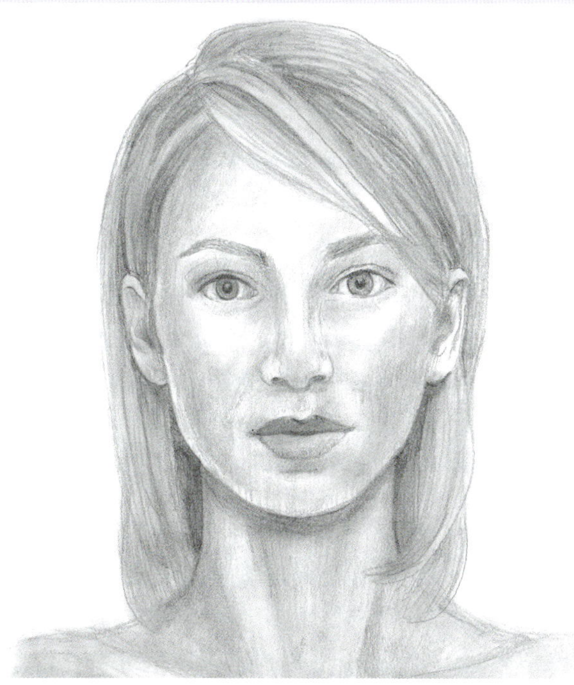

Add Tone
4. Add a light layer of tone to the face. Define the cheekbones, neck, ears, and eye area with shadows. Add dimension to the hair. The eyebrows, irises, pupils, upper lip, and nostrils should be the darkest tones.

Smooth & Blend
5. Smooth tones with a tissue on the larger areas and use a blending tool on smaller areas.

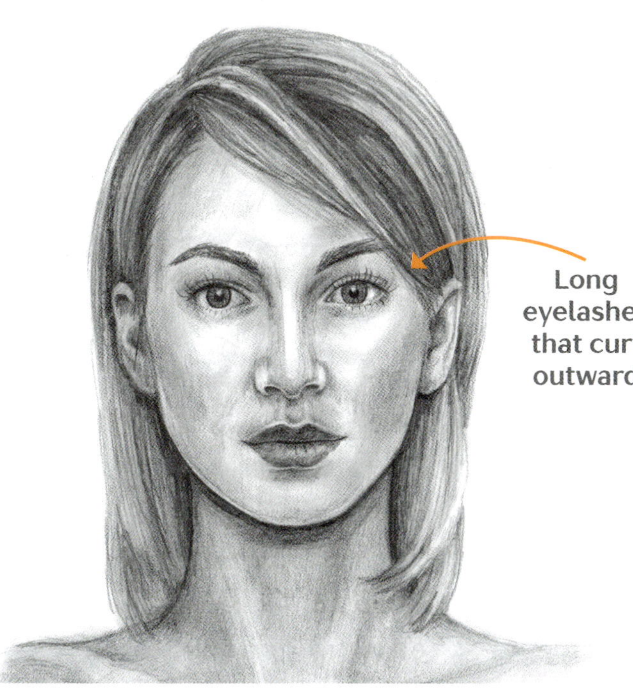

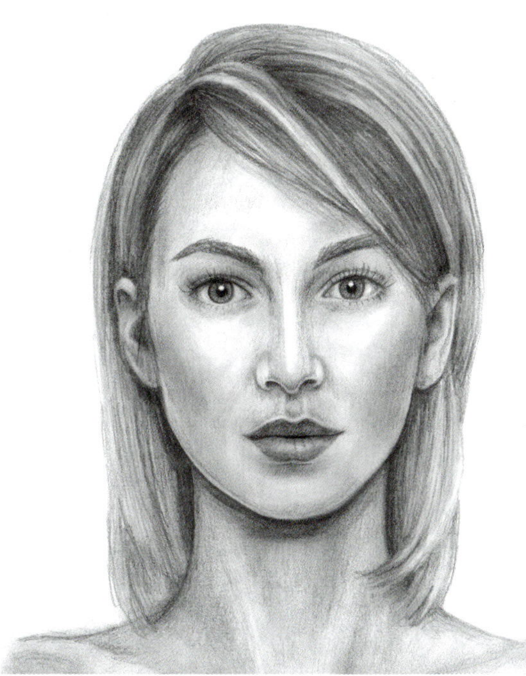

6. Soften the shadows along the edges and corners to help make the face rounder. Add another layer of tone, concentrating on the darkest areas. Use a kneaded eraser to create highlights. Add eyelashes and continue to refine features.

Build Contrast
7. Add more contrast, keeping the shadows and facial features smooth.

PROFILE VIEW

On feminine faces, there often isn't a strong line that defines the chin and jaw but rather subtle shading. Don't use a heavy pencil line to define it.

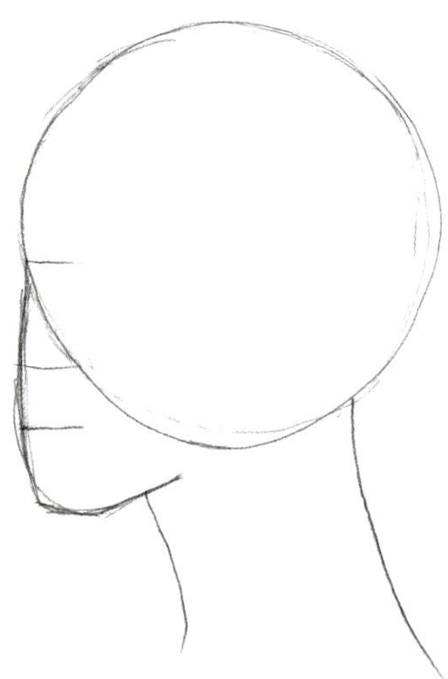

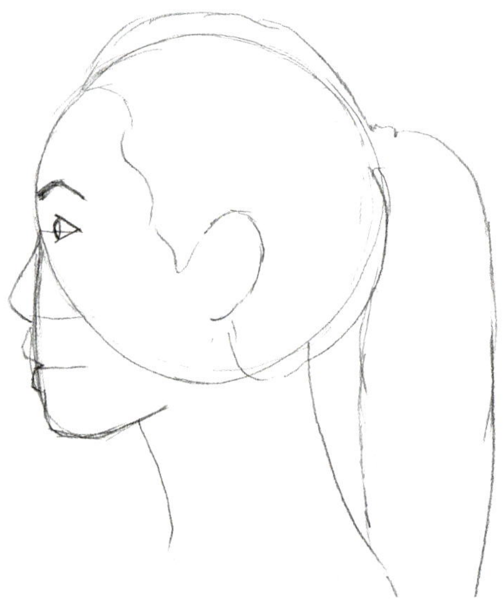

Draw the Basics

1. Draw a head following the steps on page 40. Include all necessary guidelines for the eyes, mouth, and nose. For a feminine face, the chin and jawline should be softer and more rounded. Sketch the neck and shoulders.

2. Draw a sideways triangle for the eye and add a narrow oval for the pupil. Using the guidelines, sketch the outline of the nose, lips, and chin. Add the eyebrow and the ear. Sketch the shape of the hair.

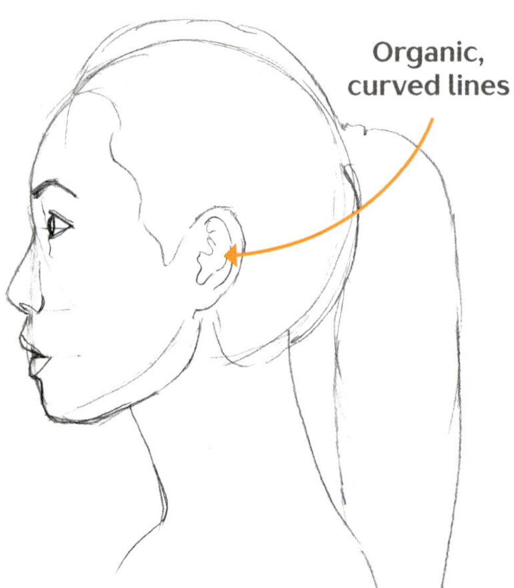

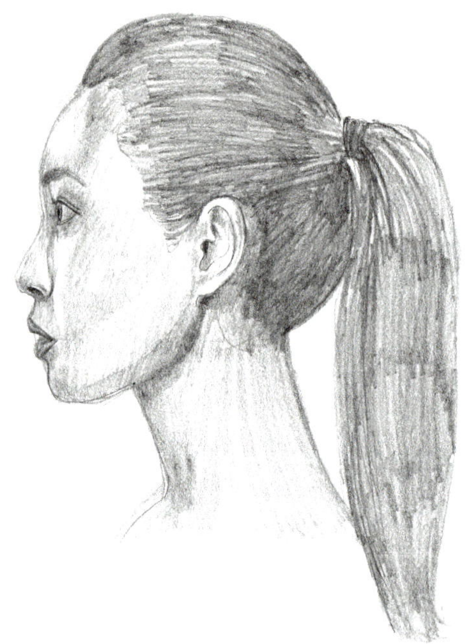

Refine the Features

3. Erase the guidelines no longer needed. Refine the features, including the shape of the forehead, lips, jawline, and neck. Thicken the eyebrows. Add details to the ears, eye area, and nose. Delineate a shadow area under the chin, which should follow the jawline up to the ear.

4. Erase the remaining guidelines. Add a light layer of tone to the face. Define the area under the chin, around the eye, inside the ear, the nose, and the lips with shading. Darken the hair, eyebrow, and pupil.

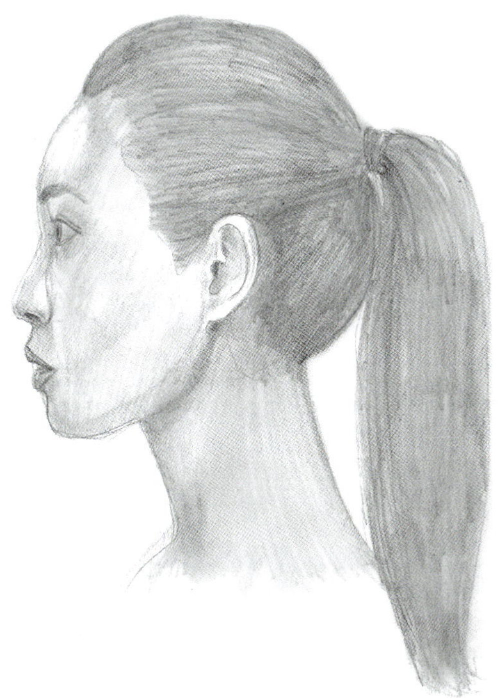

Smooth & Blend

5. Smooth tones with a tissue on the larger areas and use a blending tool on smaller areas.

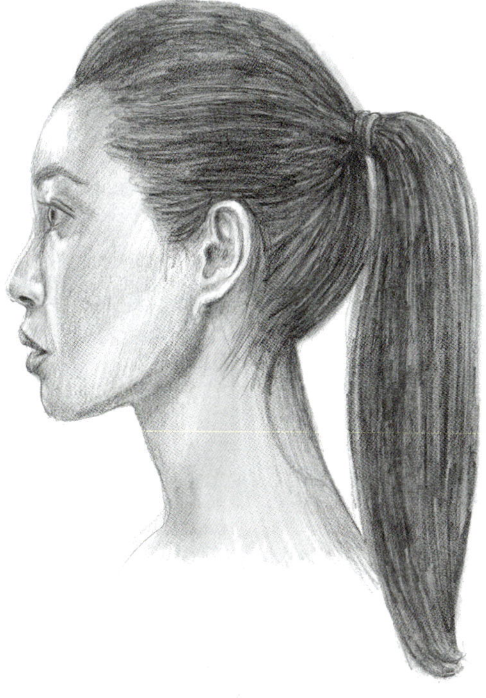

6. Add another layer of tone, concentrating on contrast. Deepen shading and lines on the face, giving each shadow sharp, angular edges. Pay attention to where there should be highlights and keep those areas light. Use short strokes to define the eyebrows, and add texture to the hair. Draw the eyelashes.

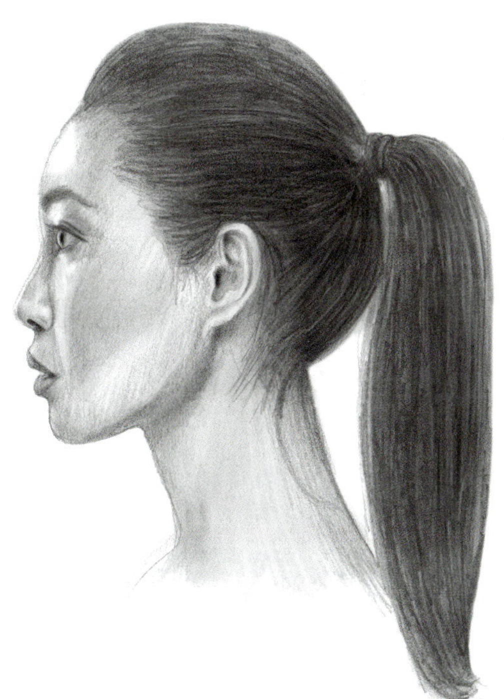

Accentuate Highlights

7. Smooth and blend tones further. Use a kneaded eraser to accentuate the highlighted areas.

TIP
You will generally see deeper shadows around the eye since it sits within the eye socket.

3/4 VIEW

The highlights in this drawing really help to bring the portrait to life, so be mindful to keep those areas lighter when adding tone and shading.

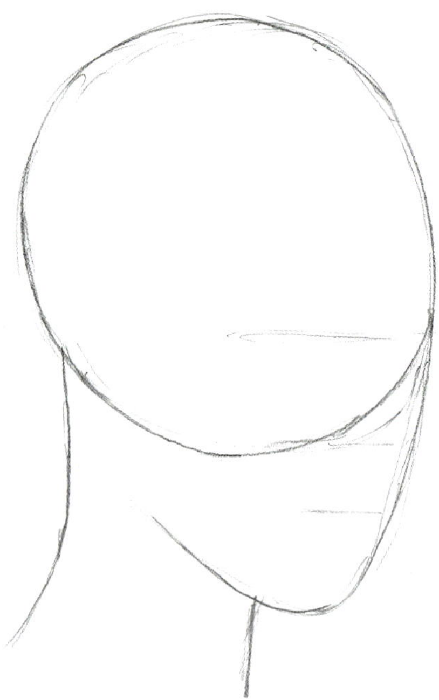

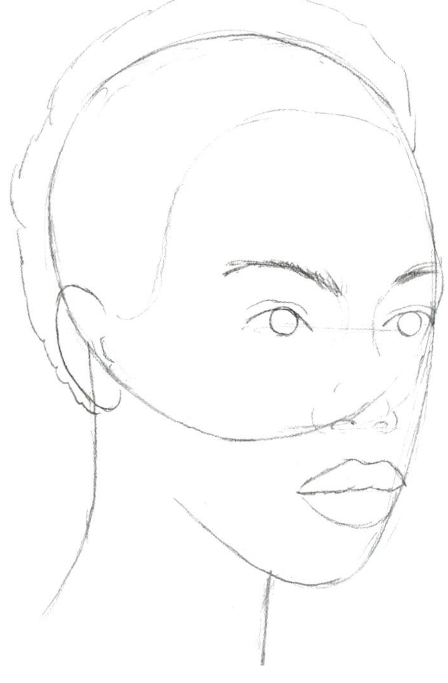

Draw the Basics

1. Draw a head following the steps on page 41. Include all necessary guidelines for the eyes, mouth, and nose. For a feminine face, the chin and jawline should be softer and more rounded. Sketch the neck.

2. Using the guidelines, draw two rounded football shapes for the eyes. Draw circles for the pupils. Sketch the eyebrows. Draw in the hairline. Sketch the nose, including the bridge and the nostrils. Sketch the mouth. Draw the ears. Begin to refine all the features: add eyelids and adjust the shape of the face to enhance the cheekbone and brow.

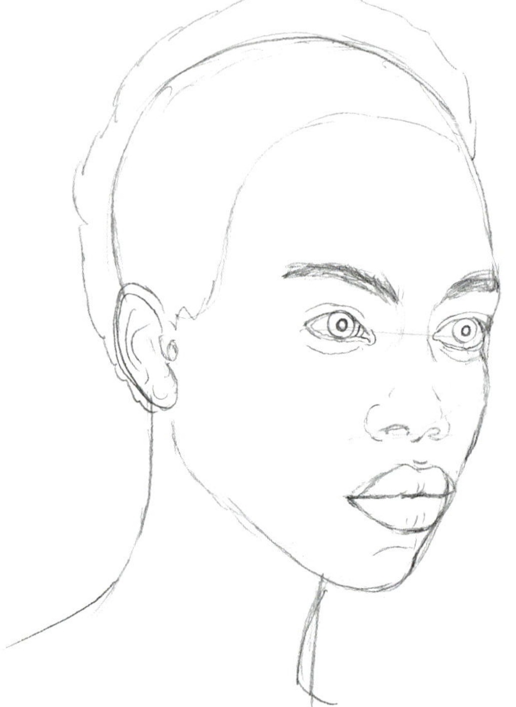

3. Erase any unneeded guidelines. Draw the ear details and lower eyelid. Refine the curve of the neck. Add definition to the mouth and chin area.

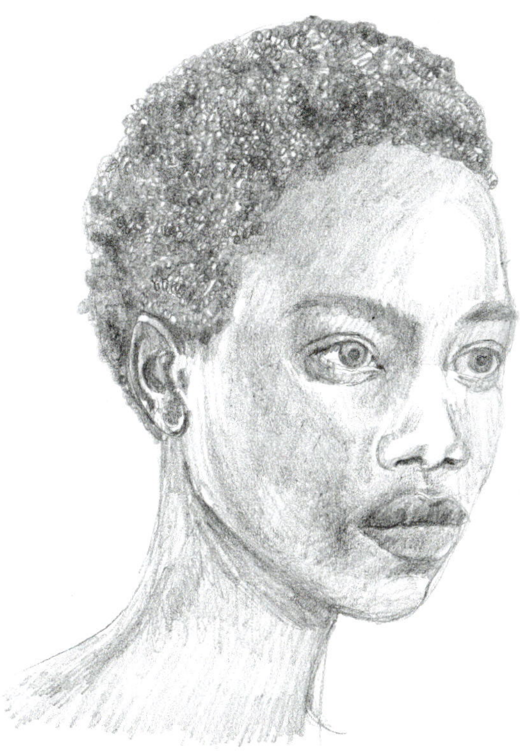

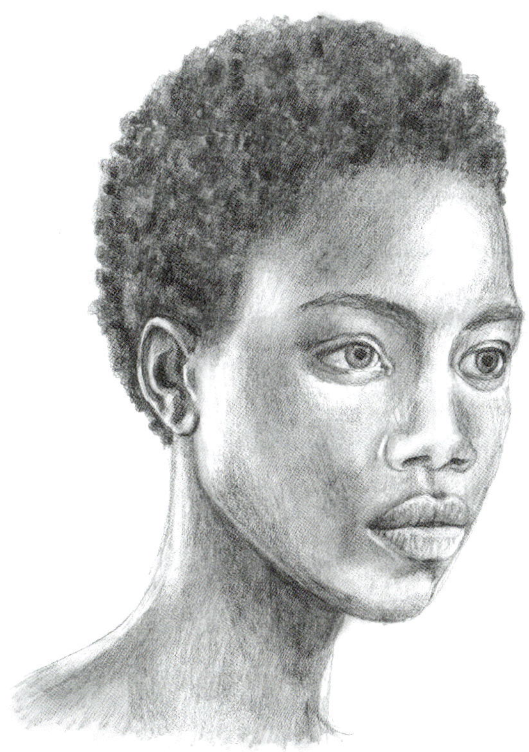

Use Scumbling

4. Use scumbling to add texture to the hair. Add a light layer of tone, concentrating in the areas that will be darkest, like under the chin, inside the ear, the pupils, and any hair. Leave areas that will be highlighted lighter.

5. Add another layer of tone, concentrating on dark and light contrast. Deepen shadows and contours of the face. Pay attention to where there should be highlights and keep those areas light. Use short strokes to define eyebrows. The hair, lips, eyes, inner ear, and nostrils should be among the darkest tones.

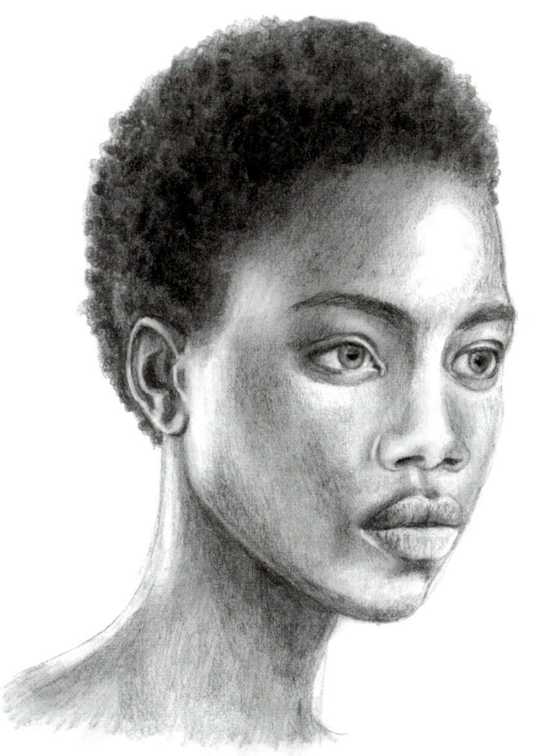

TIP
Cheekbones may be more prominent or rounder depending on the person. When shading, hint at cheekbones with value, not line.

Smooth & Blend

6. Smooth and blend tones further. Use a kneaded eraser to accentuate the highlighted areas.

OLDER FACE

One of the most important things to master when drawing an older person is creating realistic wrinkles and skin texture.

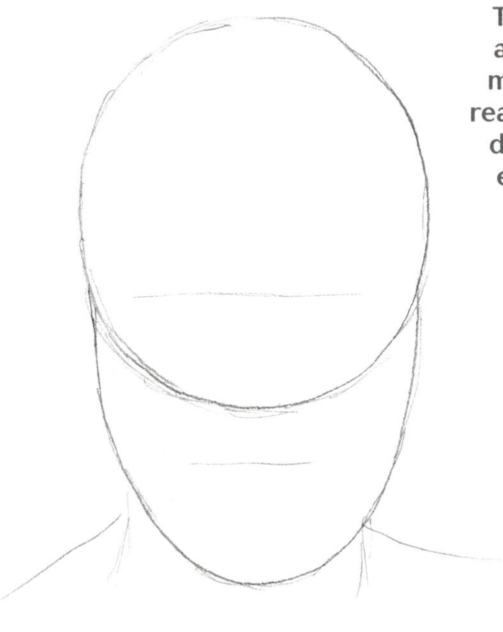

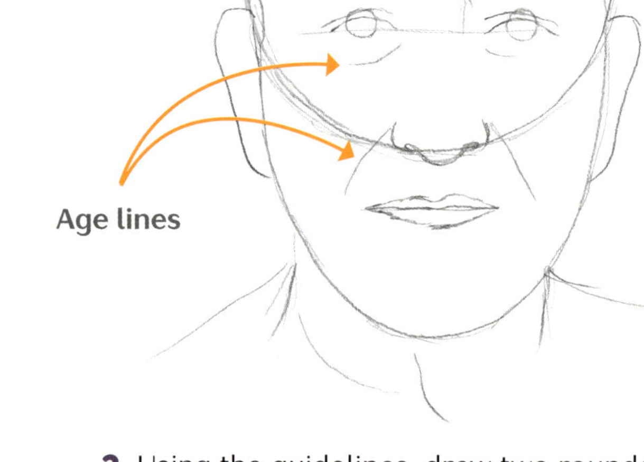

Draw the Basics

1. Draw a head following the steps on page 38. Include all necessary guidelines for the eyes, mouth, and nose. Sketch the neck and shoulders.

2. Using the guidelines, draw two rounded football shapes for the eyes. Draw circles for the irises. Sketch the nose and nostrils. Sketch the mouth. Draw the ears. Draw the hairline. Begin to refine all the features: add eyelids and draw a guideline for the eyebrows. Sketch the nostrils, and add definition to the neck.

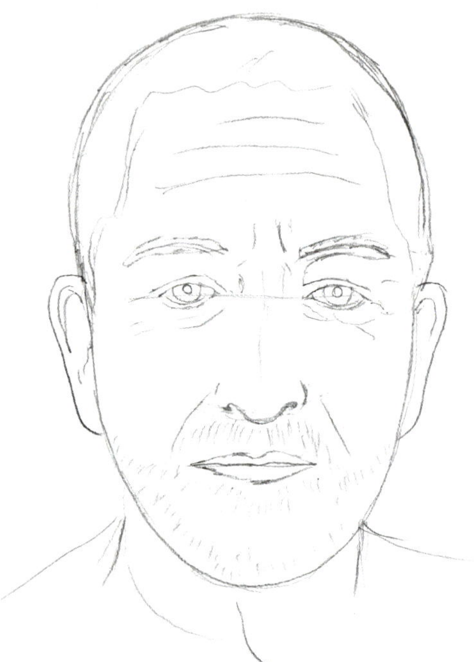

3. Add more details to the features. Thicken the eyebrows and add the pupils and lower eyelids. Erase any unneeded guidelines, including the tops of the irises. Draw contours and add definition to the ears, forehead, and around the eyes. Begin sketching in facial hair with short lines. For more information on facial hair, see page 93.

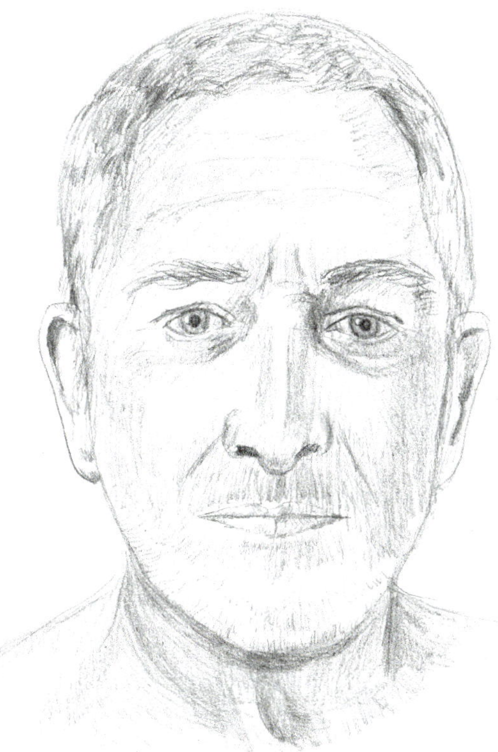

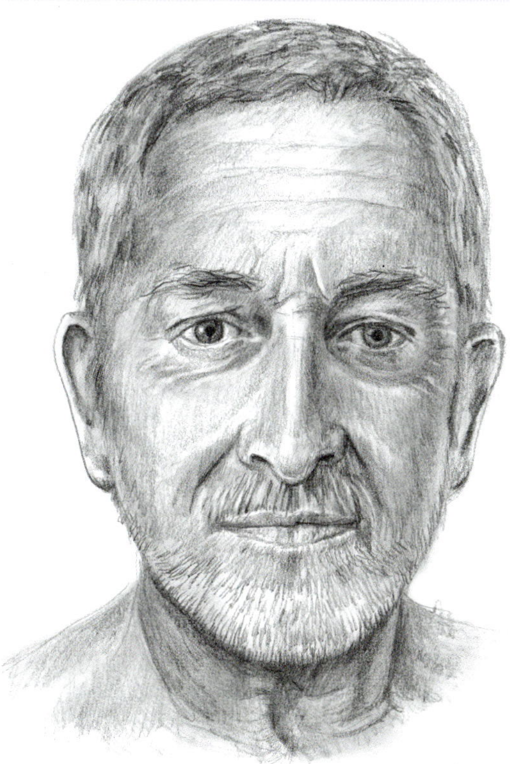

Add Tone

4. Add a light layer of tone to the face, focusing on shadows and highlights. The hair, eyebrows, irises, pupils, nostrils, and shadows around the eyes and under the chin should be the darkest tones. Use short strokes for the eyebrows.

5. Smooth tones with a tissue on the larger areas and use a blending tool on smaller areas. Continue to add more tone, building shadows and highlights. Add more definition to the hair and beard.

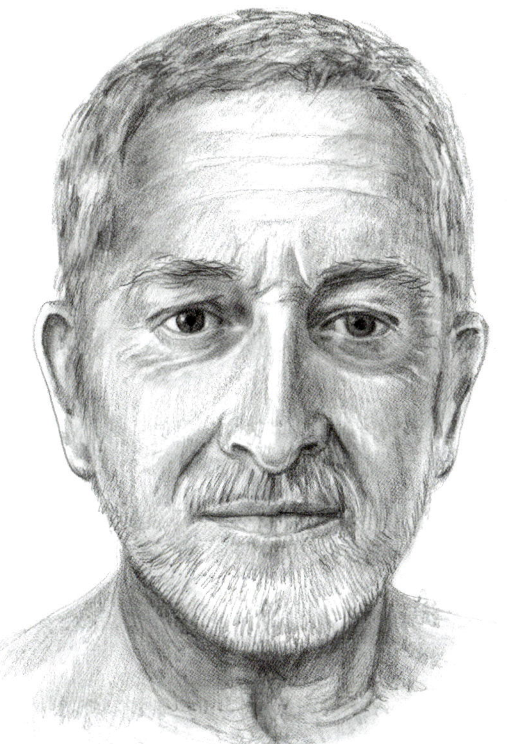

Build Contrast

6. Add another layer of tone, concentrating on contrast. Deepen shadows and lines on the face. Pay attention to where there should be highlights and use a kneaded eraser to remove tone. Smooth and blend tones further. These eyes are deeply set so the shadows are darker and the eyelashes are nonexistent.

WRINKLES & AGE LINES

Wrinkles are not linear and they have curves made of thin and thick lines. Shade only the edges, above or below the wrinkle. The more you mark the line, the deeper the wrinkle will be.

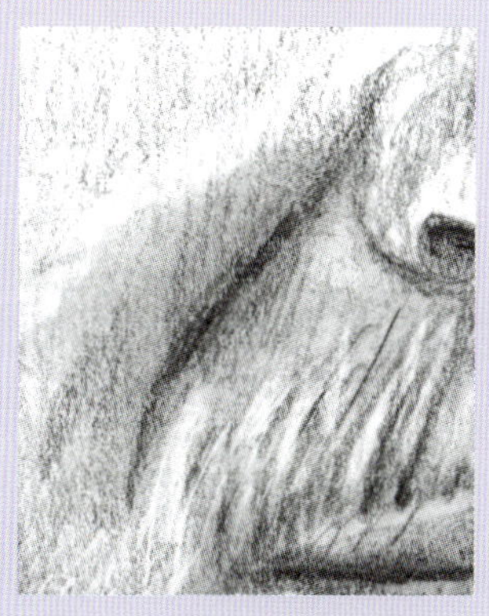

YOUNGER FACE

A child's face won't have as much texture to the skin, but making sure there are highlights and shadows will give your portrait dimension and make it feel lifelike.

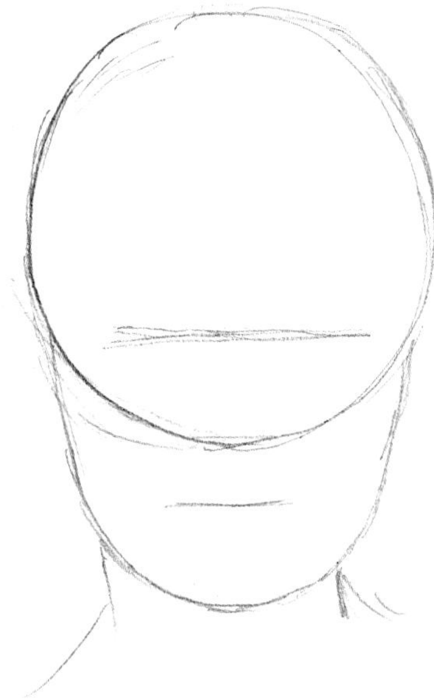

Draw the Basics

1. Draw a head following the steps on page 38. Include all necessary guidelines for the eyes, mouth, and nose. For a child's face, the chin and jawline should be rounded. Sketch the neck and shoulders.

2. Using the guidelines, draw two circles for the irises. Draw curved lines for the tops of the eyes and the eyebrows. Sketch the nose and nostrils along the nose guideline. Sketch the mouth. Draw the ears.

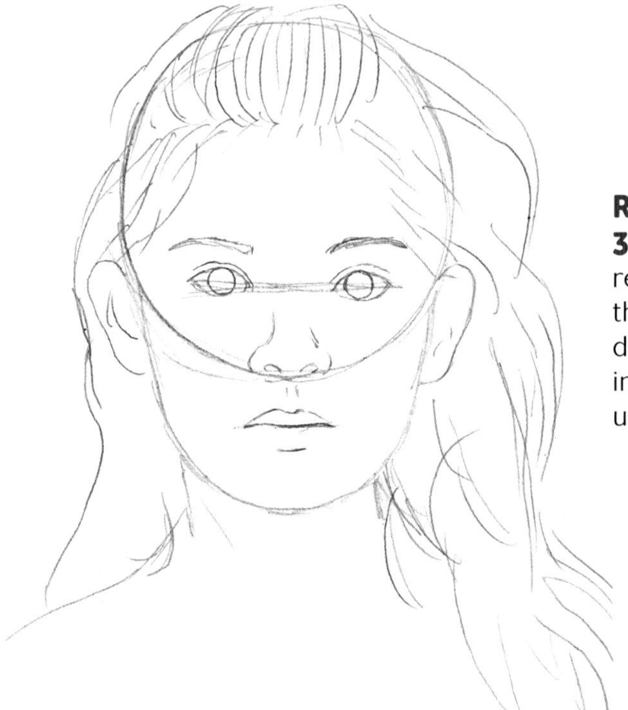

Refine the Features

3. Complete the shape of the eyes. Begin to refine all the features: add eyelids and thicken the eyebrows. Add the bridge of the nose and define the mouth area. Give definition to the inside of the ears. Sketch the outline of the hair using organic, wispy strokes for the strands.

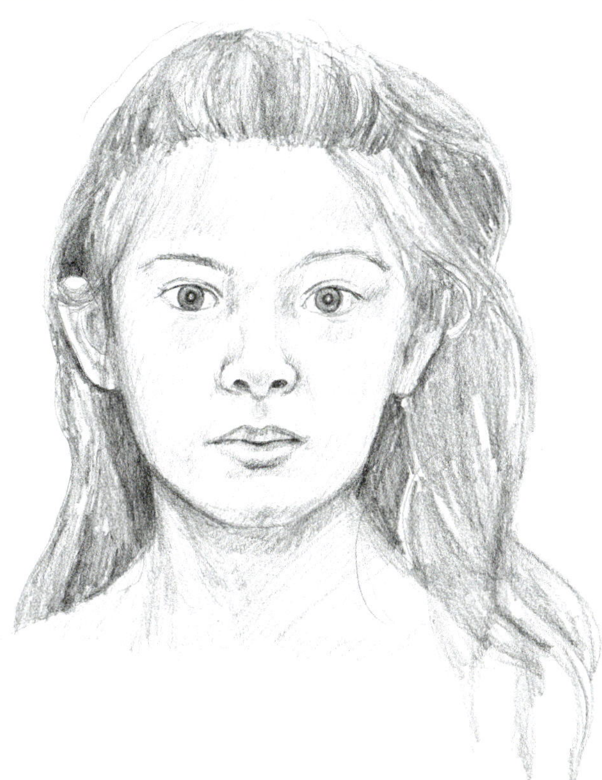

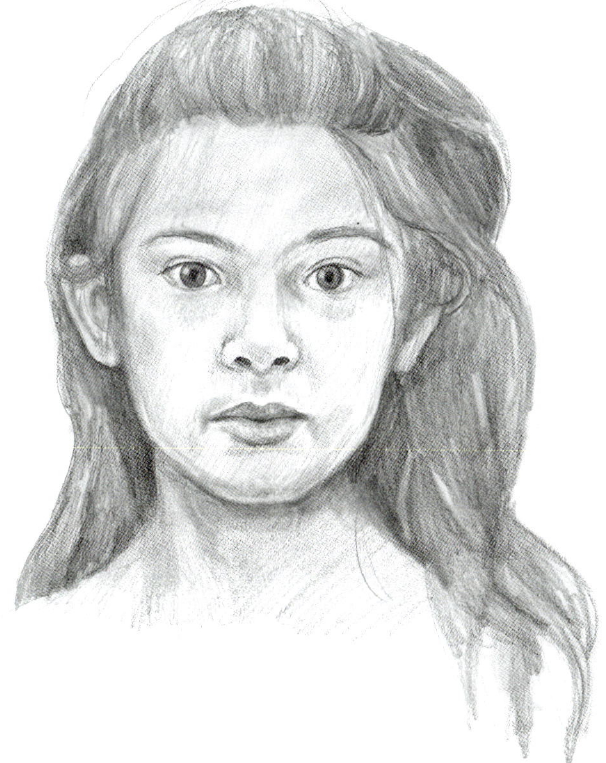

4. Complete the eyes by adding circles for the pupils. Erase any unneeded guidelines. Add a light layer of tone to the face, focusing on shadows and highlights. The hair, eyebrows, irises, pupils, nostrils, inner ear, and shadows around the eyes and under the chin should be the darkest tones. Use short strokes for the eyebrows.

5. Continue to add more tone, building shadows and highlights. Add more contrast to the hair, eye area, and mouth area.

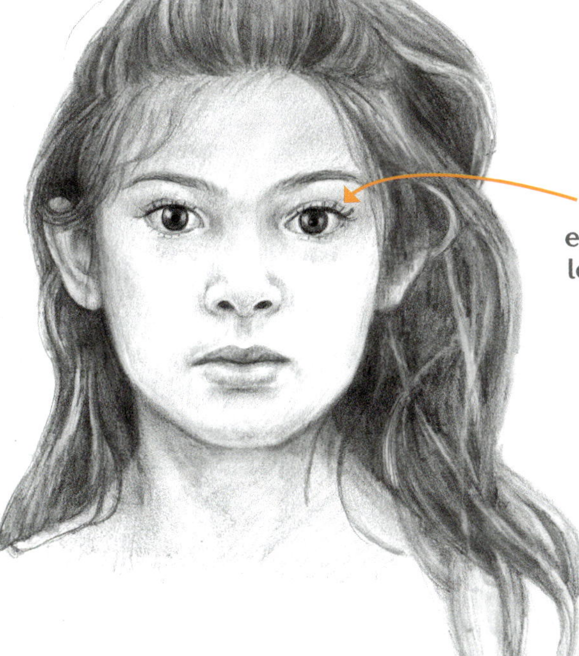

The eyelashes are long and curl outward.

Build Contrast

6. Add another layer of tone, concentrating on contrast. Deepen shadows and lines on the face. Pay attention to where there should be highlights and use a kneaded eraser to remove tone. Smooth and blend tones further. Add final details to the features, including the eyelashes.

BABY FACE

Babies' faces have different proportions than adults, so refresh your memory on page 34 and take a look at the sidebar for tips before beginning this drawing.

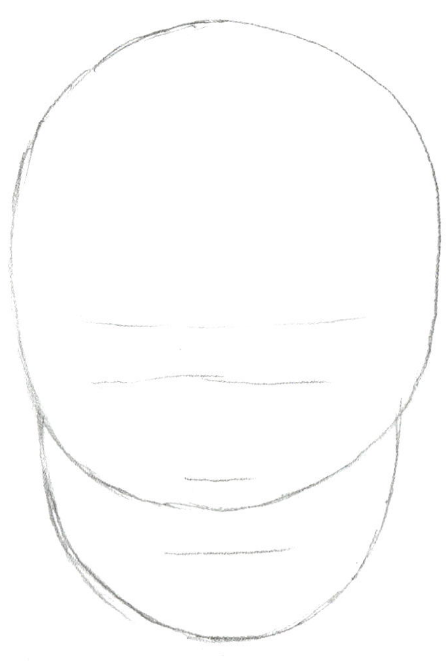

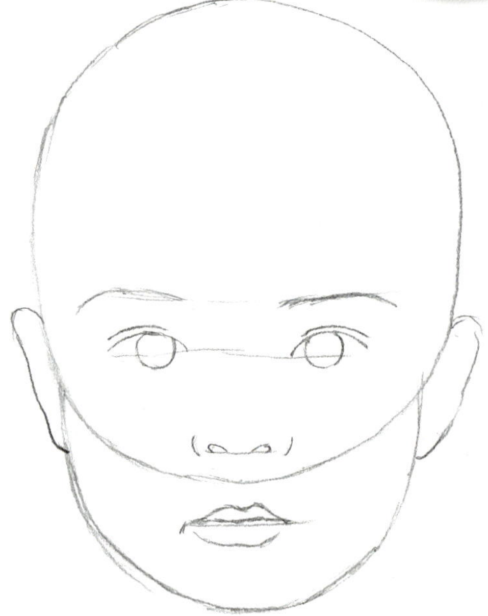

Draw the Basics

1. Draw a head following the steps on page 38. Include all necessary guidelines for the eyes, mouth, and nose. For a baby's face, the chin and jawline should be rounded.

2. Using the guidelines, draw two circles for the irises. Draw curved lines for the tops of the eyes, upper eyelids, and the eyebrows. Sketch the nose and nostrils along the nose guideline. Sketch the mouth. Draw the ears.

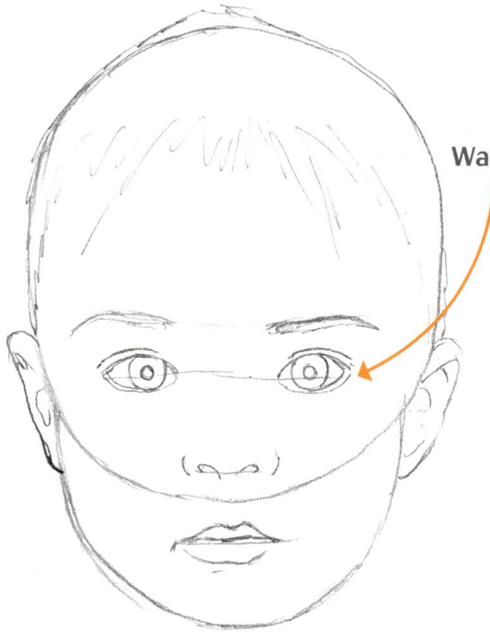

3. Add circles for the pupils. Complete the shape of the eyes, adding the waterline. Thicken the eyebrows. Sketch in the hairline. Begin to add definition to the inside of the ears.

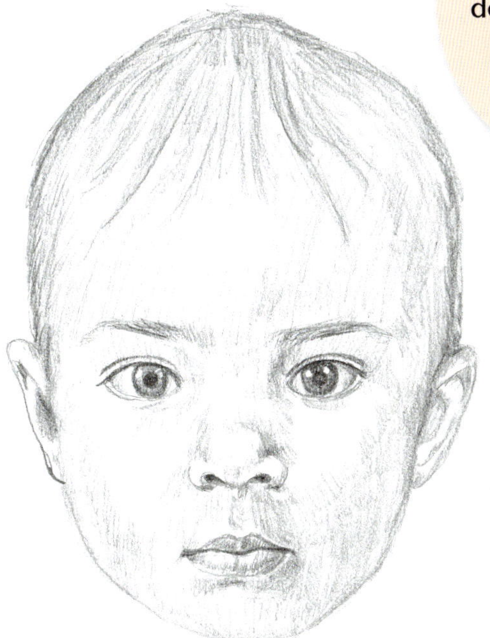

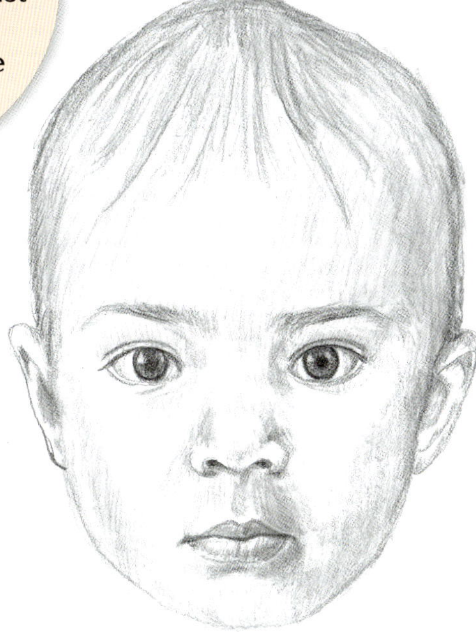

Add Tone

4. Erase any unneeded guidelines. Add a light layer of tone to the face, focusing on mid- to light tones. The value shifts are subtle since the features are not as defined as an adult's. Use short strokes for the eyebrows.

5. Smooth tones with a tissue on the larger areas and use a blending tool on smaller areas. Clean up muddy areas with a kneaded eraser. Add more tone, making sure the transitions from dark to light are subtle. The irises and pupils, lips, hair, inner ears, and nostrils should be among the darkest tones.

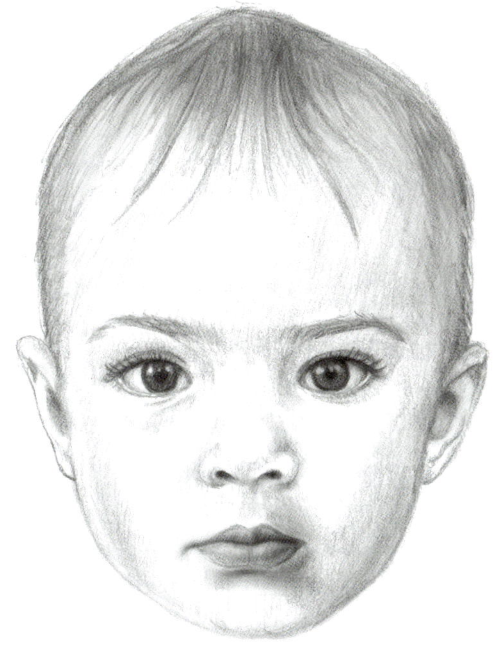

Add Final Details

6. Smooth and blend tones further. Add final details to the features, including the eyelashes.

DRAWING BABY FEATURES

- Eyes are large and in the center of the face.
- Upper eyelids are thin and almost nonexistent.
- Eyebrows are closer to the eyes than on a mature face.
- The bridge of the nose is barely perceptible, so draw as few lines as possible to suggest the base of the nose.
- Lips are slightly wider than the base of the nose. The lower lip is fuller, giving a puckered or pursed appearance.

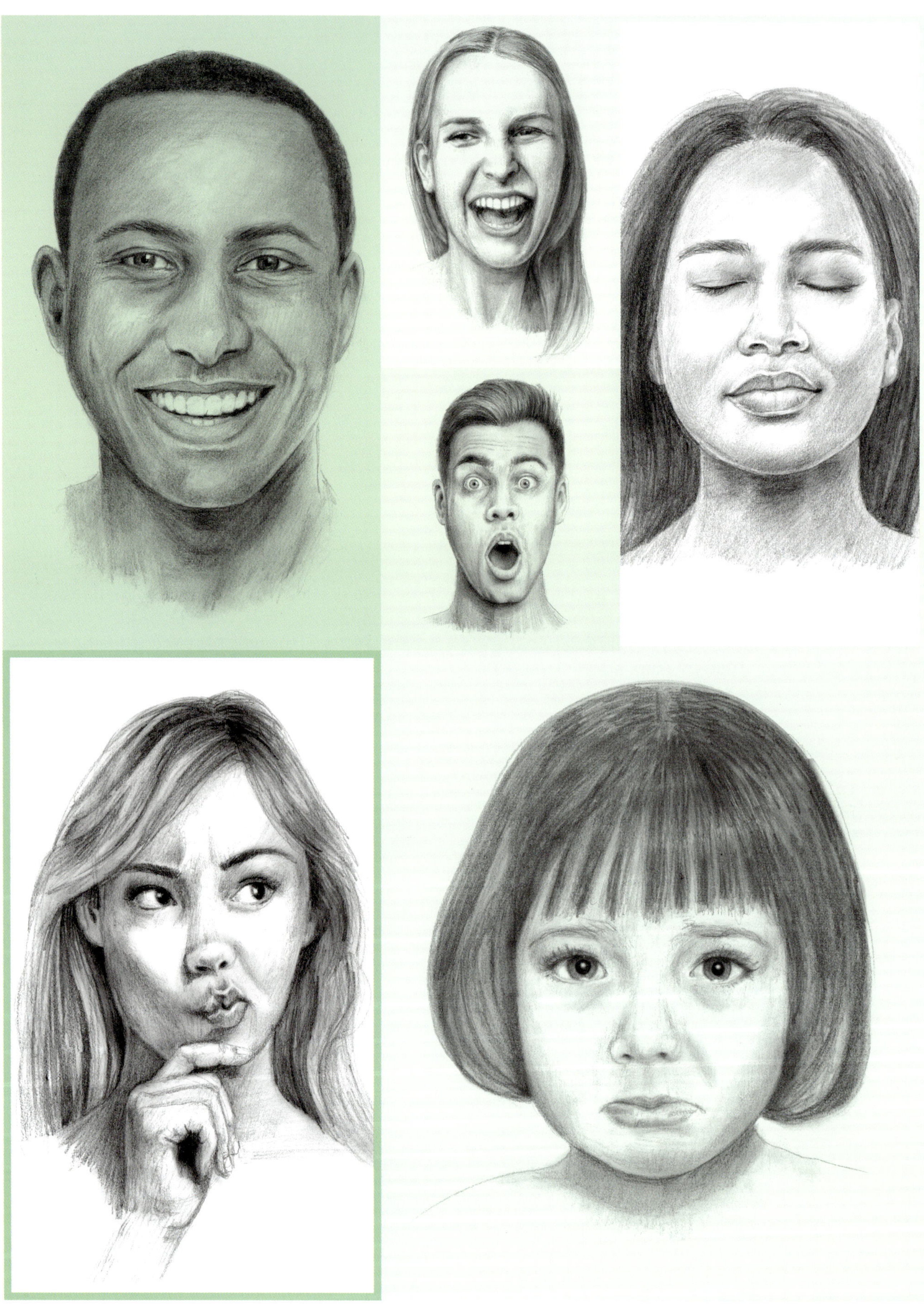

Chapter 3

DRAWING EMOTIONS & EXPRESSIONS

Different emotions can completely change the way a face looks because of the array of muscle movements involved. The cheeks, brows, eyes, nostrils, and mouth will all move in some manner to convey what a person is feeling.

In this chapter, I'll give a quick overview of what this idea looks like before we dive into the step-by-step demonstrations. These tutorials build on skills learned in the previous chapters and focus on the specifics of drawing emotions and expressions, not just faces.

Express Yourself!

One of the many challenging aspects of drawing human faces is that it's not really just one expression you need to grasp, but many. And one of the best ways to learn how to draw expressions is to make faces in the mirror and observe what happens to different features and muscles. You can even take a selfie to study, or a short video and then review it frame by frame to see the subtle changes.

Here are a bunch of self-portraits I drew that capture different emotions, and the main takeaways from each that may be helpful when trying to capture emotions through drawing.

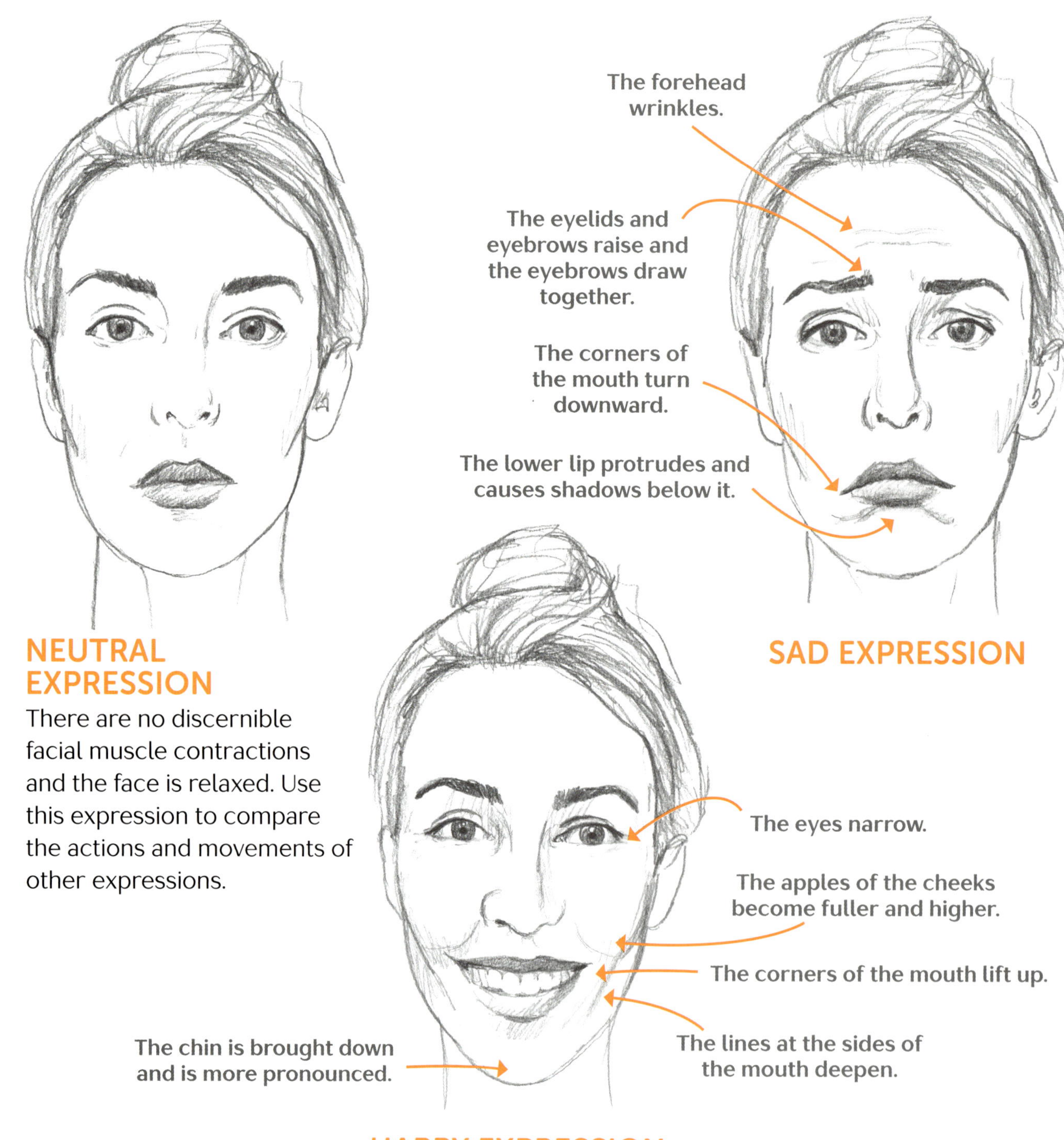

NEUTRAL EXPRESSION

There are no discernible facial muscle contractions and the face is relaxed. Use this expression to compare the actions and movements of other expressions.

SAD EXPRESSION

HAPPY EXPRESSION

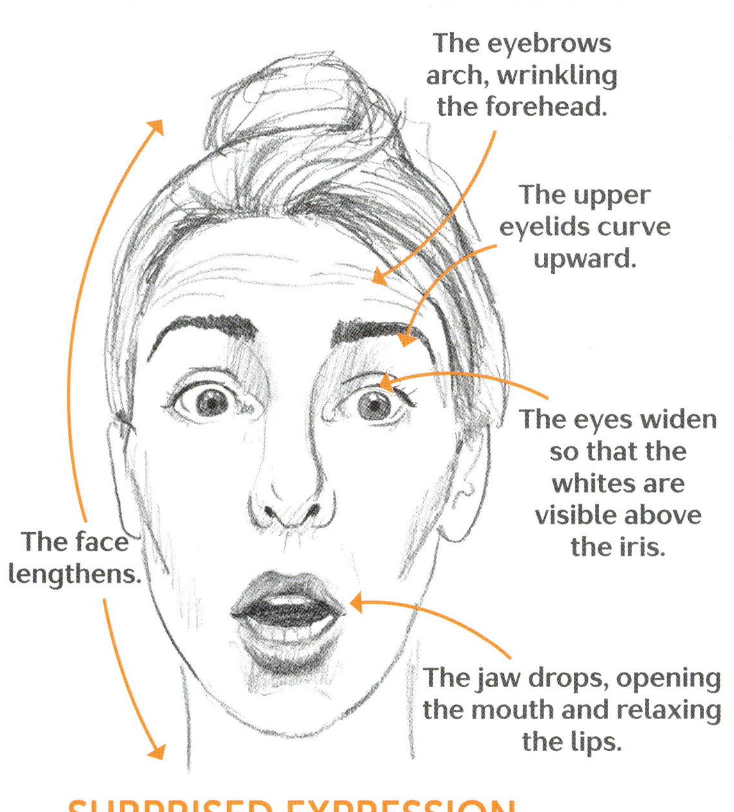

SURPRISED EXPRESSION

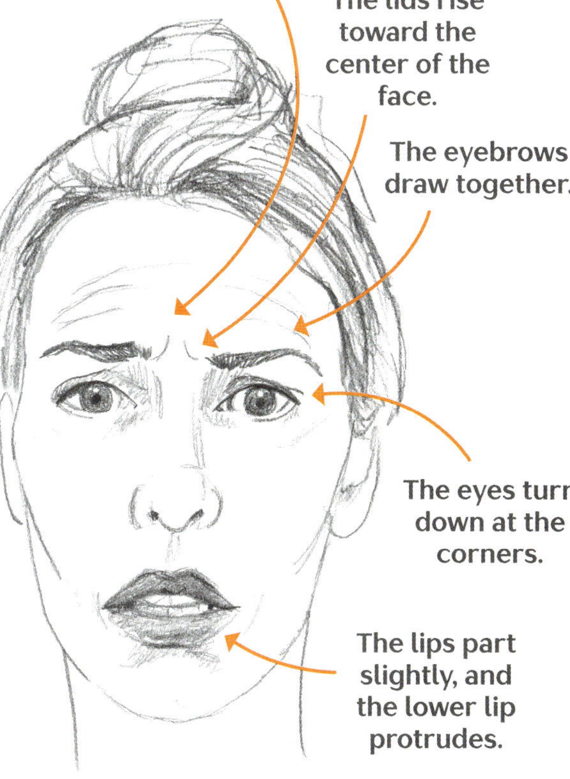

AFRAID EXPRESSION

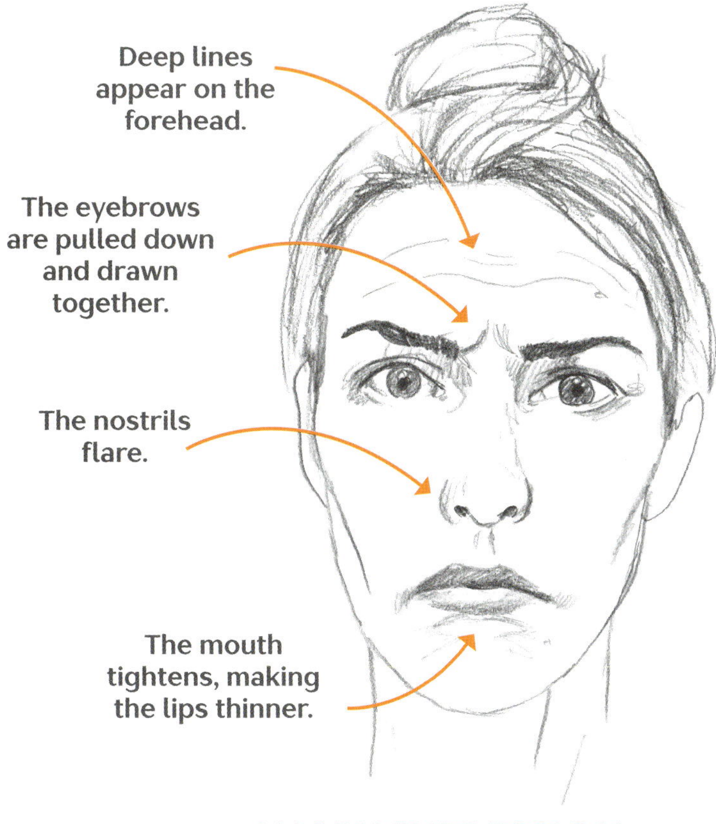

ANGRY EXPRESSION

RELAXED

A relaxed, serene expression is close to the neutral position of the face. Here, there aren't lots of shadows or wrinkles.

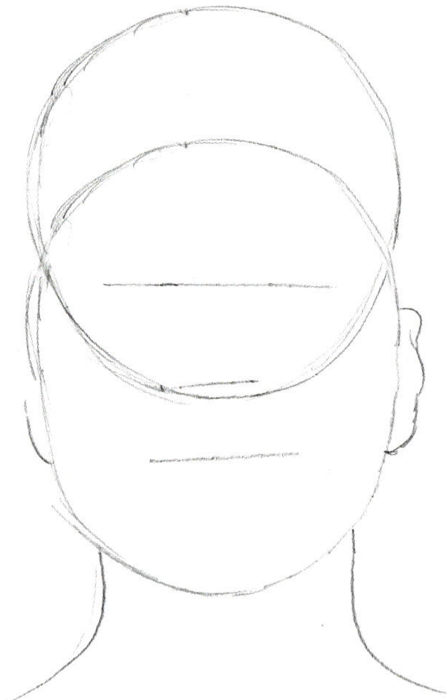

Draw the Basics

1. Draw a head following the steps on page 38. The shape is different than usual because the head is slightly tilted upward. Include all necessary guidelines for the eyes, mouth, and nose. Draw the ears and the neck and shoulders.

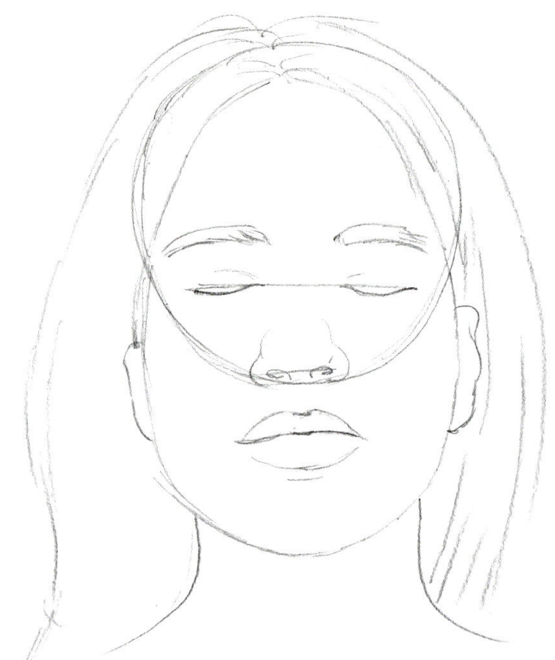

2. Draw the basic features, referring back to pages 42–47 for guidance. Even though the eyes are closed, you should draw the outline of the eye shape to use as guides for shadows, wrinkles, and highlights. Begin to refine the ears, eyebrows, and hair.

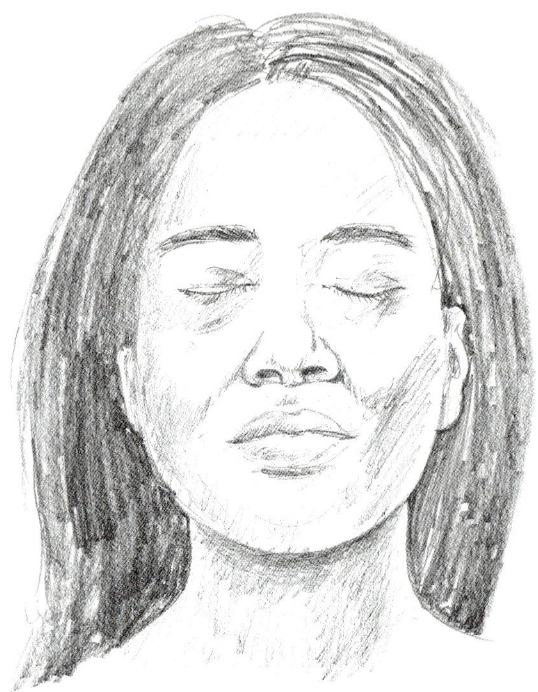

Add Tone

3. Erase any unnecessary guidelines. Add a light layer of tone and quickly block in the dark and midtones, including the hair, eyebrows, and shadows on the face and neck.

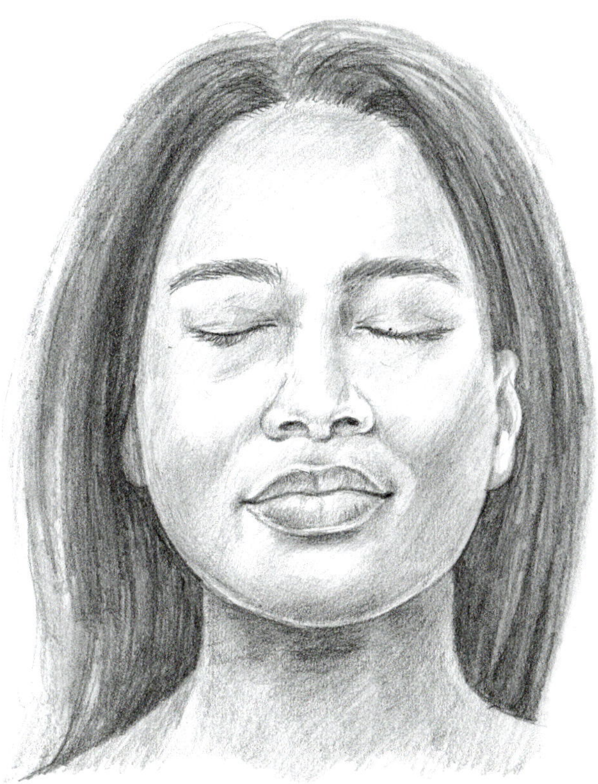

4. Blend, then add more tones as needed, concentrating on contrast. Smooth any harsh edges or dark lines.

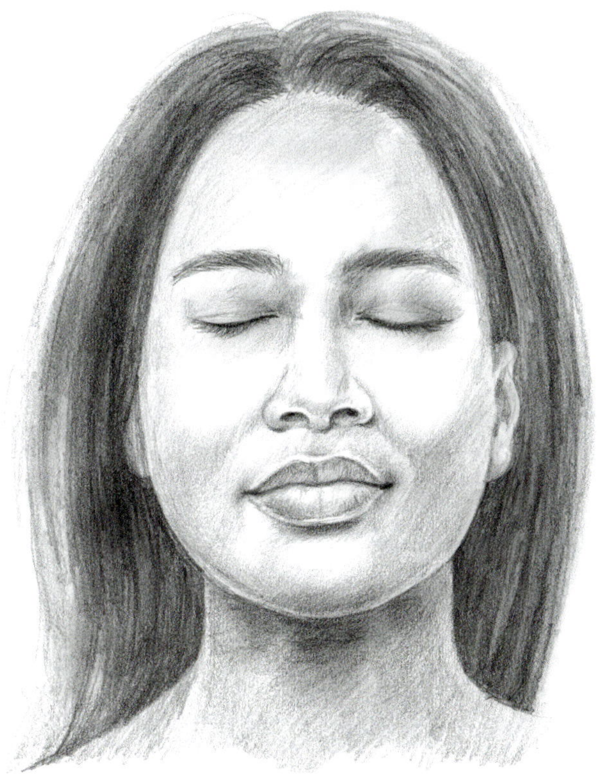

USE LIGHTING TO ENHANCE A MOOD

The direction of a light source helps emphasize specific facial features and can create different moods.

- Light coming from the front will evenly illuminate a face and reduce shadows.
- Side lighting, where light comes from the left or right, will add depth and dimension by casting shadows on one side of the subject.
- Backlighting, when the light comes from behind the subject, creates a silhouette effect or a halo around the edges, giving a dramatic look.

Understanding how to manipulate lighting helps artists control what their work looks like and can help convey a specific emotion or mood.

Build Contrast

5. Deepen the darks to add more contrast. Use a kneaded eraser to clean up any smudges and to highlight areas as needed.

BORED

This person may be bored, but this portrait is anything but boring. In it, we combine drawing a face (page 50) with drawing a hand (page 31).

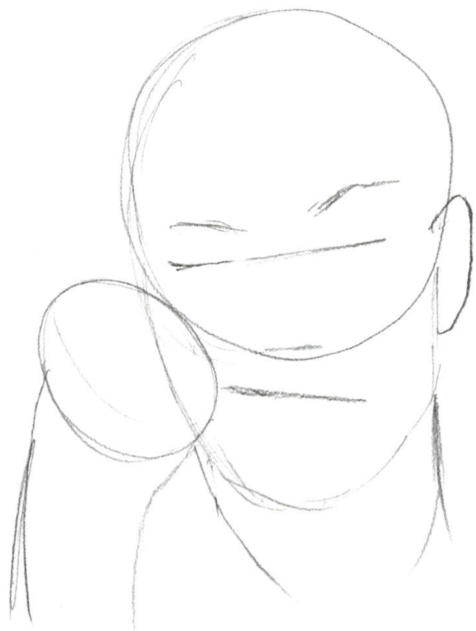

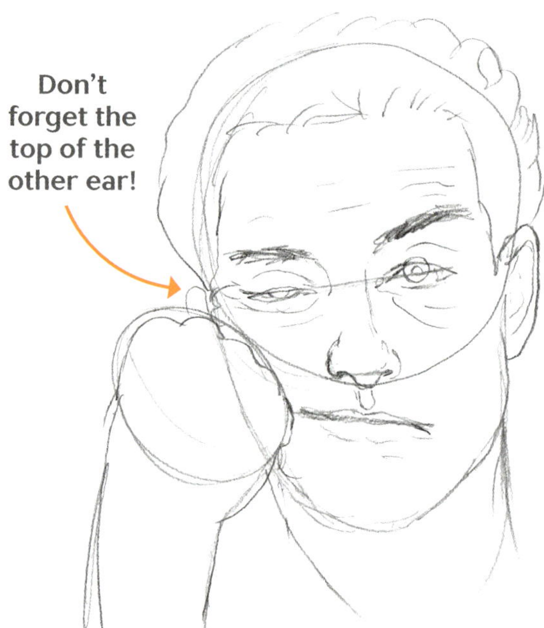

Draw the Basics

1. Draw a head following the steps on page 38. Include guidelines for the eyes, mouth, and nose. The guidelines for the mouth and nose are at an angle to show positioning. Sketch in the eyebrows. Draw an oval for the fist and lines for the arm. Draw the one full ear.

2. Draw the basic features, referring back to pages 42–47 for guidance. Sketch one eye slightly closed and pushed upward by the fist. Add lines on the face and the mouth to indicate the skin being pulled upward by the fist. Draw the other eye open, but blank with lack of expression. Sketch the nose, lips, eyebrows, and outline of hair. Round the knuckles. Add ear detail.

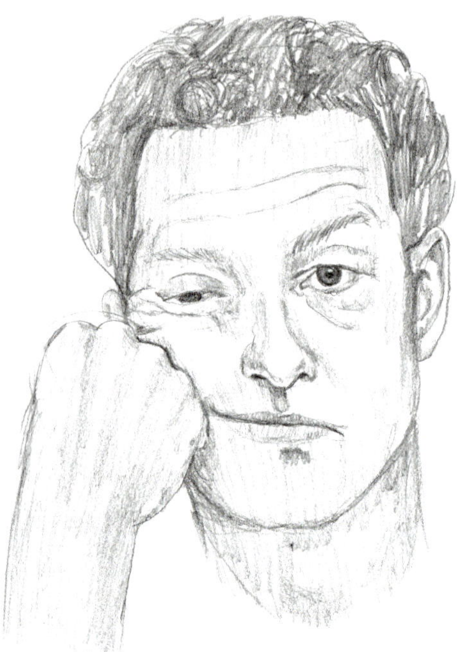

Add Tone

3. Erase any guidelines no longer needed and add a layer of tone. Focus on the wrinkles around the eyes where the skin is pushed up.

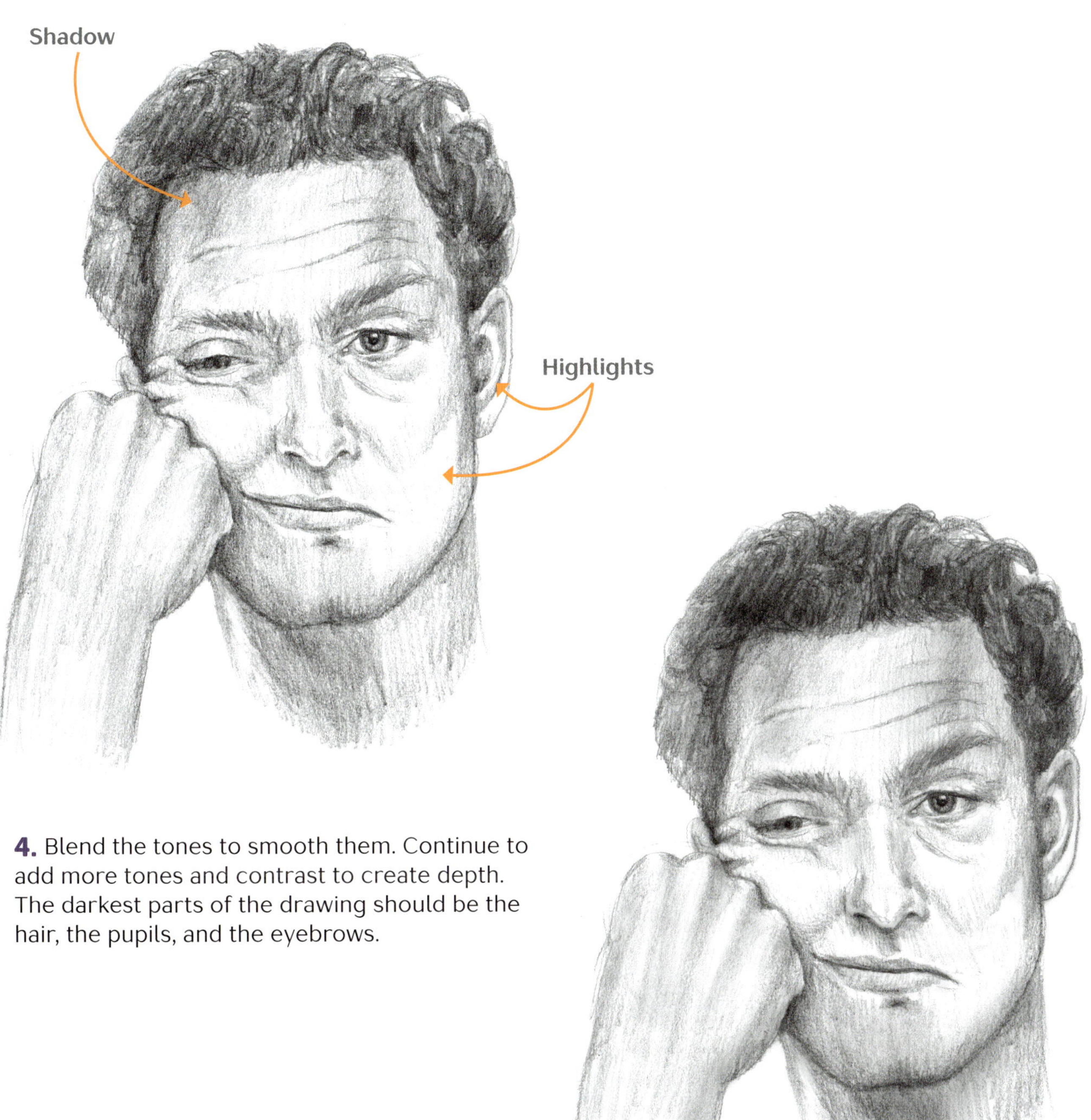

4. Blend the tones to smooth them. Continue to add more tones and contrast to create depth. The darkest parts of the drawing should be the hair, the pupils, and the eyebrows.

Finish the Drawing
5. Smooth and blend the tones further. Add more tone to create contrast, especially in the wrinkles and lines of the face. Clean up smudges, and soften any hard lines using a kneaded eraser.

SMILING

"Say Cheese!" You'll likely have plenty of smiling faces to choose from when it comes to portraits, so make sure you've really practiced drawing a mouth (page 46) and teeth (page 47).

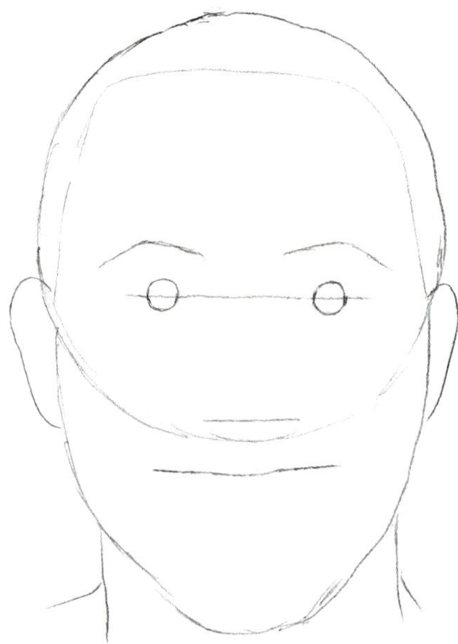

Draw the Basics

1. Draw a head following the steps on page 38. Include all necessary guidelines for the eyes, mouth, and nose. The guidelines for the nose and mouth should be slightly higher than usual to accommodate a big smile. Draw the hairline, the ears, and the neck and shoulders.

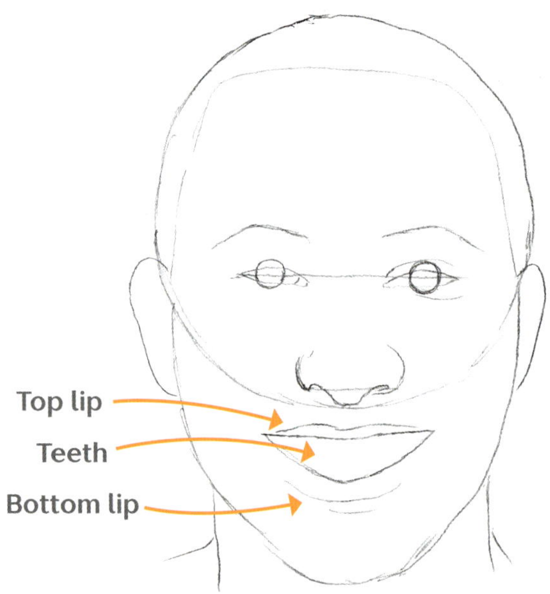

2. Draw the basic features, referring back to pages 42–47 for guidance. Because the eyes are squinting, the shape of the eye will overlap the circles for the irises. Draw the mouth. Smiling stretches the lip, so the top lip is thinner than usual.

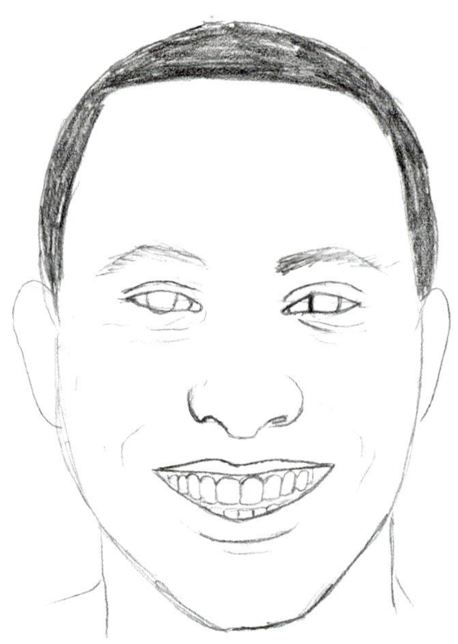

Refine the Features

3. Erase any guidelines no longer needed, including parts of the iris. Begin to refine the features. Draw a few lines to indicate wrinkles from the way the face moves with a smile. Most definition will be done with light shading later. Add creases at the bottoms of the eyes from the smile pushing the cheeks up.

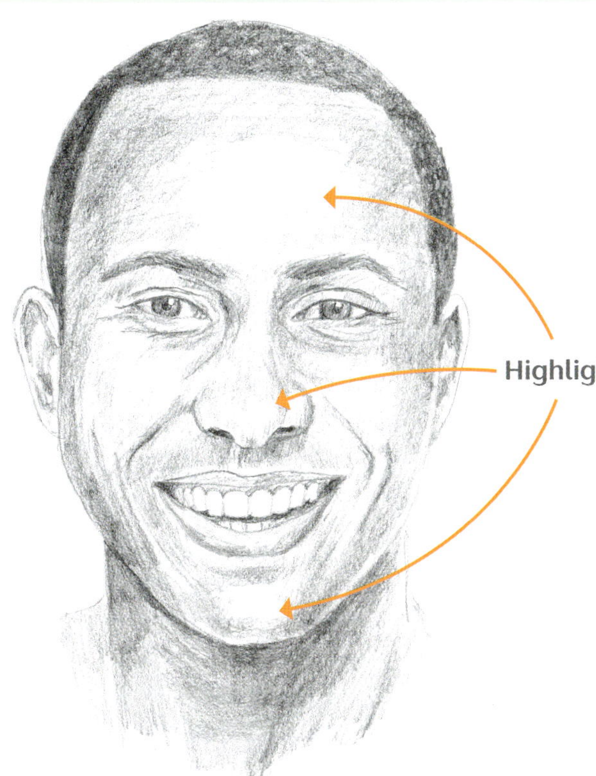

4. Add a layer of tone and more details to the features. Pay attention to highlighted areas and leave them light. Make the laugh lines more pronounced, and add some lines to show the creases along the side of the mouth toward the sides of the nose. Add a secondary line under the lower eyelid formed by the cheeks pushing upward. Add the ear detail.

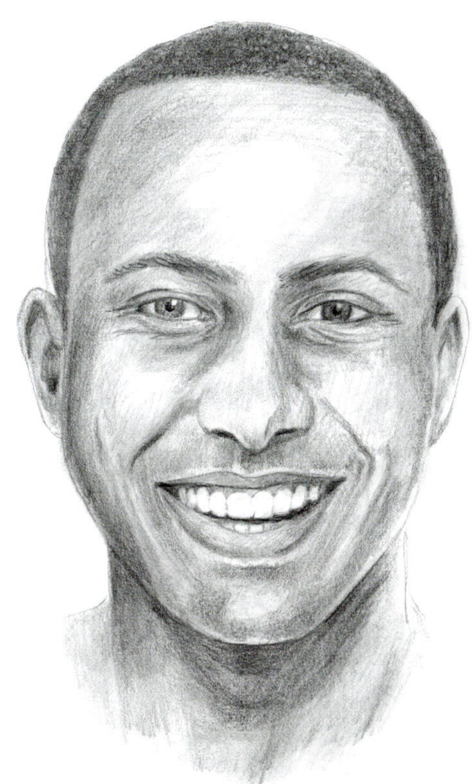

Blend & Build Contrast

5. Blend, then continue to add more contrast. The smile stretches the lips, reducing the amount of shadow that's showing underneath the upper lip. The eyes, inside of the mouth, inner ears, nostrils, and hair should be among the darkest tones.

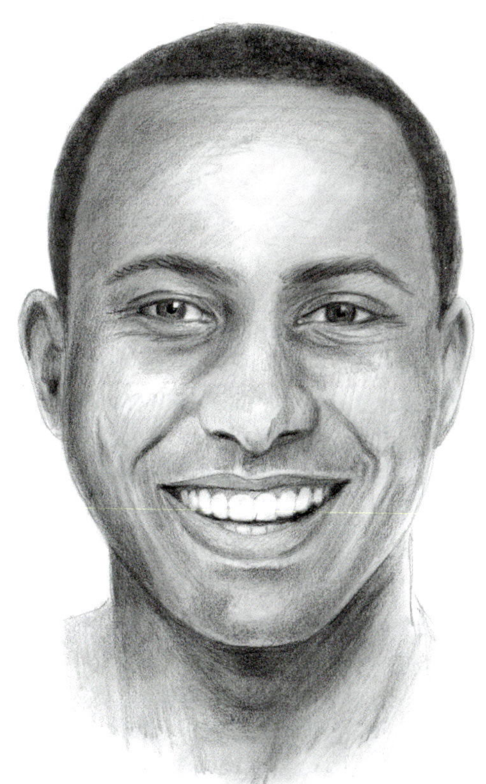

6. Refine the artwork by adding more contrast between highlights and shadows. Use a kneaded eraser to clean up and highlight areas as needed.

LAUGHING

Drawing someone who is laughing will take your mouth-drawing skills to the next level. Pay attention to the different shadows and dark areas inside the mouth—it's not just black—which makes it feel realistic.

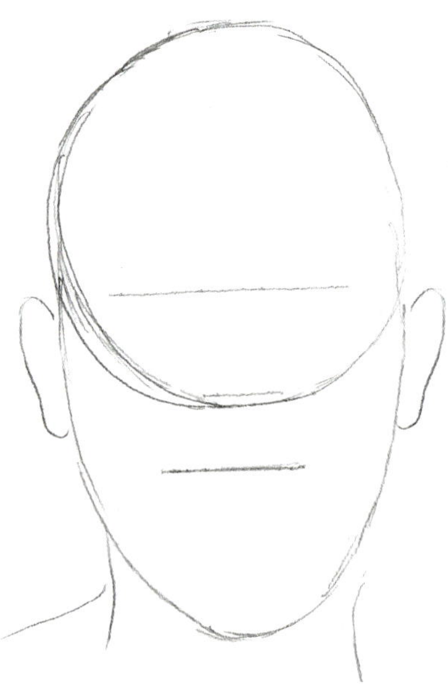

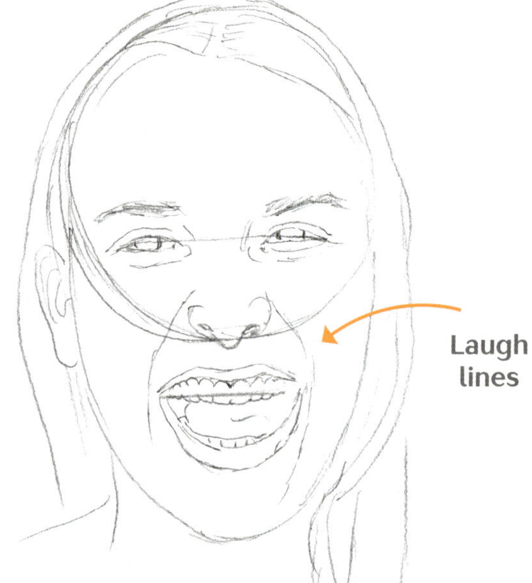

Draw the Basics

1. Draw a head following the steps on page 38. Include all necessary guidelines for the eyes, mouth, and nose. Draw the ears and the neck and shoulders.

2. Draw the basic features, referring back to pages 42–47 for guidance. Because the eyes are squinting, the shape of the eye will overlap the circles for the irises, and the skin under the eyes will bunch. The eyebrows are slightly raised. Draw a nose with flared nostrils, and an open mouth with its corners tilting upward. Draw the teeth and outline the tongue. Sketch curved lines around the mouth. Begin to refine the ears, eyebrows, and hair.

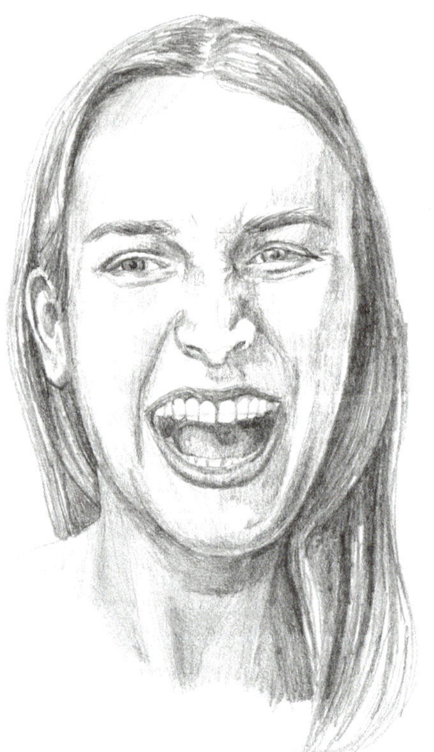

Add Tone

3. Erase any guidelines no longer needed. Add a light layer of tone, concentrating on the subtle wrinkle lines at the top of nose, around the mouth, and under the eyes. Thicken the eyebrows and add contrast to the hair.

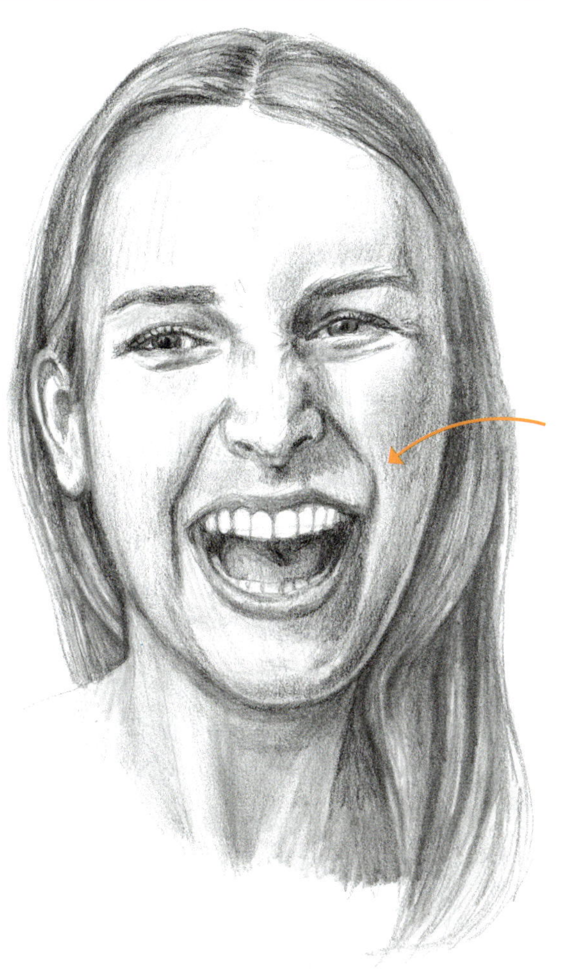

4. Blend, then build up tones and continue to add contrast. The hair, eyes, inside of mouth, and inner ears should be among the darkest tones.

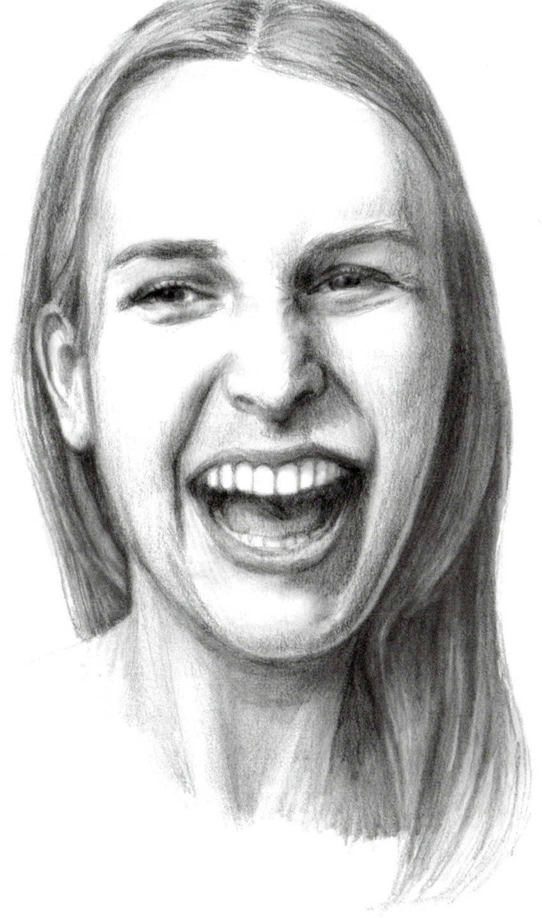

KEEP IN MIND

When drawing a portrait of someone laughing, pay special attention to the mouth and eyes, which are where you'll be able to show their joy. The mouth should be wider than usual and slightly open, with the corners turned up. Draw the eyes squinting or crinkled at the edges to convey genuine happiness. Pay attention to the lines around the eyes and mouth, as they deepen during laughter. Add some lines or wrinkles to show movement. Remember, laughter is contagious, so enjoy the process!

Finish the Drawing

5. Refine the artwork by adding more contrast between highlights and shadows. Clean up smudges, and soften any hard lines using a kneaded eraser.

SURPRISED

Notice the way the placement and size of features change in this portrait when compared to a more neutral expression.

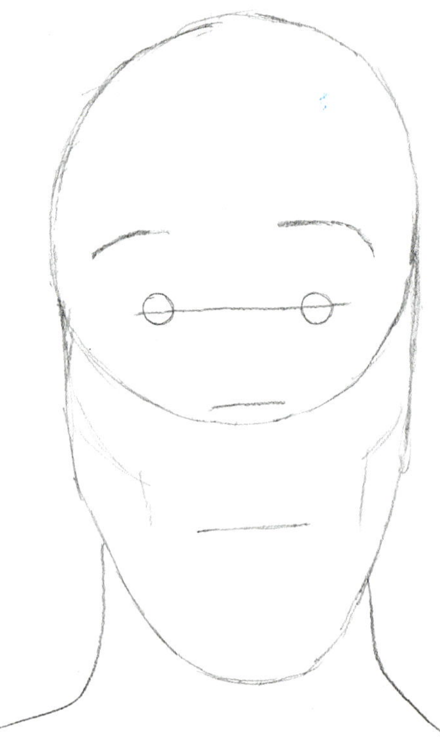

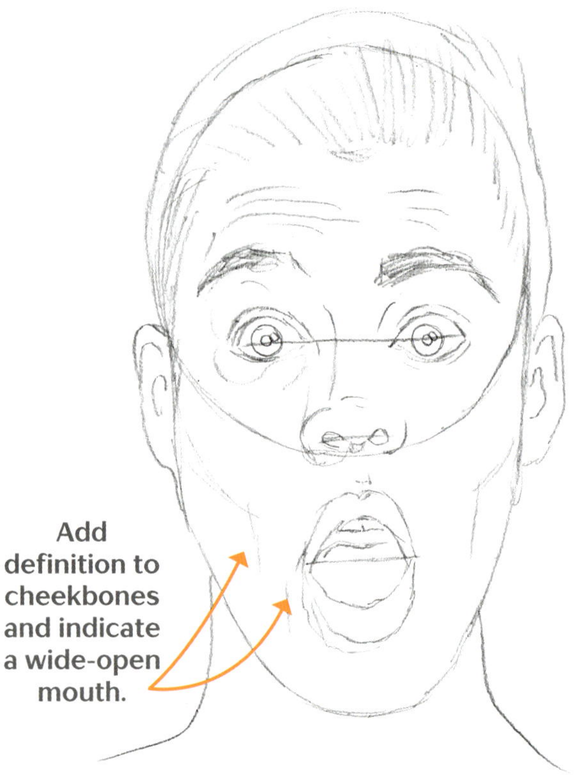

Draw the Basics

1. Draw a head following the steps on page 38. Include all necessary guidelines for the eyes, mouth, and nose. Draw the neck and shoulders. The oval for the bottom half of the face should be elongated, and the guideline slightly higher to accommodate the way the open mouth stretches the jawline. Add circles for the irises and raised eyebrows high above them. Add lines on the cheeks to indicate an open mouth.

2. Draw the basic features, referring back to pages 42–47 for guidance. Draw the eyes rounded and wide open. Draw the mouth open in an "O" shape. Thicken the eyebrows, and add wrinkles to the forehead since the skin wrinkles when eyebrows push upward.

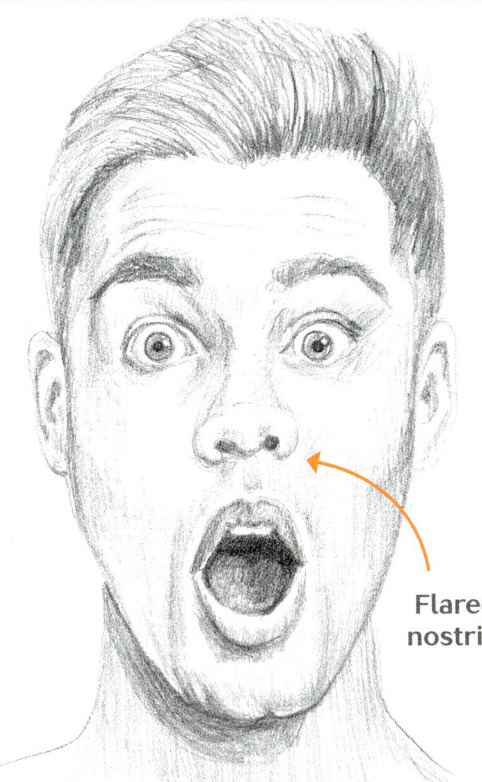

Add Tone

3. Add a layer of tone, shading under and around the eyes so they look open wide. Don't add too much shadow between the brows because the area is stretched. Add a few pull lines around the mouth and deepen the wrinkles in the forehead. Refine the rest of the features.

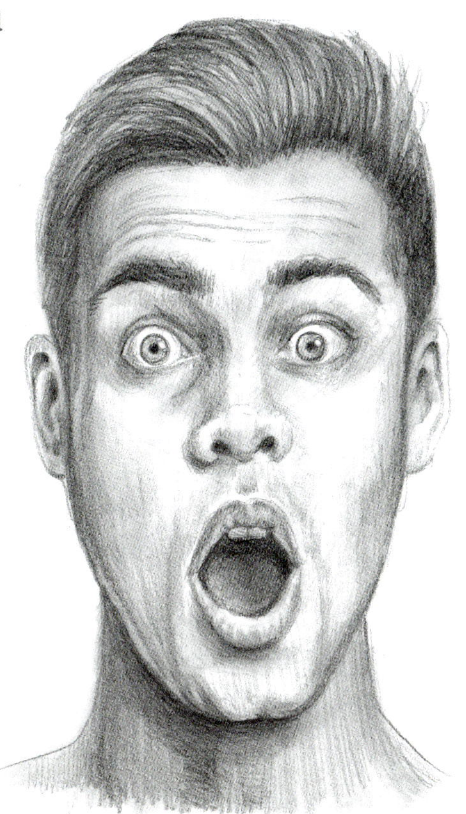

4. Blend, then add more tone, including subtle shadows around the mouth. The eyes, hair, inside of the mouth, nostrils, and inner ears should be among the darkest tones.

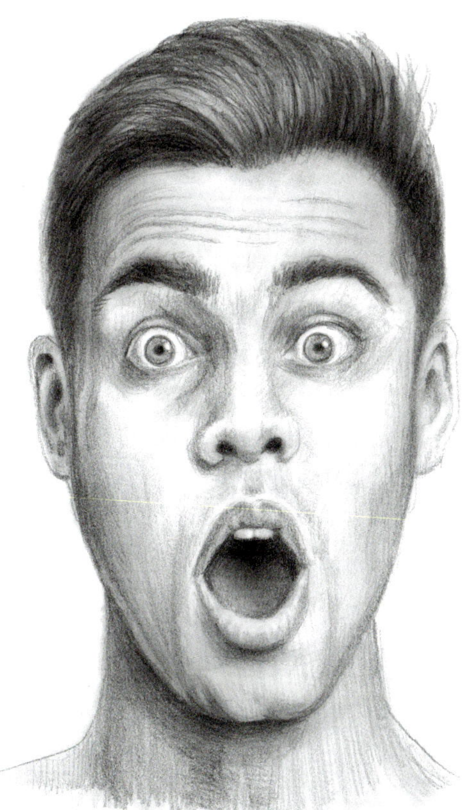

Refine the Drawing

5. Refine the artwork by adding more contrast between highlights and shadows. Use a kneaded eraser to clean up and highlight areas as needed.

CONCENTRATING

In this demonstration, a lot of the emotion is shown in the mouth. This person purses their lips as they concentrate. Some people furrow their brows, and others bite their lips. How does your face behave when you're concentrating?

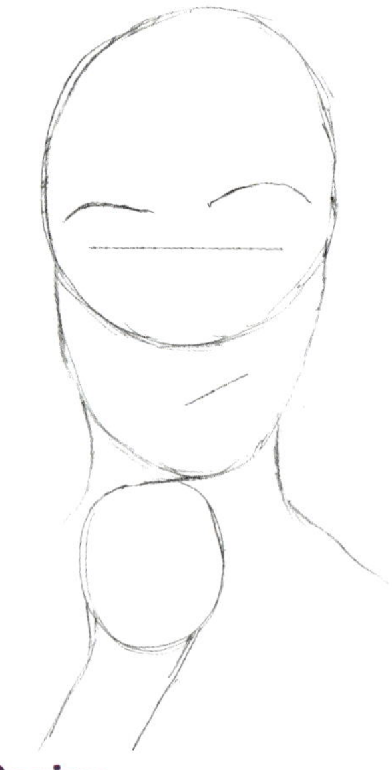

Draw the Basics

1. Draw a head following the steps on page 38. Include all necessary guidelines for the eyes, mouth, and nose. The guideline for the mouth is at an angle to show positioning. Sketch in the eyebrows. Draw an oval for the hand and lines for the arm.

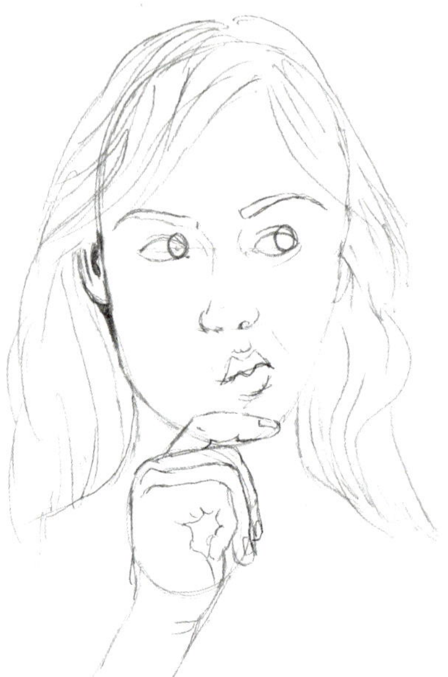

2. Draw the basic features, referring back to pages 42–47 for guidance. Draw both of the ears before covering them with the hair. The eyes are squinting and looking to the right, so draw the circles for the irises at the right of the eye shape and have the eyelids around them. The mouth is puckered and set off to the right. Add lines for the fingers.

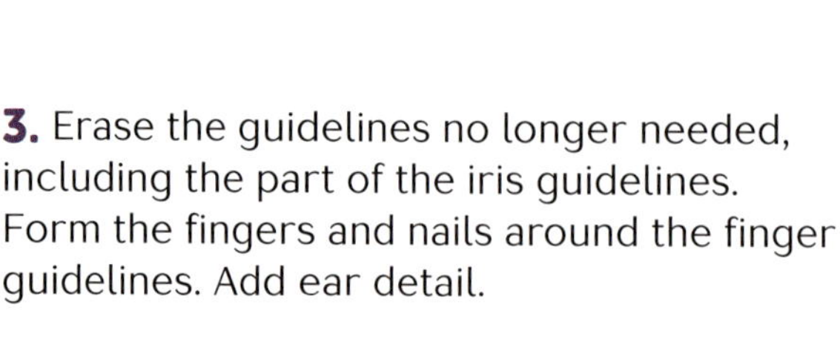

3. Erase the guidelines no longer needed, including the part of the iris guidelines. Form the fingers and nails around the finger guidelines. Add ear detail.

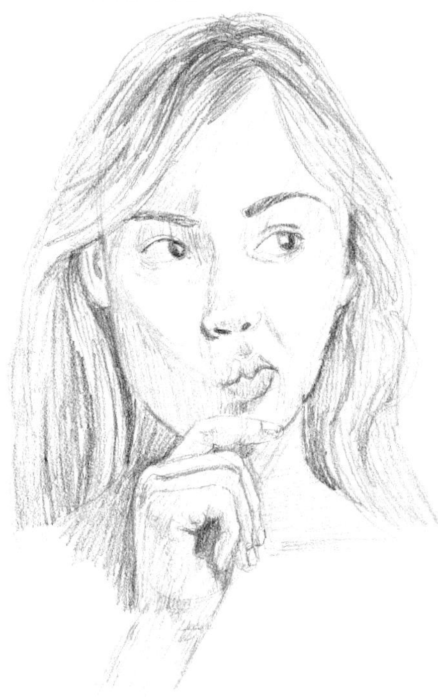

Add Tone

4. Add a light layer of tone to the entire drawing. Add lines next to the nose to show the mouth twisting. Use shading to define the pursed lips and furrowed brow.

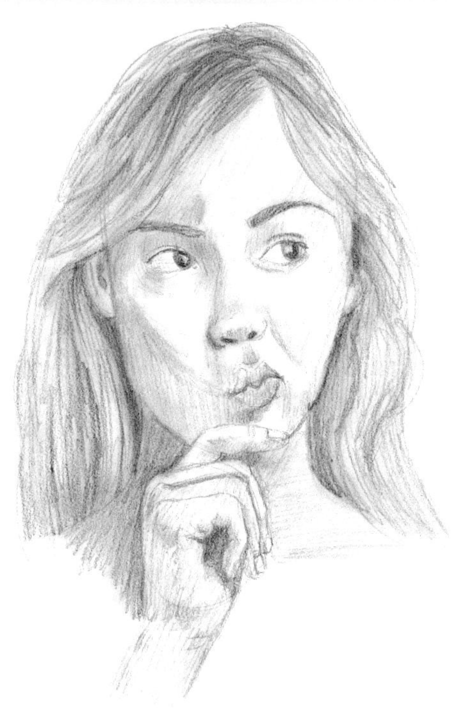

5. Smooth tones using a tissue on larger areas and a blending tool on the smaller areas.

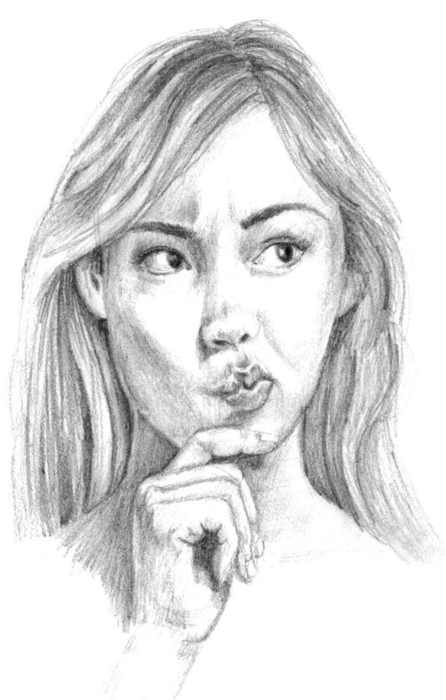

Add Shadows

6. Add another layer of tone, darkening the eyebrows, irises, and the shadows in the hand, hair, and lips. Add subtle shadows around the mouth so that it looks twisted but not harshly so. Notice how half of the face is in shadow.

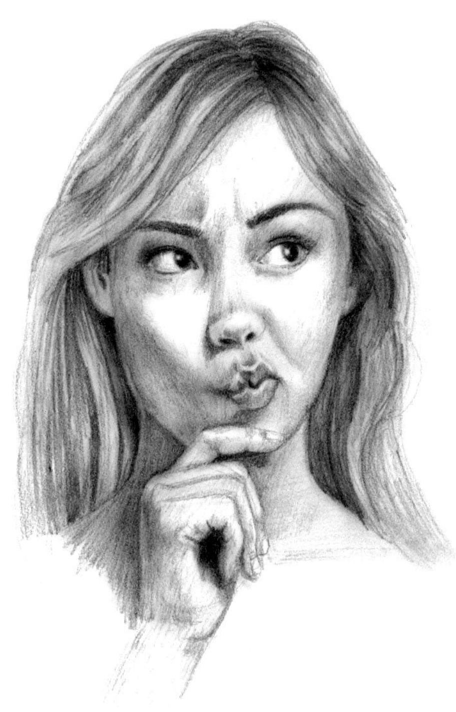

7. Refine the artwork by adding more contrast between highlights and shadows. Clean up smudges and soften any hard lines using a kneaded eraser.

SAD

Once you've successfully completed this portrait, try your hand at drawing a sad expression on someone who is a bit older. Take note of the way the proportions and placement of the features change.

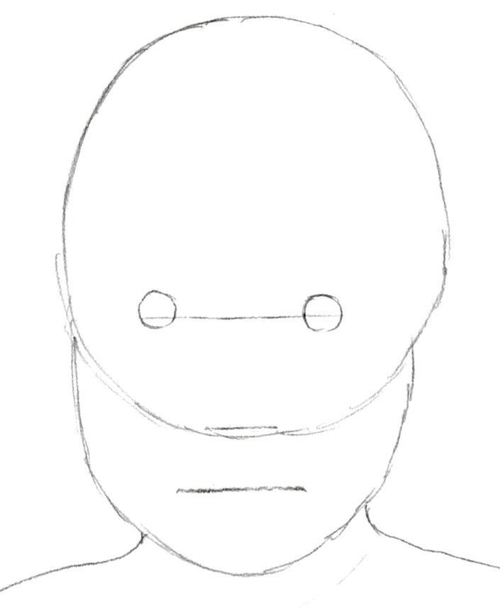

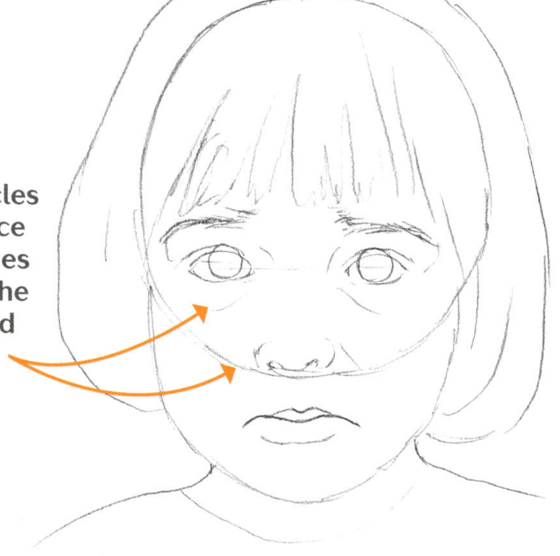

Draw the Basics

1. Draw a head following the steps on page 38. Include all necessary guidelines for the eyes, mouth, and nose. Draw circles for the irises. Draw the neck and shoulders.

2. Draw the basic features, referring back to pages 42–47 for guidance. The eyes, eyebrows, and the mouth should angle downward at the sides to convey sadness. The top lip should be thinner and the bottom larger, since the mouth is pouting.

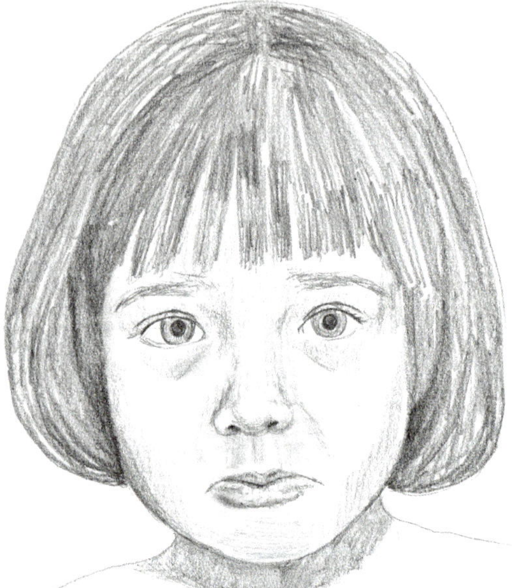

Add Tone

3. Erase any unnecessary guidelines. Refine the features. Add a layer of tone to the whole drawing. The darkest areas should be the hair and eyebrows, pupils, lips, and shadows under the chin.

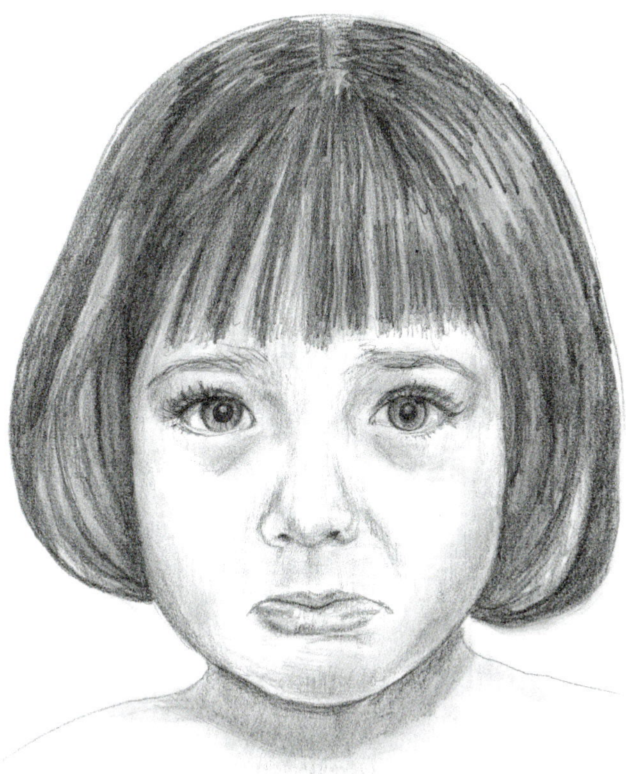

Smooth & Blend

4. Smooth tones using a tissue on larger areas and a blending tool on the smaller areas. Create subtle shadows under the eyes to show they're swollen from crying. Draw the eyelashes. Build up shadows under the lower lip and lashes and continue to deepen tones.

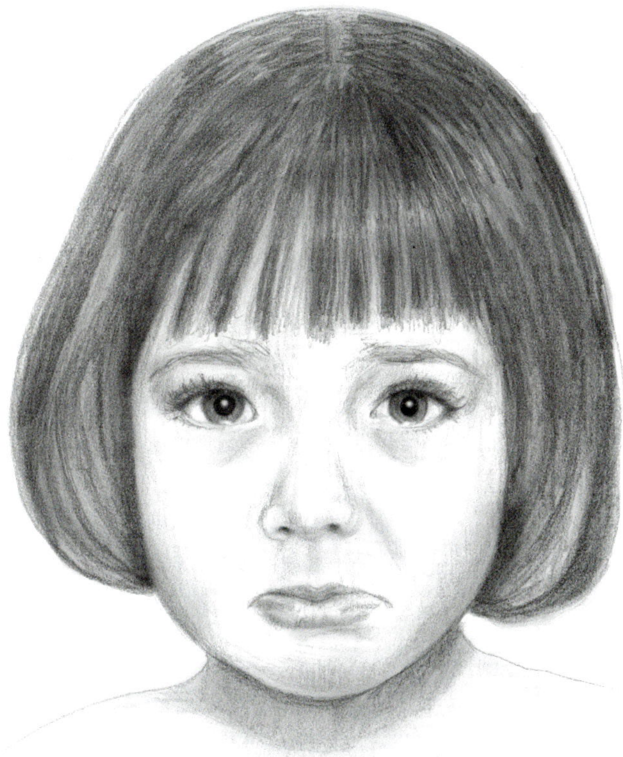

5. Deepen the darks and use a kneaded eraser to add more contrast. Use a stick eraser to add shiny spots beneath the irises to show tears pooling.

KEEP IN MIND

When drawing a sad adult, pay attention to their features. Sketch downturned corners of the mouth, droopy eyelids, and furrowed brows.

ANGRY

Faces reflect anger in different ways. Some are much more subtle than this portrait, but this over-the-top reaction helps accentuate some of the hallmarks of anger and is good practice.

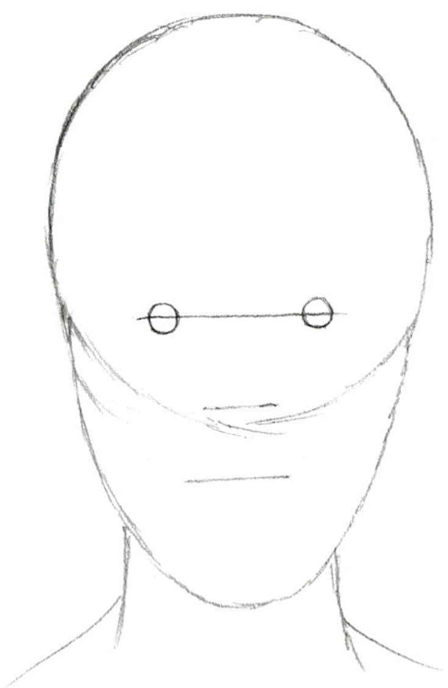

Draw the Basics

1. Draw a head following the steps on page 38. Include all necessary guidelines for the eyes, mouth, and nose. Add circles for the irises. Draw the neck and shoulders.

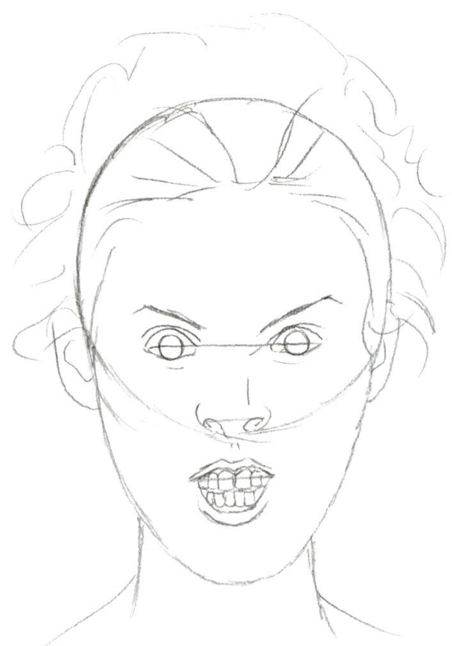

2. Draw the basic features, referring back to pages 42–47 for guidance. Draw a curled upper lip, flared nostrils, and slanted eyebrows. Sketch the eyes. Notice that the white above the iris is visible with this expression because the eyebrows are raised. Draw the bared teeth. Add the ears and an outline of the hair.

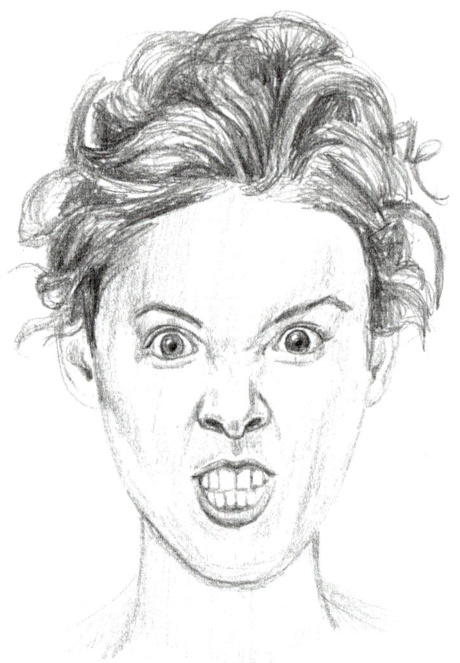

Add Tone

3. Erase any guidelines no longer needed and add a layer of tone. Press hard in areas of darkness including the wrinkles and lines caused by the expression. Add details and definition to the ears.

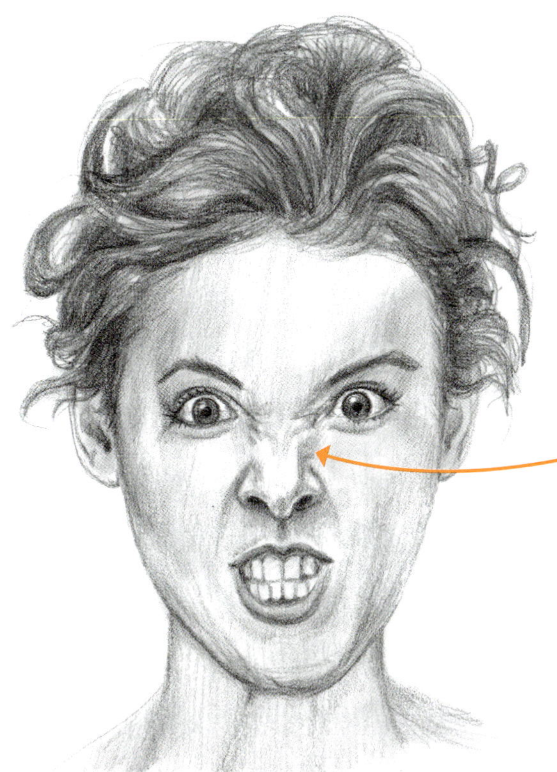

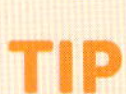

Blend & Define

4. Blend the tones to smooth, and add more tone to the drawing, building up the shading as needed. Concentrate on defining the lines around the mouth, the nose wrinkles, and the eyebrows to help solidify the mood being presented.

TIP

To draw someone angry, emphasize sharp lines and tense muscles. Sketch furrowed brows, narrowed eyes, and a clenched jaw. Add bold strokes to show intensity and frustration in their expression.

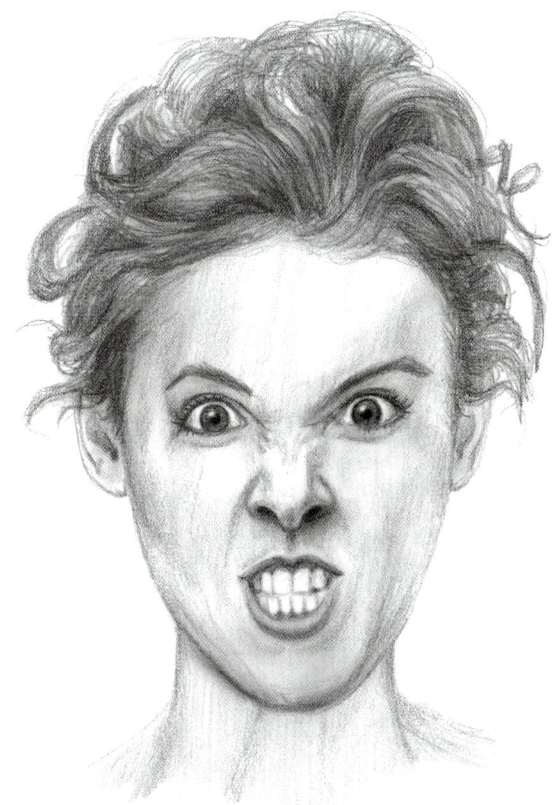

5. Deepen the darks to add more contrast for depth and realism. Add highlights to the eyes, and use a kneaded eraser to highlight the face and add shine to hair.

SCARED

Because the mouth is open, there are some similarities between the scared expression you're drawing here, the surprised expression (page 80), and the portrait of someone laughing (page 78).

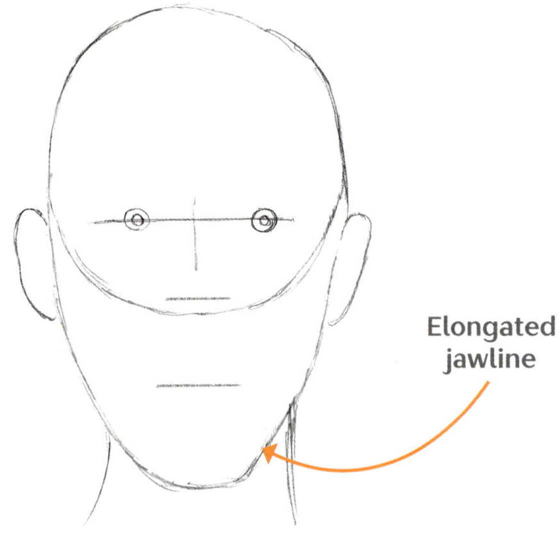

Draw the Basics
1. Draw a head following the steps on page 38. Include all necessary guidelines for the eyes, mouth, and nose. Draw the ears and the neck.

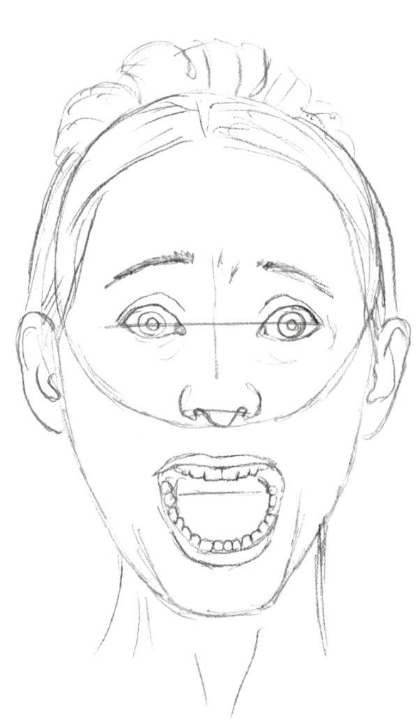

2. Draw the basic features, referring back to pages 42–47 for guidance. The mouth is wide open, so the lips will be stretched over the teeth. Angle the eyebrows downward and flare the nostrils. Some of the whites of the eyes should be visible above the irises because they are wide open. Draw lines for a strained neck and chin. Add ear detail, and the outline of the hair.

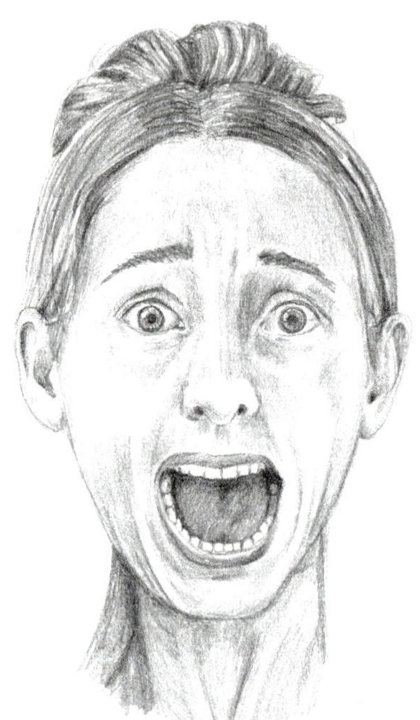

Add Tone
3. Erase any guidelines no longer needed and add a light layer of tone to help define subtle lines without actually outlining them. Add light lines between the eyebrows, under the eyes, and around the mouth with shading. Shade the muscles and veins in the neck.

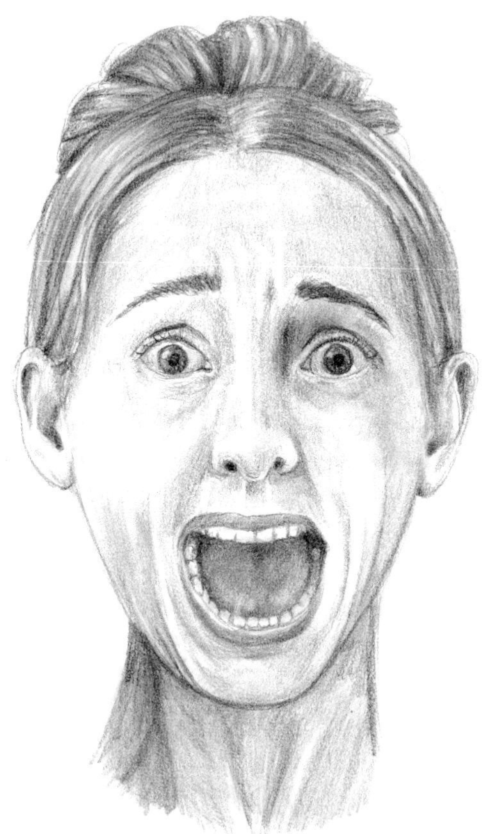

4. Smooth tones using a tissue on larger areas and a blending tool on the smaller areas.

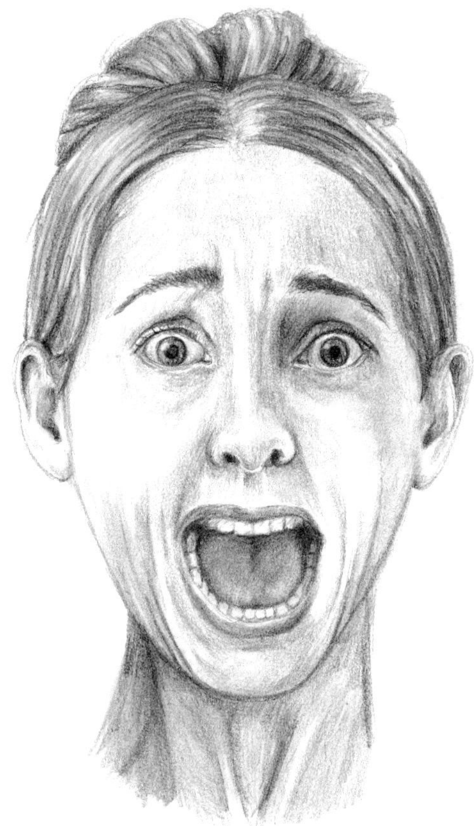

Build Contrast
5. Add more tone to the entire drawing and deepen the shadows. The eyes, hair, inside of the mouth, inner ear, and nostrils should be among the darkest tones.

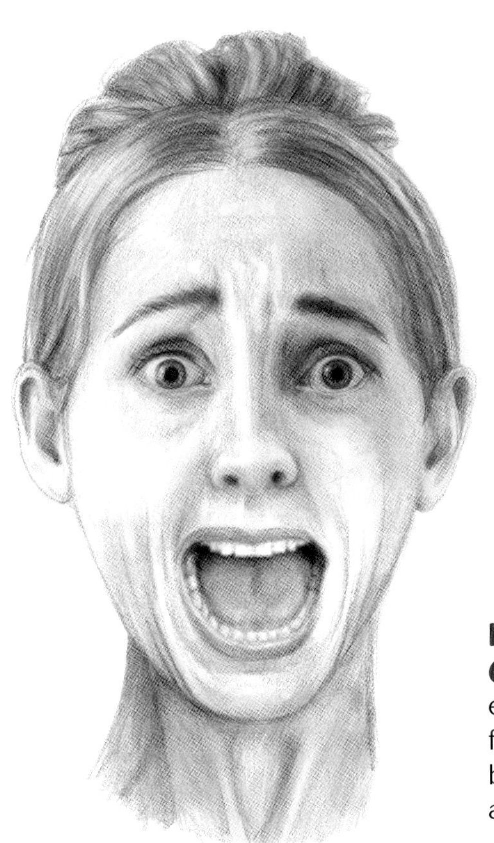

Refine the Drawing
6. Add highlights to the eye. Use a kneaded eraser to remove tone to add highlights to the face and make the hair shine. Refine the artwork by adding more contrast between highlights and shadows.

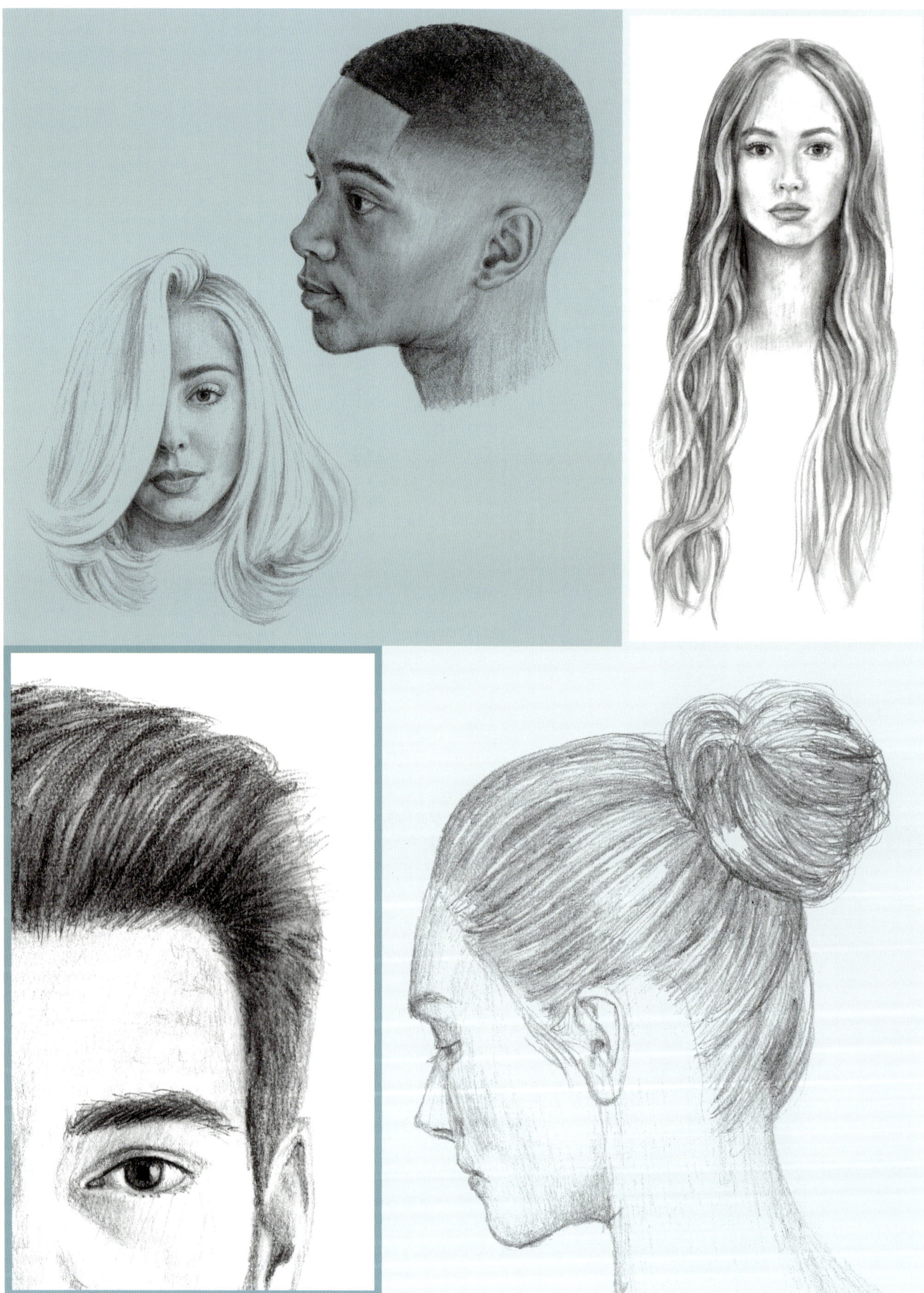

Chapter 4

DRAWING HAIRSTYLES

In this chapter, we're diving into the art of drawing various hairstyles, whether you're sketching flowing locks, intricate braids, or shorter styles. Just as a haircut can transform a person, your hair drawing will breathe life into your characters, giving them a unique identity.

The main focus of these portraits is the steps that are used to draw the hair, so you'll want to turn back to chapters 2 and 3 if you need more guidance for drawing faces and features.

SHORT HAIR

Paying attention to the direction the strands of hair are growing or styled in helps give a short hairstyle volume and movement and makes it look realistic.

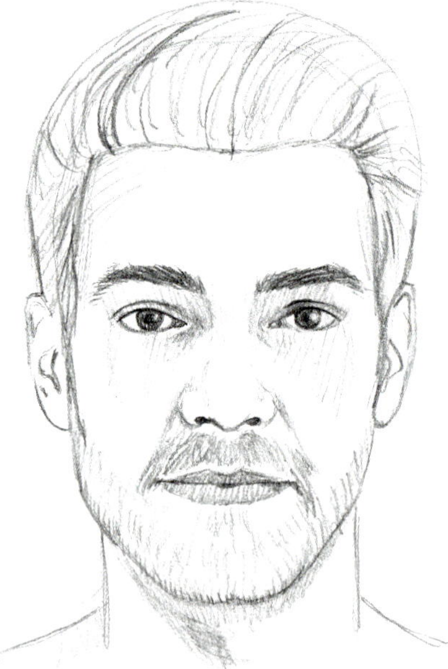

Draw the Basics

1. Draw a head following the steps on pages 38–39. Include all necessary guidelines for the eyes, mouth, and nose. Draw the basic features, referring back to pages 42–47 for guidance. Begin the hairline slightly higher than halfway between the brow line and the top of the head. Outline the hairstyle and begin sketching strands.

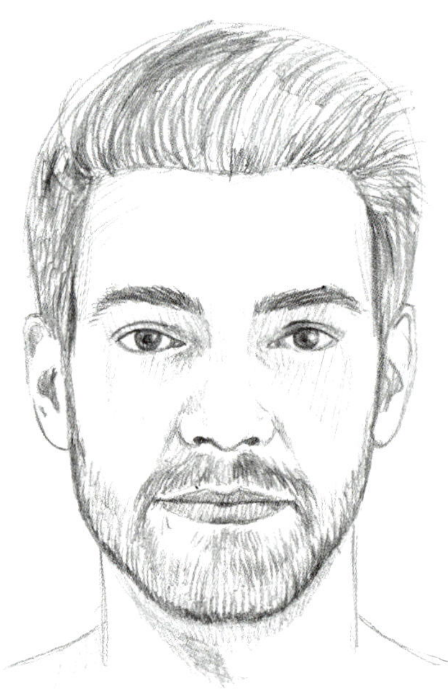

2. Add more lines to fill in the hair, paying attention to the direction of each section to create a style and provide movement.

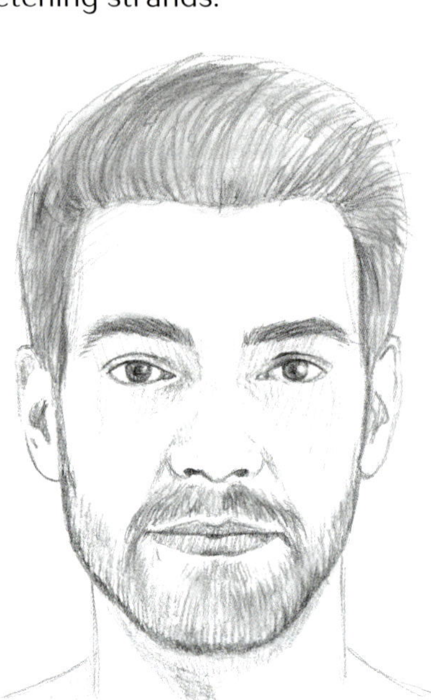

Blend & Smooth

3. Add a layer of tone to the drawing. Use a blending tool to smooth the lines of individual hairs so that each one does not stand out too much.

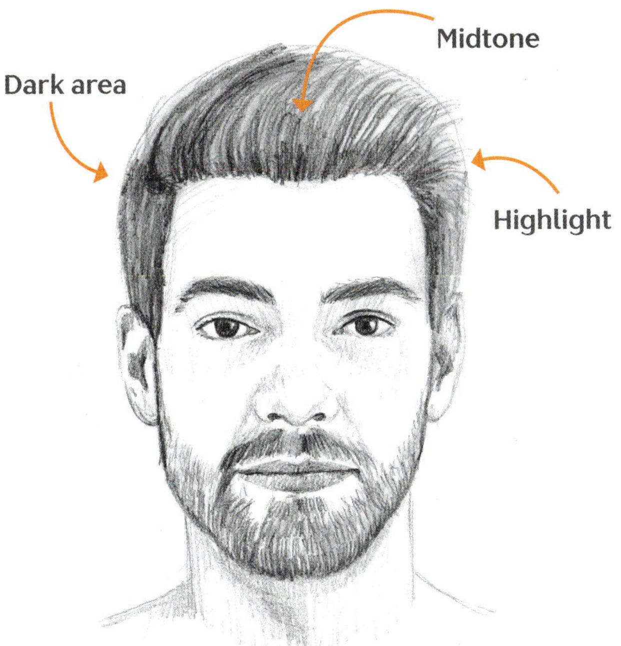

4. Identify the dark areas, midtones, and highlights, and add tone to reflect them. As the hair darkens, the shadows on the face should be darkened according to where the light is coming from.

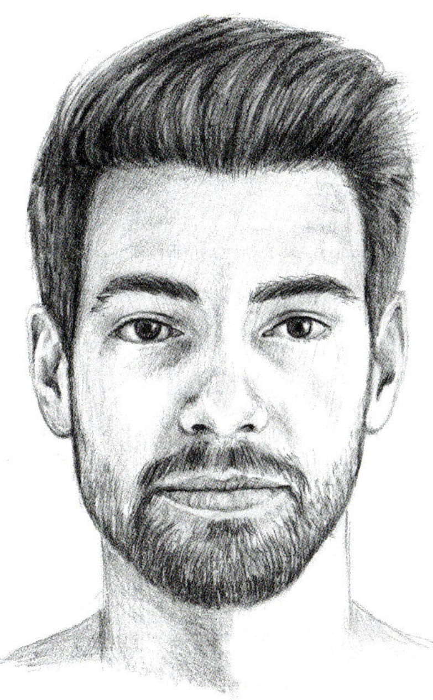

5. Add a few short strands at the hairline to make it look more realistic. It is not necessary to draw every single hair. Take artistic license and simplify!

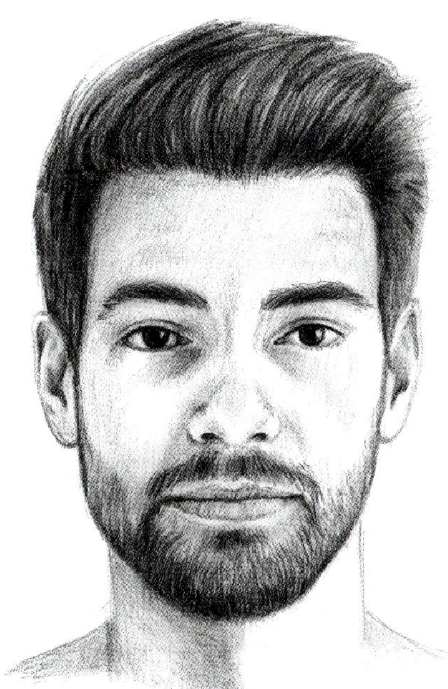

Refine the Drawing

6. Add more contrast for interest and depth. Deepen the tones in the hair. Use a kneaded eraser to remove pigment from the hairs that are highlighted.

DRAWING FACIAL HAIR

When drawing facial hair in portraits, consider its texture and shape. Start by lightly sketching the overall outline of the beard or mustache. Pay attention to the direction of hair growth and use short, flicking strokes to mimic its appearance. For a fuller beard, draw denser clusters of hair, leaving small gaps for realism. Add highlights and shadows to create depth and dimension, emphasizing areas where light hits and casting shadows where hair overlaps or recedes. Remember that facial hair varies greatly between individuals, so observe reference photos closely.

BUZZ CUT

This hairstyle is cut close to the scalp and this version of it relies on scumbling to show the texture of the hair. If you need a refresher on scumbling, see page 11.

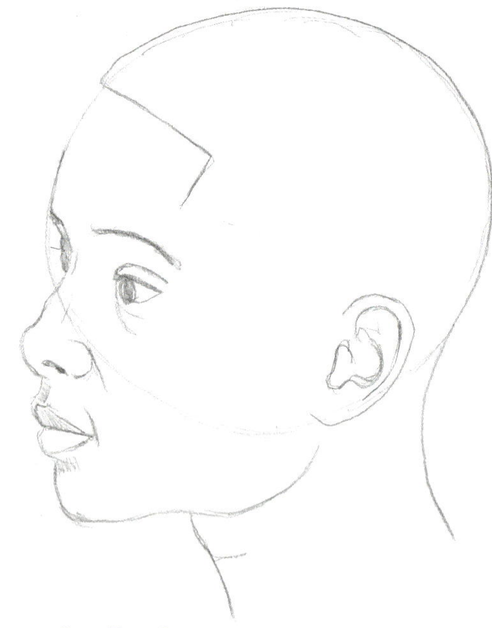

Draw the Basics

1. Draw a head in profile following the steps on page 40. Draw the basic features, referring to pages 42–47 for guidance. Draw a backward "L" as the guide for the hairline in this style.

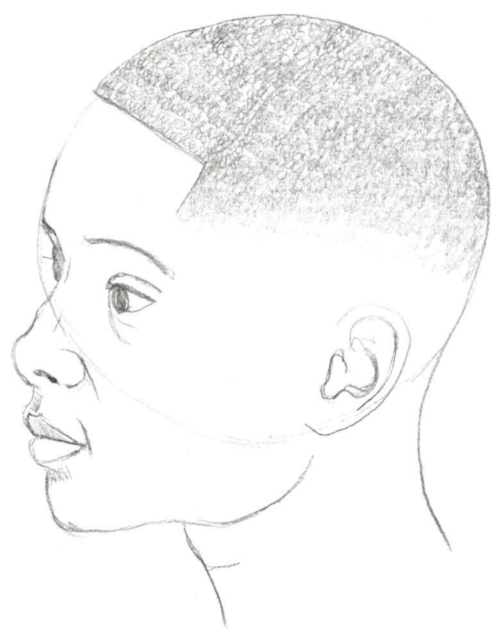

Use Scumbling

2. Lightly fill in the tone for the hair using a light layer of scumbling with the side of the pencil. The hair should gradually lighten toward the ears.

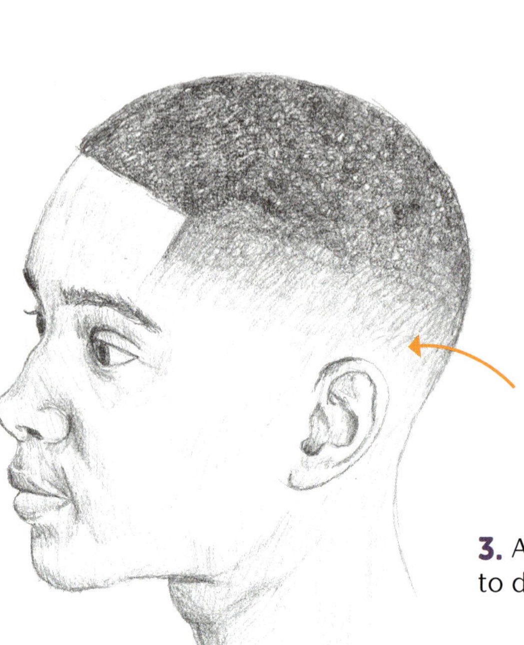

This hairstyle is also called a "fade" because of how the hair fades into the skin.

3. Add another layer of scumbling for the hair to darken it.

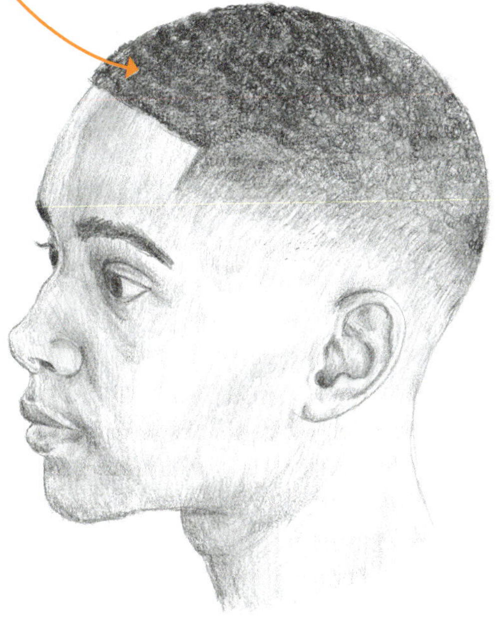

Build Contrast

4. Identify the dark areas, midtones, and highlights, and add tone to reflect them. As the hair darkens, the shadows on the face should be darkened according to where the light is coming from.

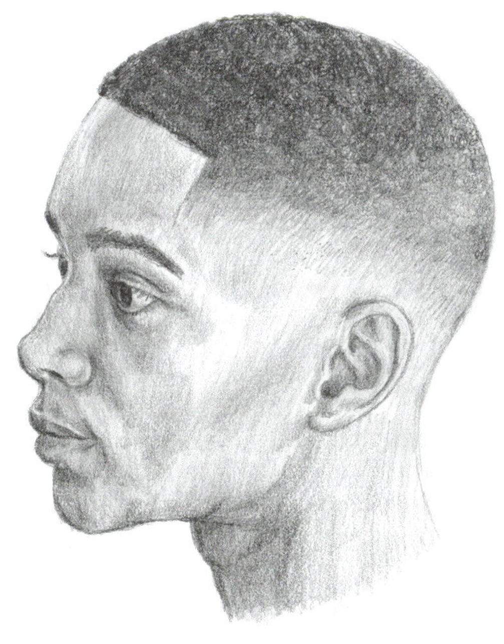

Blend & Smooth

5. Smooth the hair with a blending tool to help cover any open spots in the scumbling. Continue to add contrast between the dark areas, midtones, and highlights.

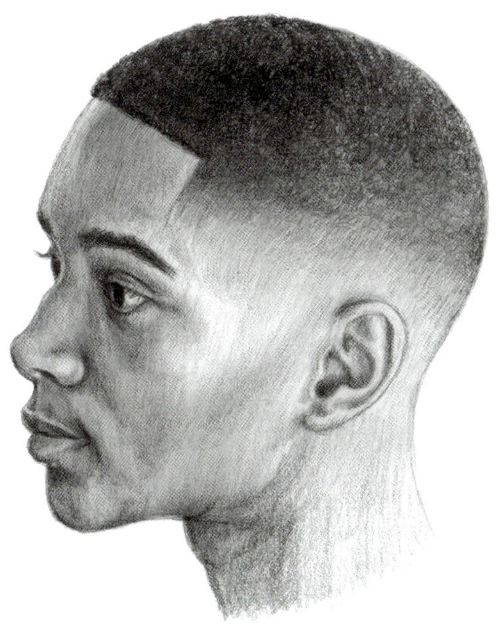

6. Add more contrast for interest and depth. Deepen tones in the hair. Use a kneaded eraser to remove pigment from the hairs that are highlighted.

SCUMBLING

Scumbling uses lots of tiny, overlapping circles. Lighter pressure and larger circles result in a rougher-looking texture, while harder pressure and smaller circles look smoother. For best results, use a sharp pencil angled on its side.

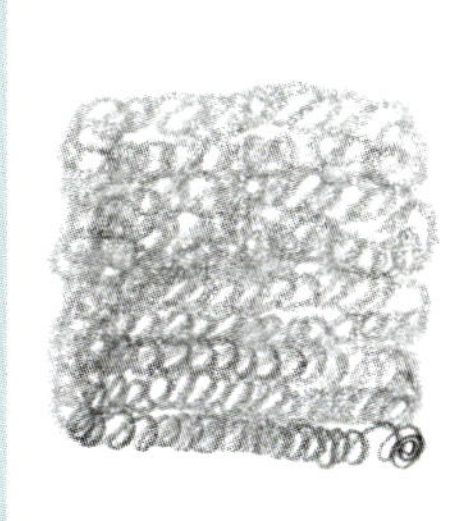
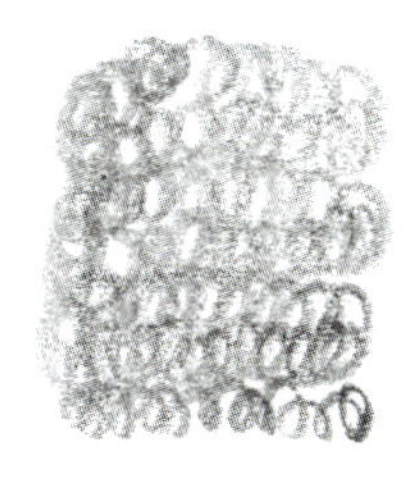

BOB HAIRCUT

A bob is a very versatile hairstyle. In this example, the hair has a bit of a wave to it, which gives an opportunity to practice creating depth. However, a person could also have a smooth, sleek bob that would rely more on contrast to show shine to help it look realistic.

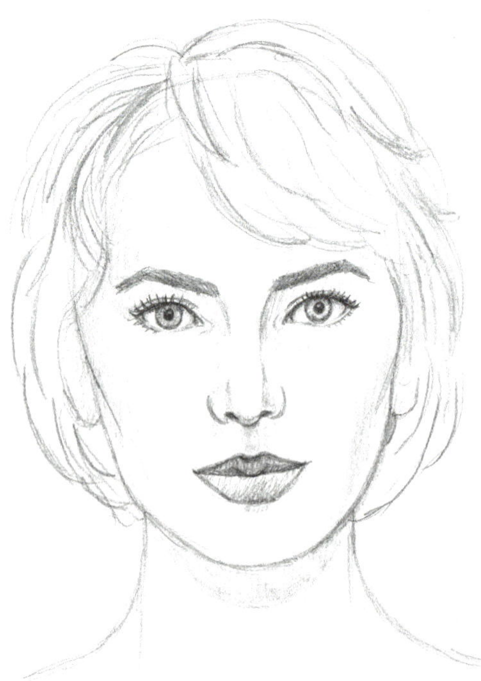

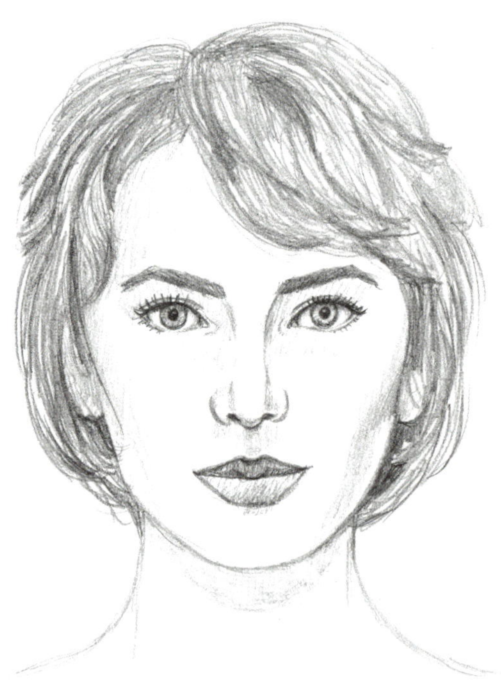

Draw the Basics

1. Draw a head following the steps on pages 38–39. Draw the basic features, referring back to pages 42–47 for guidance. With sketchy strokes, outline the basic shape of the hairstyle, starting the hairline slightly higher than halfway between the brow line and the top of the head. Add more wispy strokes to give the hair more shape and dimension.

2. Add more lines to fill in the strands of the hair. Follow the contour of each section to provide movement. Note how the hair is drawn over the ears—it doesn't block them completely from view.

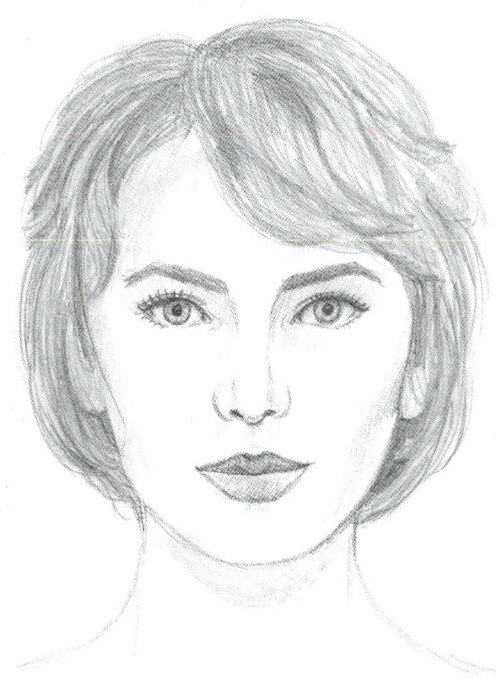

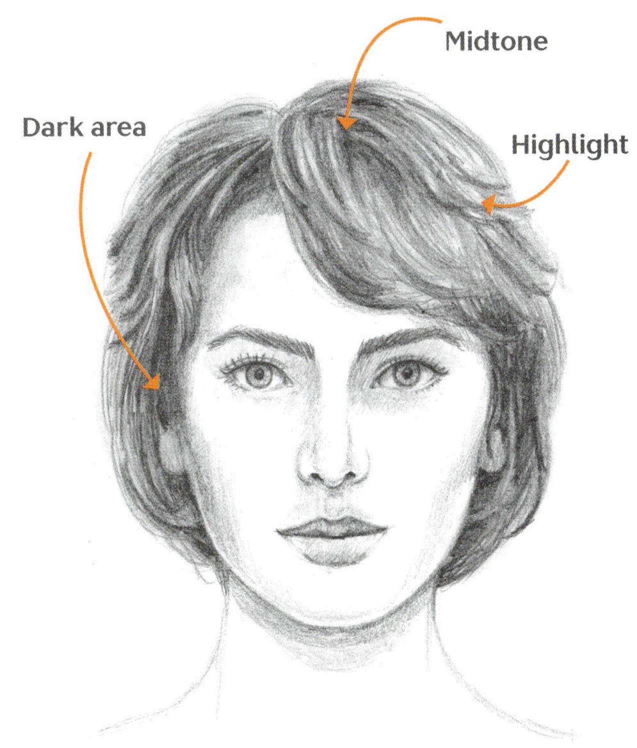

Blend & Smooth

3. Add a layer of tone to the drawing. Use a blending tool to smooth the hairs so that individual strands don't stand out too much.

Add Tones

4. Identify the dark areas, midtones, and highlights, and add tone to reflect them. As the hair darkens, the shadows on the face should be darkened according to where the light is coming from.

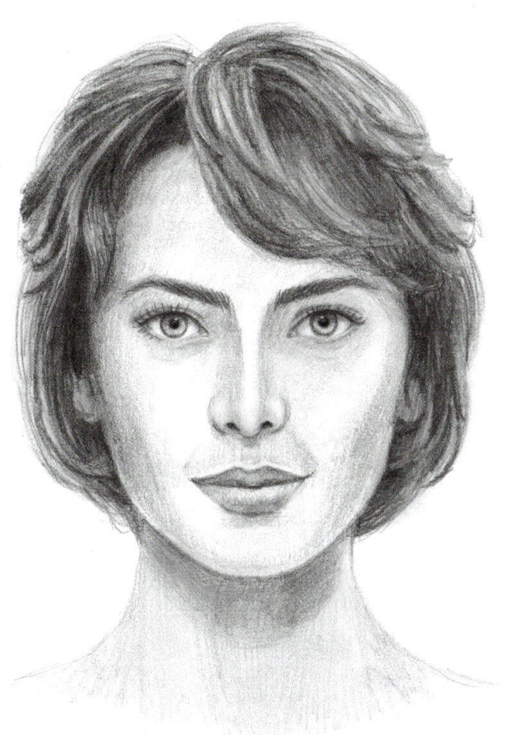

5. Continue to blend, and add another layer of tone to build contrast. Deepen the darkest tones, and use a kneaded eraser to remove pigment from the hairs that are highlighted.

SHOULDER-LENGTH HAIR

Often, a person's hair is darker than their skin tone, but this woman has very blonde hair, which has an impact on the contrast, shadows, and highlights in the drawing.

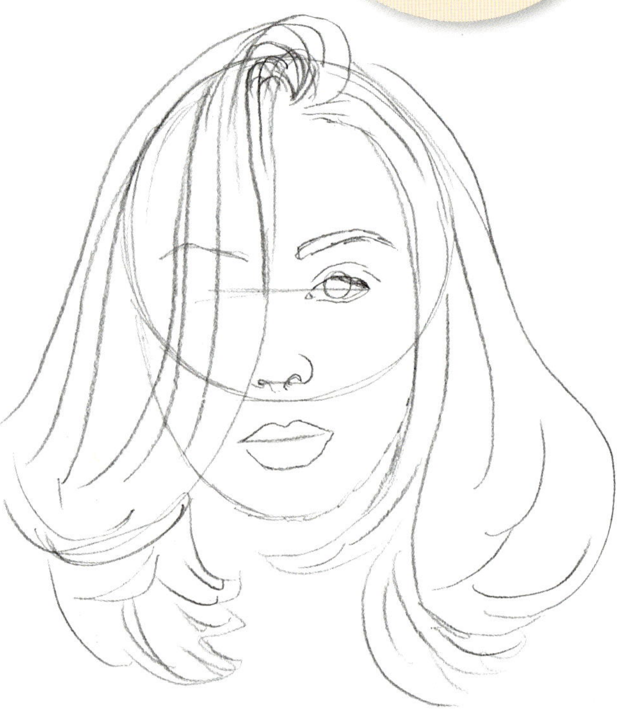

Draw the Basics

1. Draw a head following the steps on page 38. Include all necessary guidelines for the eyes, mouth, and nose. Draw the basic shape of the hairstyle.

2. Draw the basic features, referring back to pages 42–47 for guidance. Add more lines to help define the hair, showing volume and movement.

DRAWING WHAT IS HIDDEN

When drawing features like ears or eyes that are hidden by a hairstyle, start by lightly sketching them entirely. Imagine where they would be positioned under whatever is covering them, but avoid adding too much detail since they're partially obscured. Once the hidden features are sketched, draw the hairstyle over them and erase any areas that are hidden. This will give you the most realistic features and help make sure they've been placed correctly.

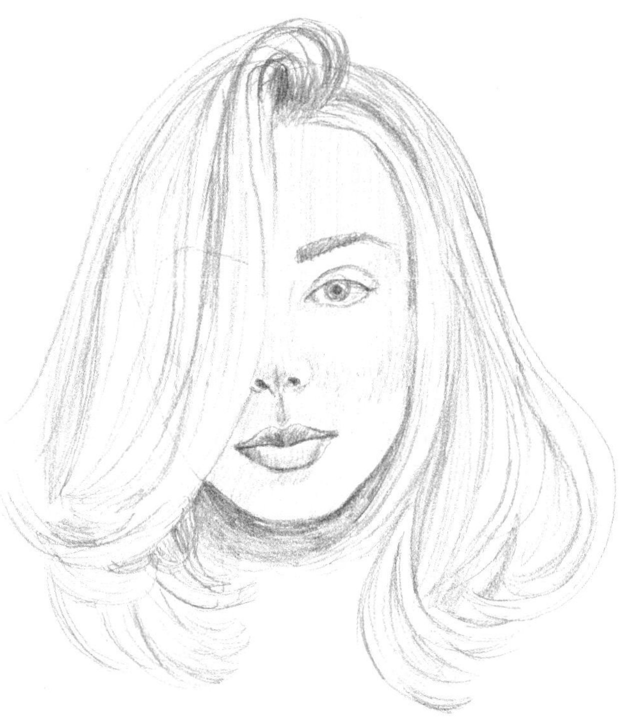

3. Draw more strands of hair. Since this hair is a very light hair color, most of it will be highlighted and few areas will be dark. Keep that in mind as you add a layer of tone to the drawing.

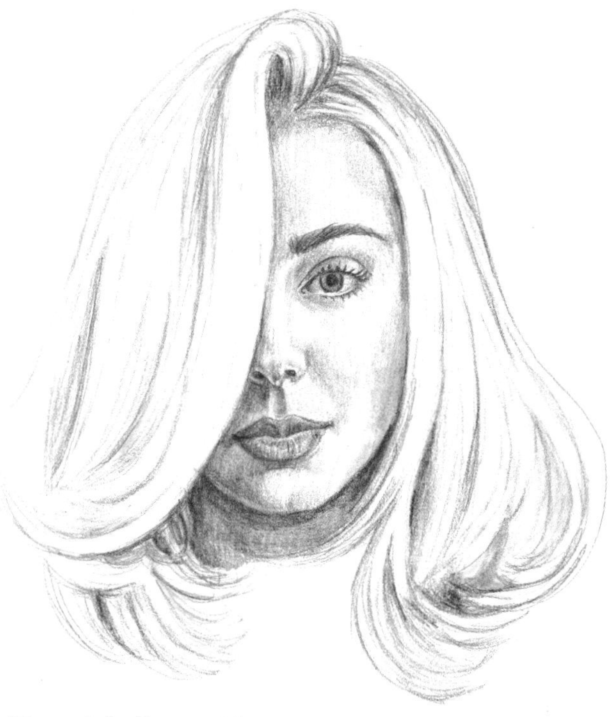

Blend & Smooth

4. Smooth hairs using a blending tool so that individual strands don't stand out too much. Continue to add contrast by deepening the dark tones.

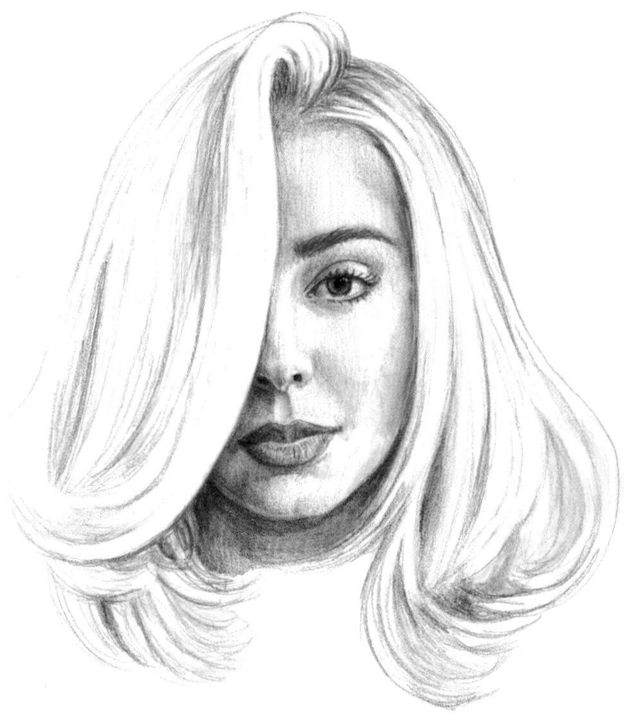

5. Use a kneaded eraser to remove pigment from large areas, and a stick eraser to remove pigment in lines to indicate strands of hair. This helps create contrast, which gives the hair dimension.

CURLY HAIR

I love how the loose curls in this example are brought to life with organic curved lines and the use of tone, highlight, and shadow. There's a huge difference between the hairstyle as it's shown in step 1 and the finished drawing!

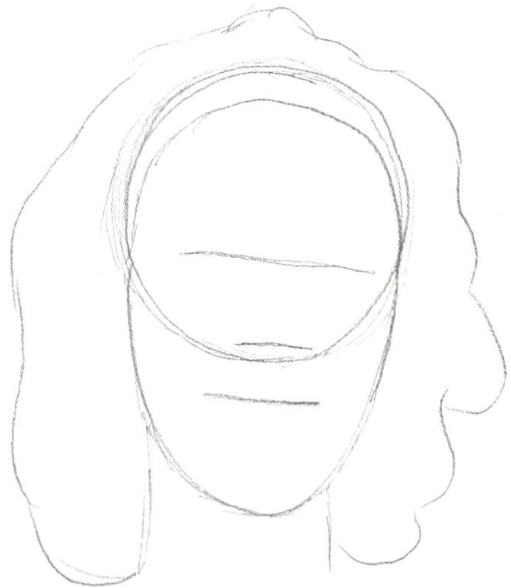

Draw the Basics

1. Draw a head following the steps on page 38. Include all necessary guidelines for the eyes, mouth, and nose. Draw the basic shape of the hairstyle.

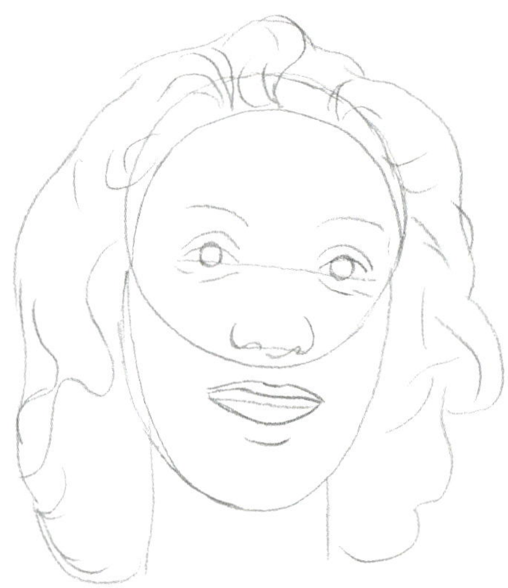

2. Draw the basic features, referring back to pages 42–47 for guidance. Add a few lines to help define the hair, showing volume and movement. Note that the hairline starts about an inch onto the forehead.

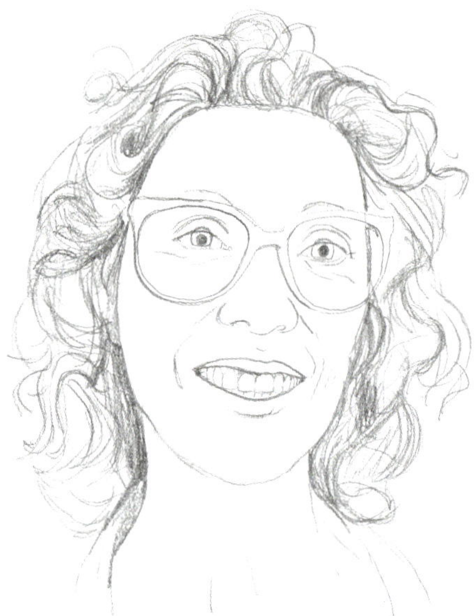

Refine the Features

3. Erase any guidelines no longer needed, and continue to refine the features. For the curls, use organic, curving lines of varying thickness and tone to convey movement and volume.

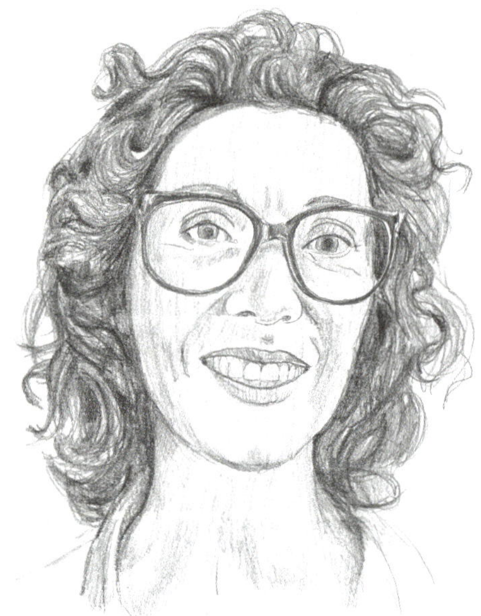

Add Tone

4. Add a layer of tone to the drawing. Identify the dark areas, midtones, and highlights, and add tone to reflect them. The darkest lines provide structure to the curls, but you don't want them to stand out too much.

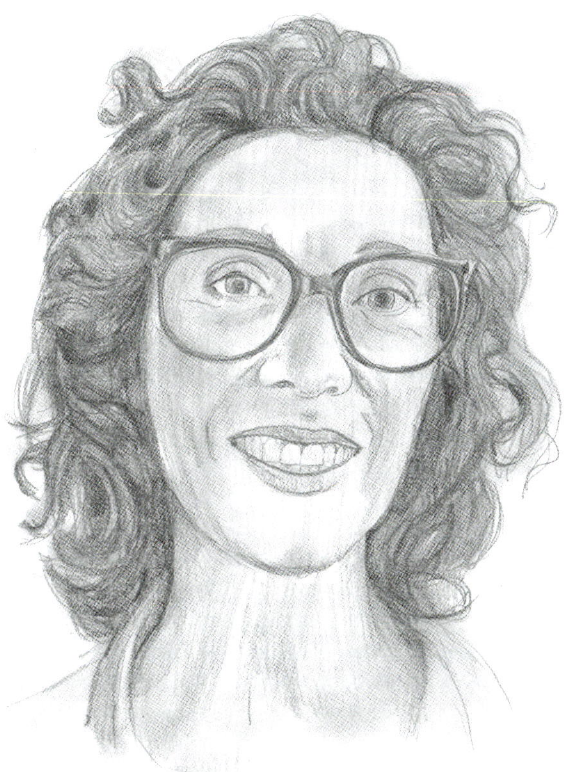

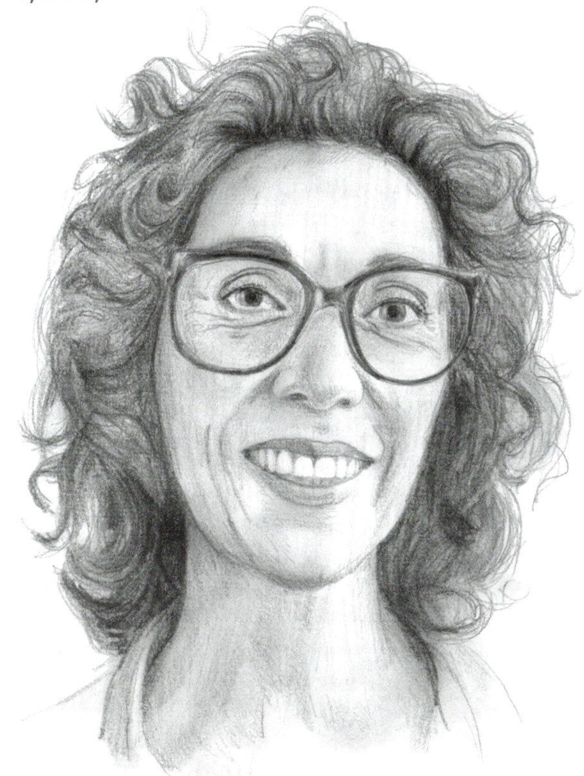

5. Blend to soften the appearance of the strands. Deepen the dark tones, making sure to pay attention to where shadows are falling on the face and neck.

Build Contrast

6. Draw more lines to further refine the curls, and continue to build up the contrast so individual curls are visible. Use a kneaded eraser to create highlighted areas.

DIFFERENT TYPES OF CURLS

Loose curls like in this example use gently curving lines of varying thickness to convey movement and volume. Shading focuses on subtle transitions between light and shadow to define the curls' form and texture.

Drawing ringlets requires more precise, uniform lines to depict tighter coils. Each ringlet is distinct, with sharper curves and consistent spacing. Shading accents the contrast between the inner and outer curves, which enhances the illusion of depth and dimension.

LONG HAIR

This portrait really comes to life when we begin to adjust the contrast—just look at the difference between steps 4 and 5!

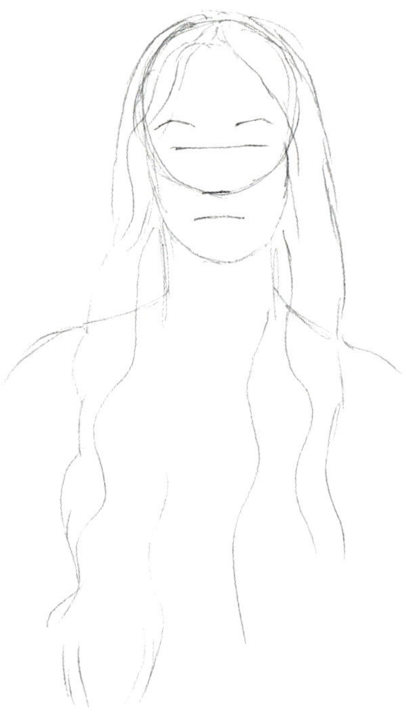

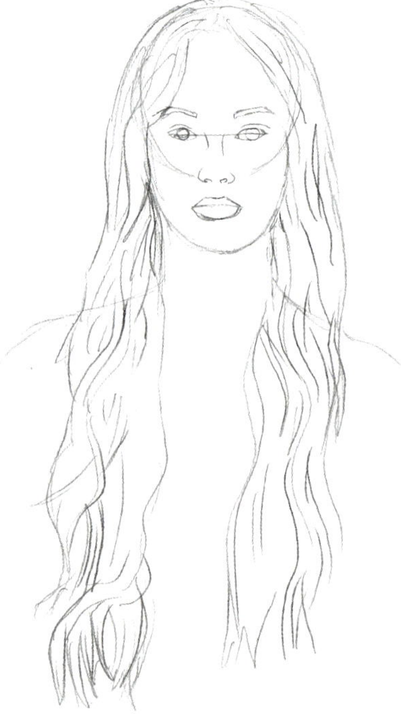

Draw the Basics

1. Draw a head following the steps on page 38. Include all necessary guidelines for the eyes, mouth, and nose. Because this hairstyle is long, we'll also want to include the neck and shoulders. Draw the basic shape of the hairstyle.

2. Draw the basic features, referring back to pages 42–47 for guidance. Add a few lines to help define the hair, showing volume and movement.

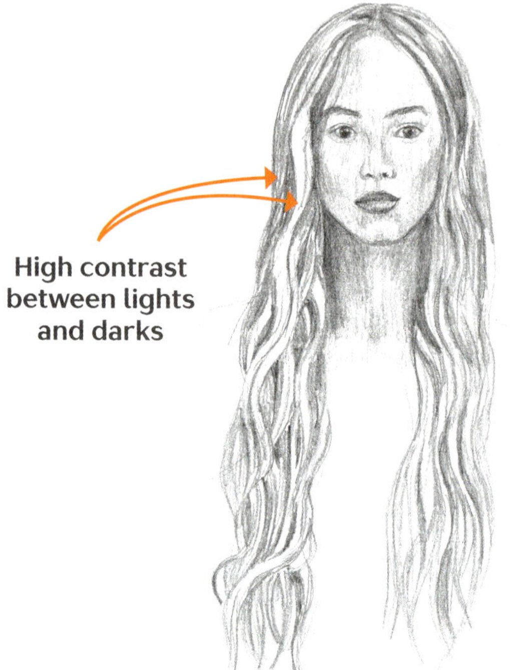

Add Tone

3. Add more details. Add a layer of tone to the drawing, focusing on adding highlights and shadows to the hair. Because this hairstyle includes face-framing highlights, the contrast between the highlights and the shadows is very high.

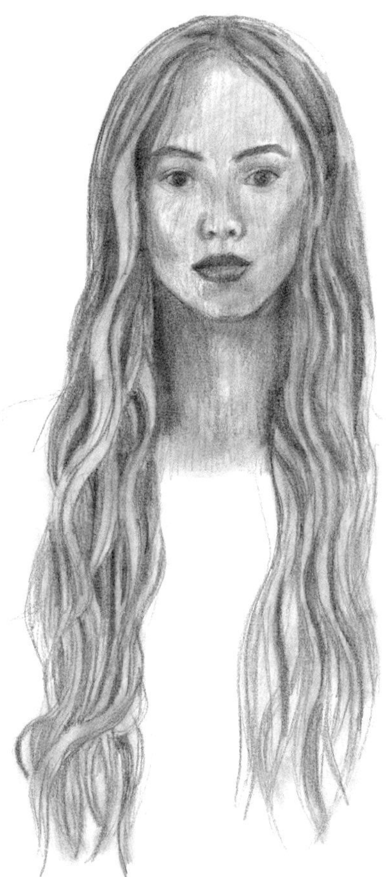

4. Using a blending tool, soften and smooth out the hair. Continue to deepen tones and build up contrast between the highlights and the shadows.

Build Contrast

5. Apply more pressure to the darker areas, and begin to remove tone in areas of highlight with a kneaded eraser.

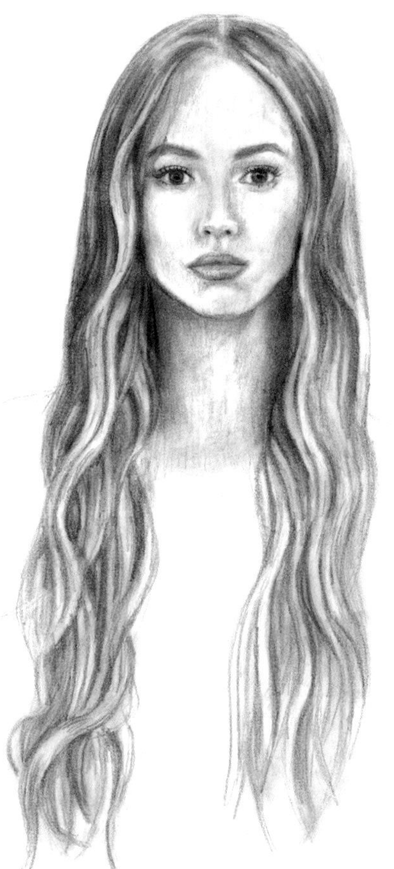

6. Continue to refine the contrast between lights and darks. This will give the hair a shiny appearance.

CORNROWS

Practicing how to draw realistic braids is important for this demonstration. See the tips in the sidebar before you begin your drawing.

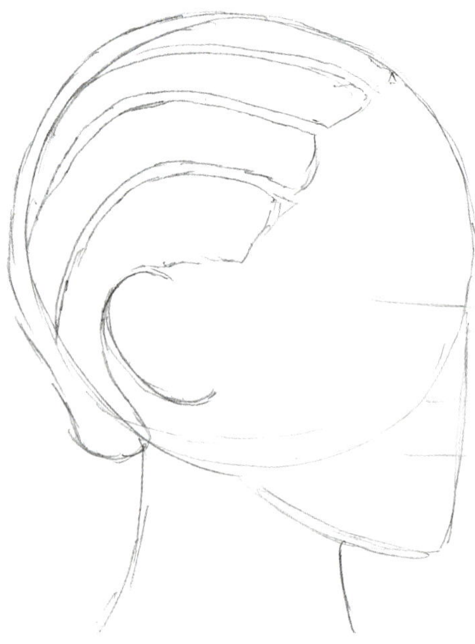

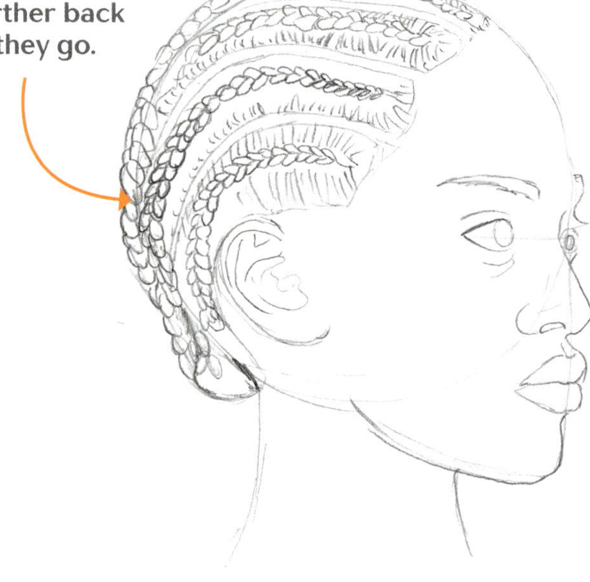

Draw the Basics

1. Draw a head in profile following the steps on page 40. Include all necessary guidelines for the eyes, mouth, and nose. Draw the outline of the hairstyle.

2. Draw the basic features, referring back to pages 42–47 for guidance. Draw the outlines of the small shapes that make up the braids. Use small lines to indicate the hair being pulled taut.

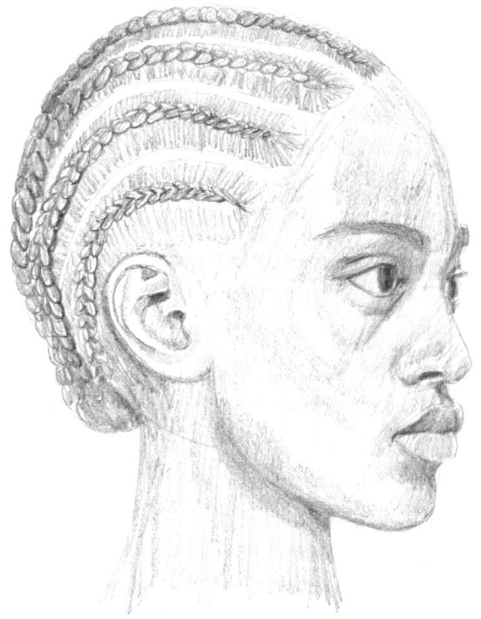

Add Tone

3. Add a light layer of tone to the entire drawing. Make sure to keep light areas light or untouched while darker areas have heavier pencil pressure.

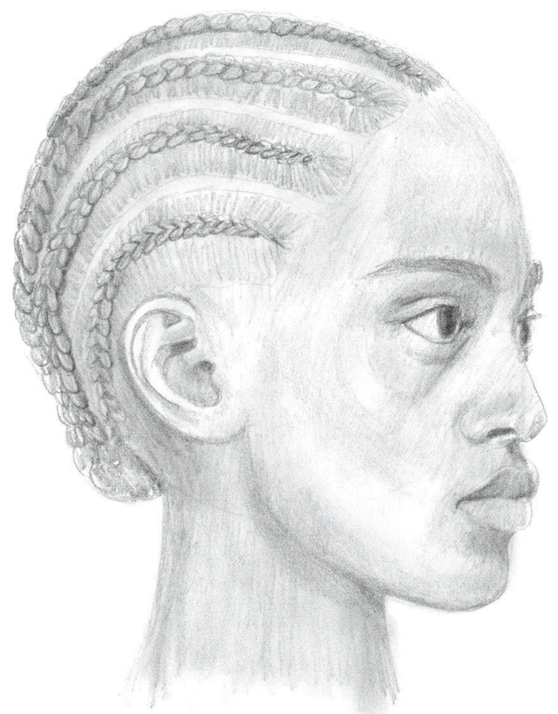

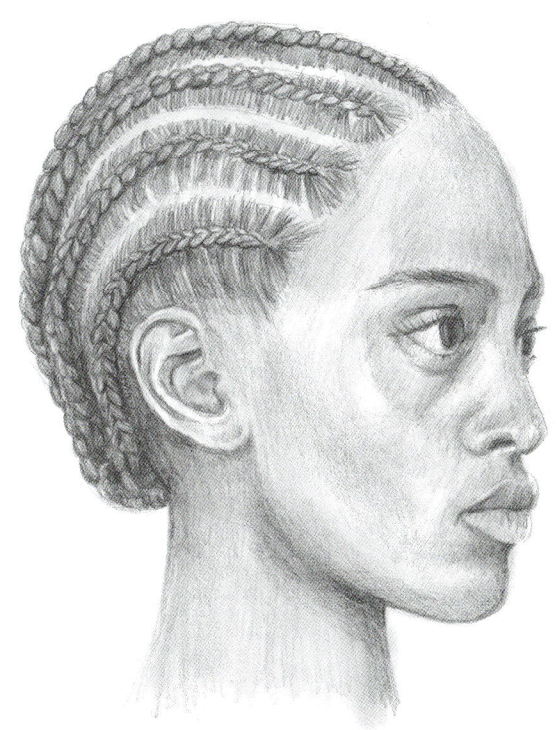

4. Smooth hairs using a blending tool so that no individual strand stands out too much.

Add Details

5. Add more detail to show the braid pattern using highlights, shadows, and lines to give texture and dimension. This will make the braids look three-dimensional.

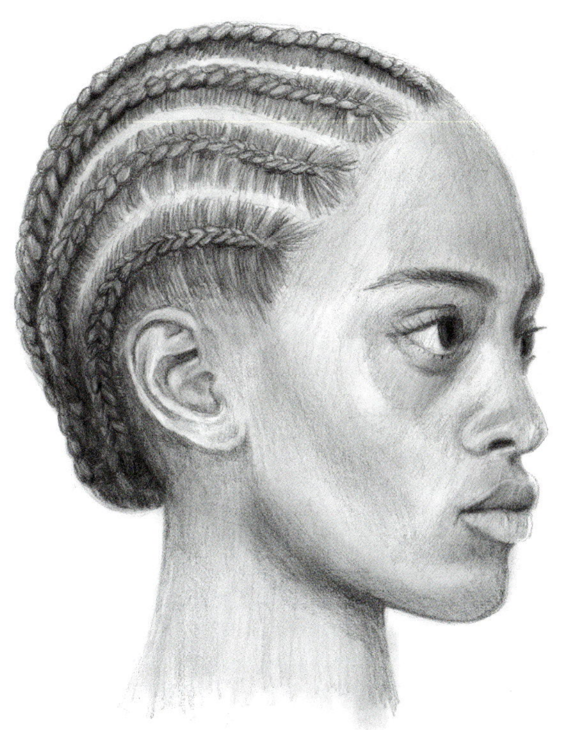

Build Contrast

6. Refine the artwork by adding more contrast between the highlights and shadows. Use a kneaded eraser to clean up any smudges and further define the highlighted areas.

DRAWING BRAIDS

When drawing braids, the starting point of the braid should be a little bit below the starting point of the hair, since the hair is being pulled into it. At the sketch stage, braids will be made up of small half-circles in pairs as seen on the side of the head, but notice that only one side of the braid is shown of the topmost braid when viewed in a profile.

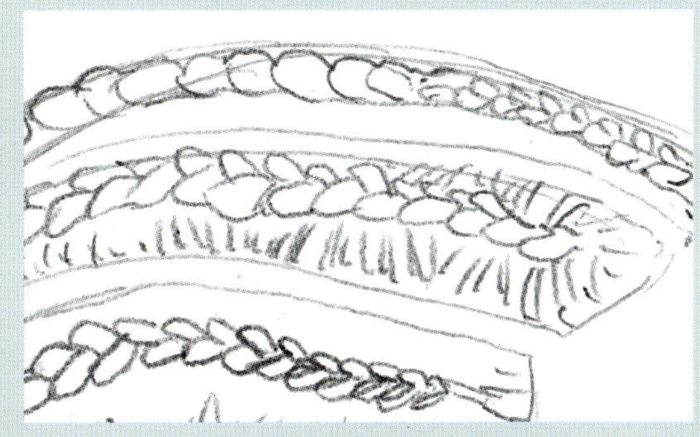

UPDO

For the sake of showing the hairstyle, this demonstration uses a 3/4 view that predominantly features the back of the head.

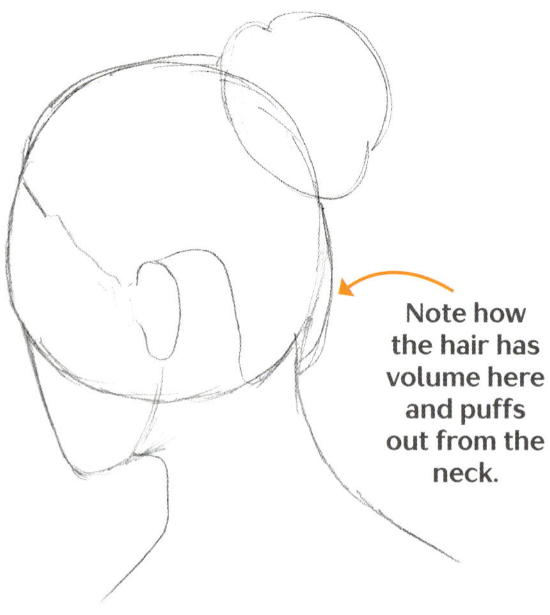

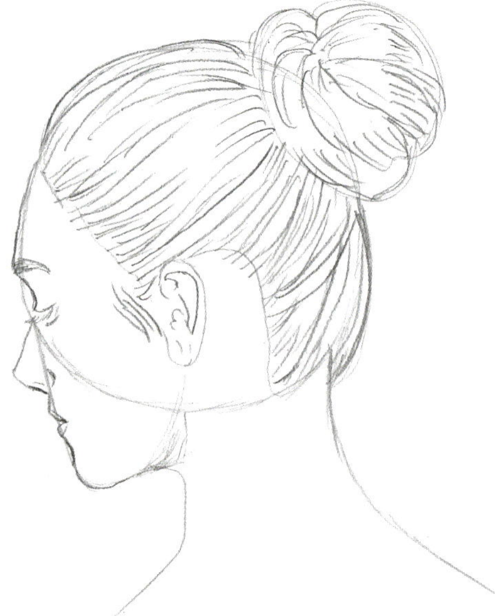

Draw the Basics

1. Draw a 3/4 view of a head following the steps on page 41. Include all necessary guidelines for the eyes, mouth, and nose. Draw the outline of the hairstyle.

2. Draw the basic features, referring back to pages 42–47 for guidance. Draw lines to indicate strands of hair, as well as their direction. Notice the difference in the directions of the lines on the head versus the lines of the bun.

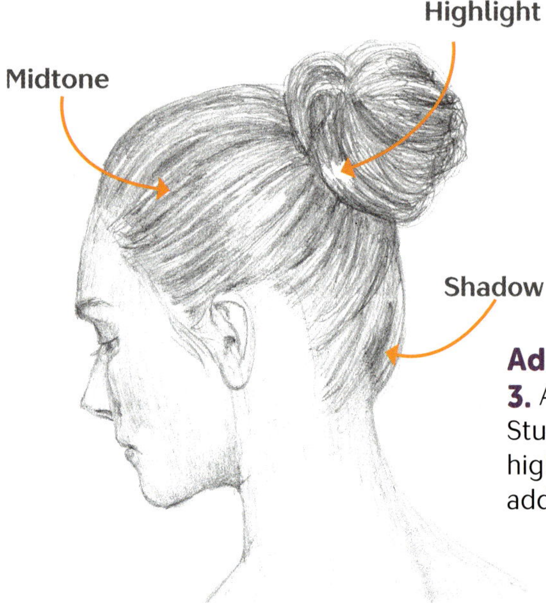

Add Tone

3. Add a light layer of tone to the drawing. Study your subject to see the areas of highlights, shadows, and midtones. Use lines to add contrast between the tones.

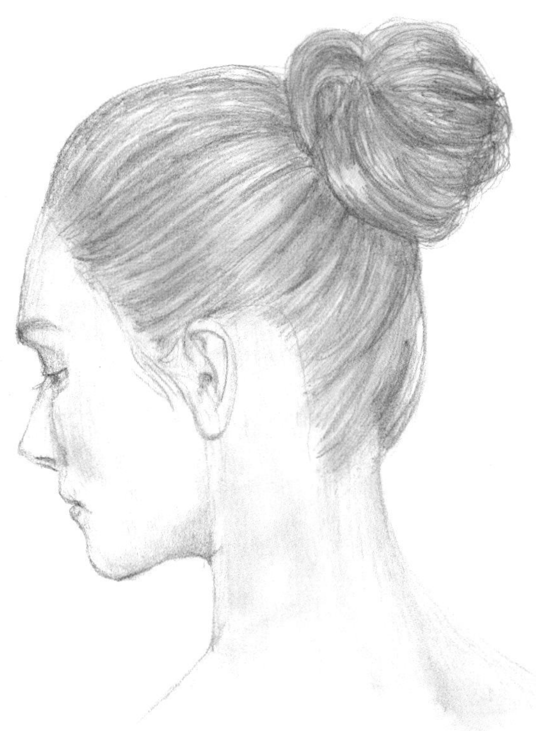

Blend & Smooth

4. Using a blending tool, soften and smooth out the hair to create a more uniform base layer. Continue to deepen tones and build up contrast between the highlights and the shadows.

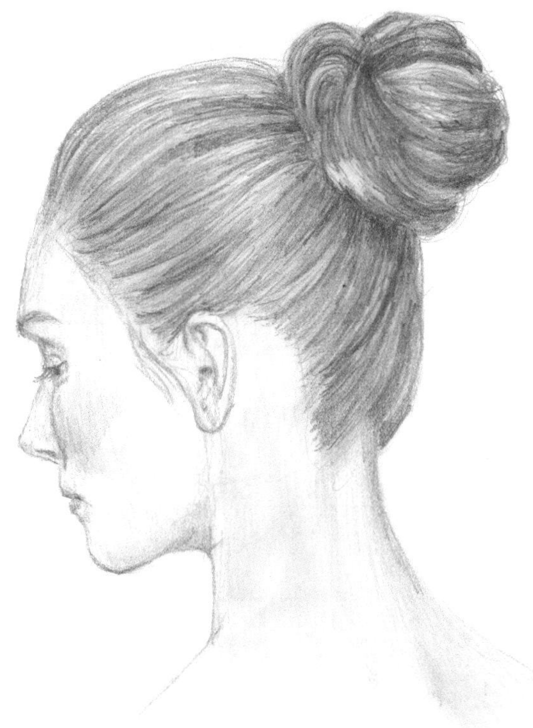

5. Draw lines to add more contrast to the strands, focusing on the darker tones and highlights.

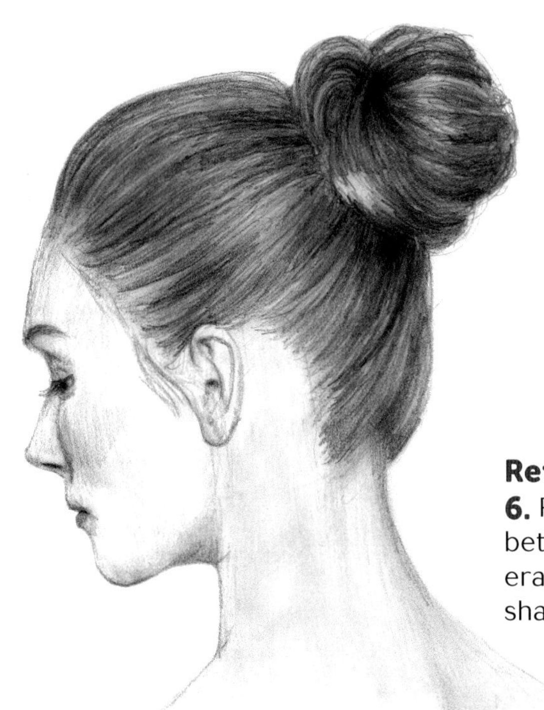

Refine Highlights & Shadows

6. Refine the artwork by adding more contrast between highlights and shadows. Use a kneaded eraser to further highlight areas, and add shading to increase the shadows.

PONYTAIL

This ponytail looks realistic because of all the loose pieces and flyaways framing the face and at the base of the neck. Including imperfections is one of the best ways to draw lifelike portraits.

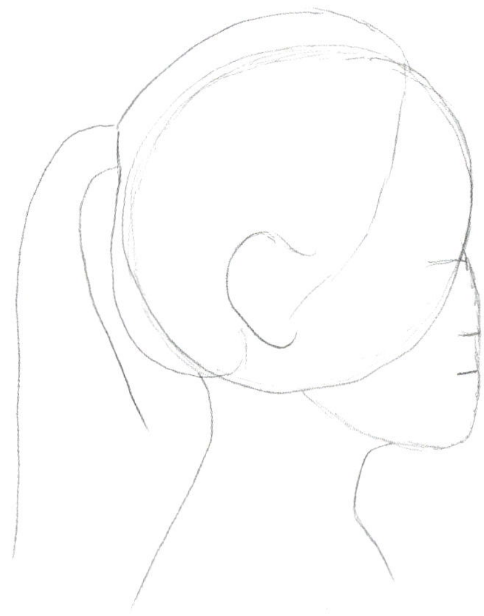

Draw the Basics

1. Draw a head in profile following the steps on page 40. Include all necessary guidelines for the eyes, mouth, and nose. Draw the outline of the hairstyle.

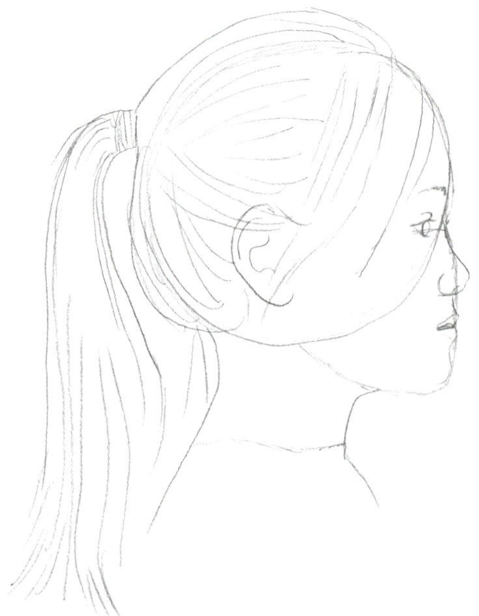

2. Draw the basic features, referring back to pages 42–47 for guidance. Draw lines to indicate strands of hair as well as their direction.

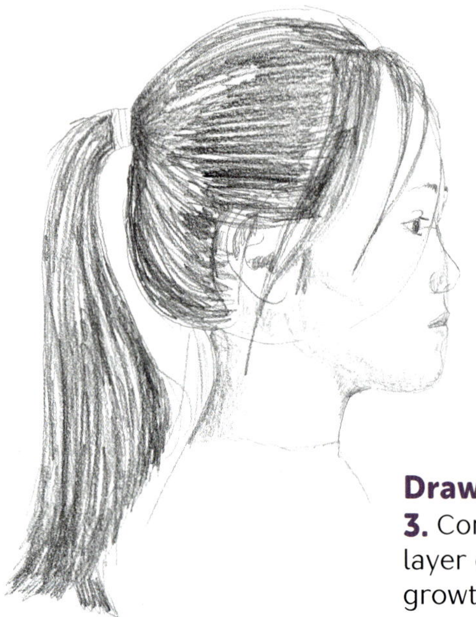

Draw Lines

3. Continue to thicken the hair by drawing a layer of lines that follow the direction of the hair growth.

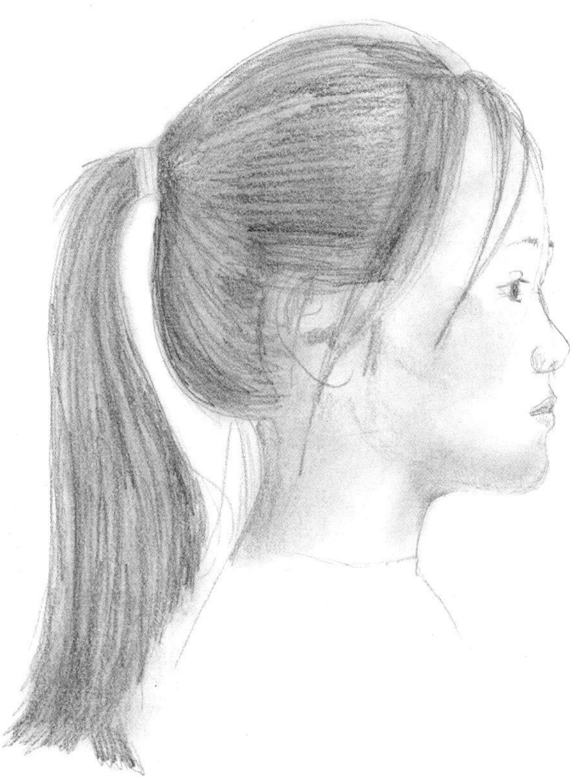

Add Tone

4. Add a light layer of tone to the drawing. Study your subject to see the areas of highlights, shadows, and midtones. Draw lines to add contrast between the tones. Then use a blending tool to soften and smooth out the hair.

Add Detail

5. Add more detail to the hair with lines that may have been blended out. Add some loose hairs and flyaways. Continue to deepen the tones and build up contrast between the highlights and the shadows.

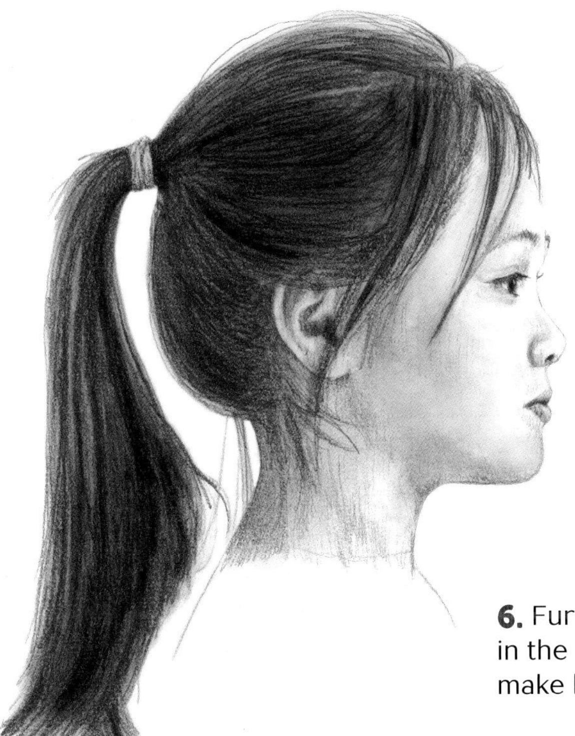

6. Further refine the contrast by using shading in the darker areas and a kneaded eraser to make highlighted areas stand out.

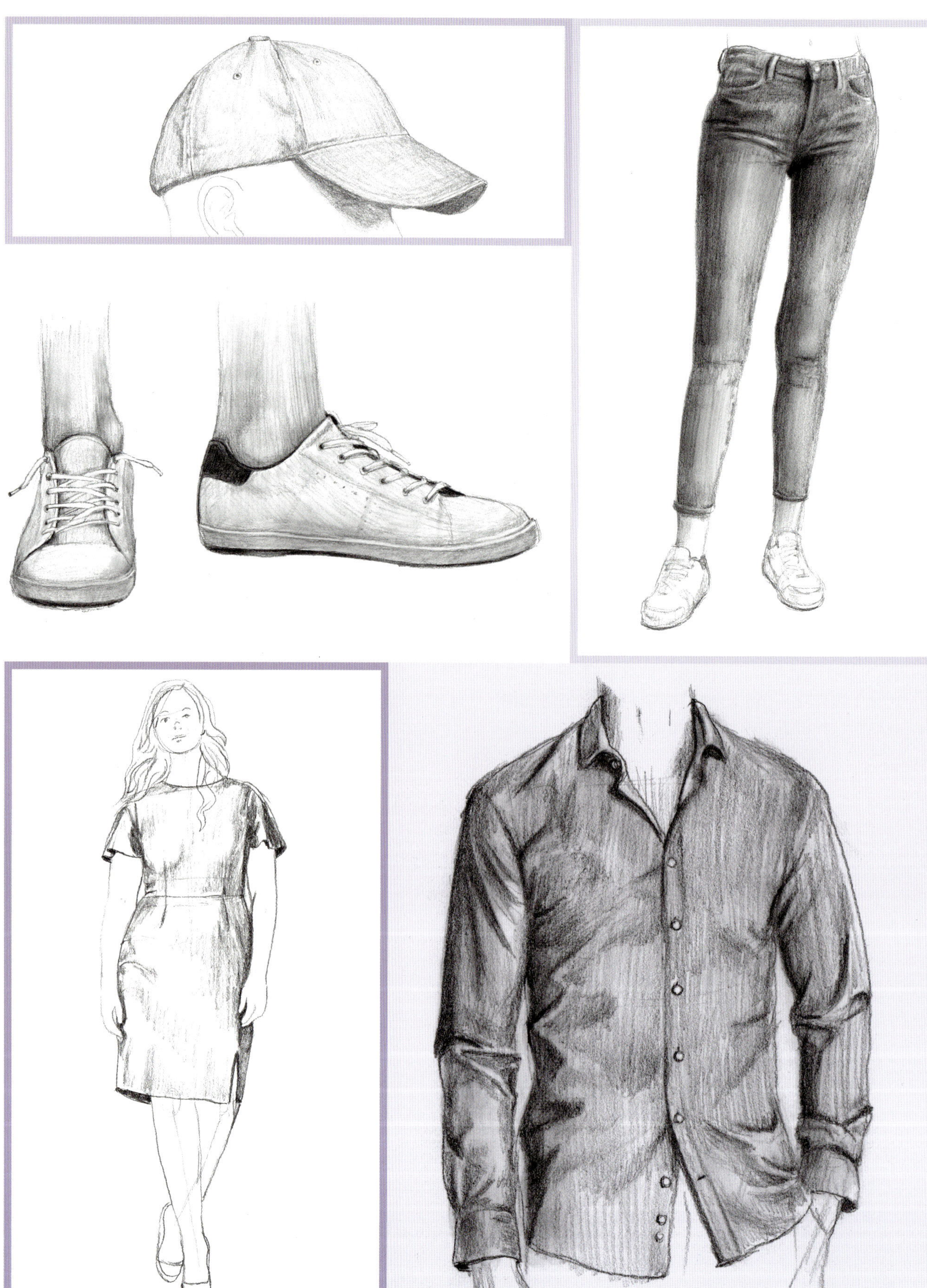

Chapter 5

DRAWING CLOTHING & ACCESSORIES

In this chapter, we'll explore how to draw various clothing items and accessories—from everyday staples like jeans and T-shirts to elegant dresses and stylish sneakers. Throughout the tutorials, you'll discover tips and tricks for drawing textures, folds, and other details that will make your portraits feel more realistic and lifelike with just a pencil and paper.

The main focus of the instructions will be the clothing and accessories, with the other features of the portrait only explained in relation to them as needed.

SLIM PANTS

With pants that fit closer to the body, there is less extra fabric to cause creases, wrinkles, and folds. This example is for a pair of jeans, but the steps could apply to any type of slim-fitting pants.

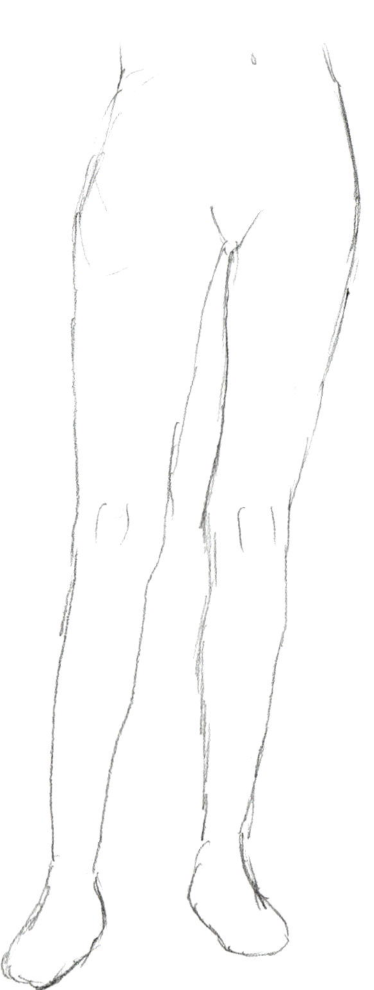

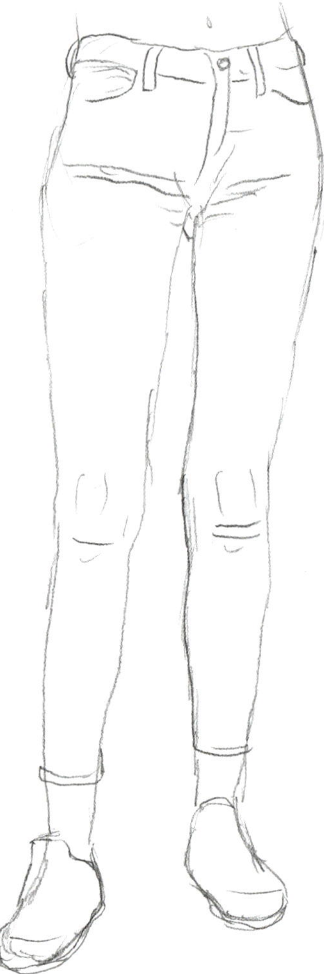

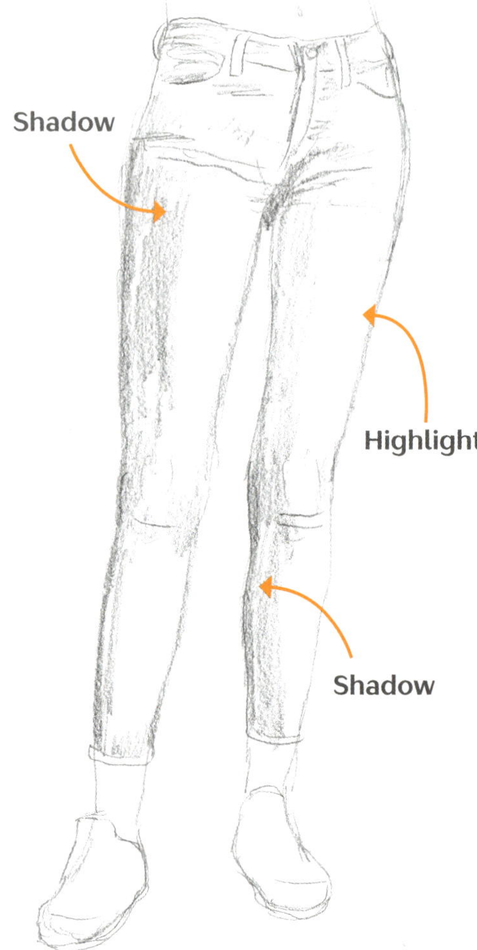

Draw the Basics
1. Draw the front view of the lower half of a body, following the steps on pages 24–25. For guidance on drawing legs, see page 32.

Add Details
2. Because these pants fit close to the body, there is no need to draw their shape extending from the legs. Sketch any details, including belt loops, pockets, cuffs, and a zipper and button. Using lines, add creases and wrinkles in the fabric at the groin and knees, or anywhere the fabric might bunch or pull.

Add Tone
3. Erase any unneeded guidelines. Add a light layer of tone, concentrating on the creases and wrinkles in the pants and areas of shadow. In this drawing, the light source is coming from the right, so the left side of the drawing is darker, including the inner thigh of the leg on the right side.

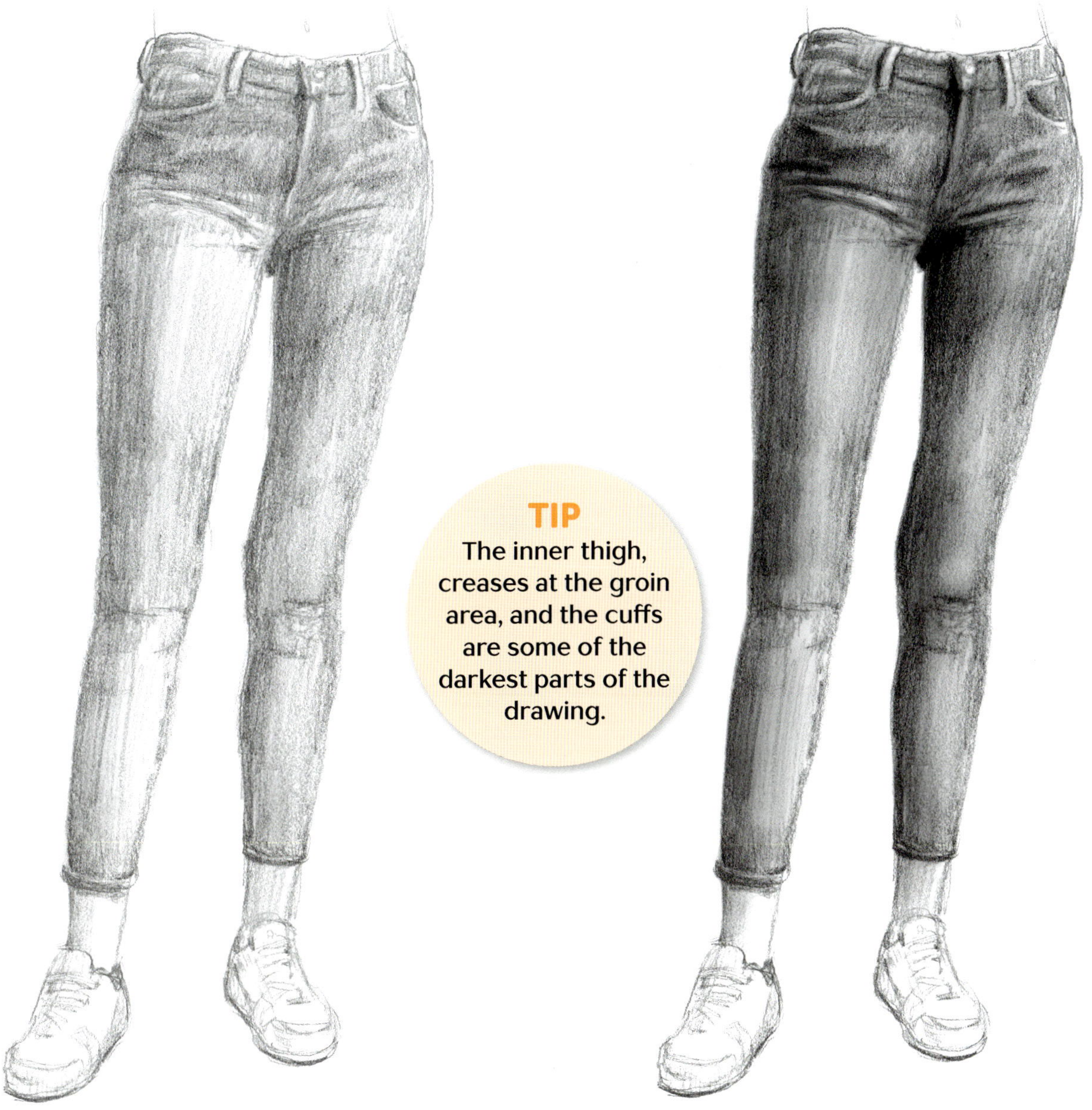

4. Add another layer of tone, and blend using a blending tool to create a more uniform base layer. Continue to deepen shadowed areas. Further define the pockets, belt loops, and button closure.

Build Contrast

5. Using shading, add more contrast. The left side of the leg and right inner thigh are in the most shadow. Use a kneaded eraser to highlight the front of the thighs and the tops of the wrinkles and folds.

PANTS

Just like in the Button-Down Shirt drawing (page 118), these pants are brought to life with creases, wrinkles, and folds in the fabric. For tighter-fitting pants, look at Slim Pants on page 112.

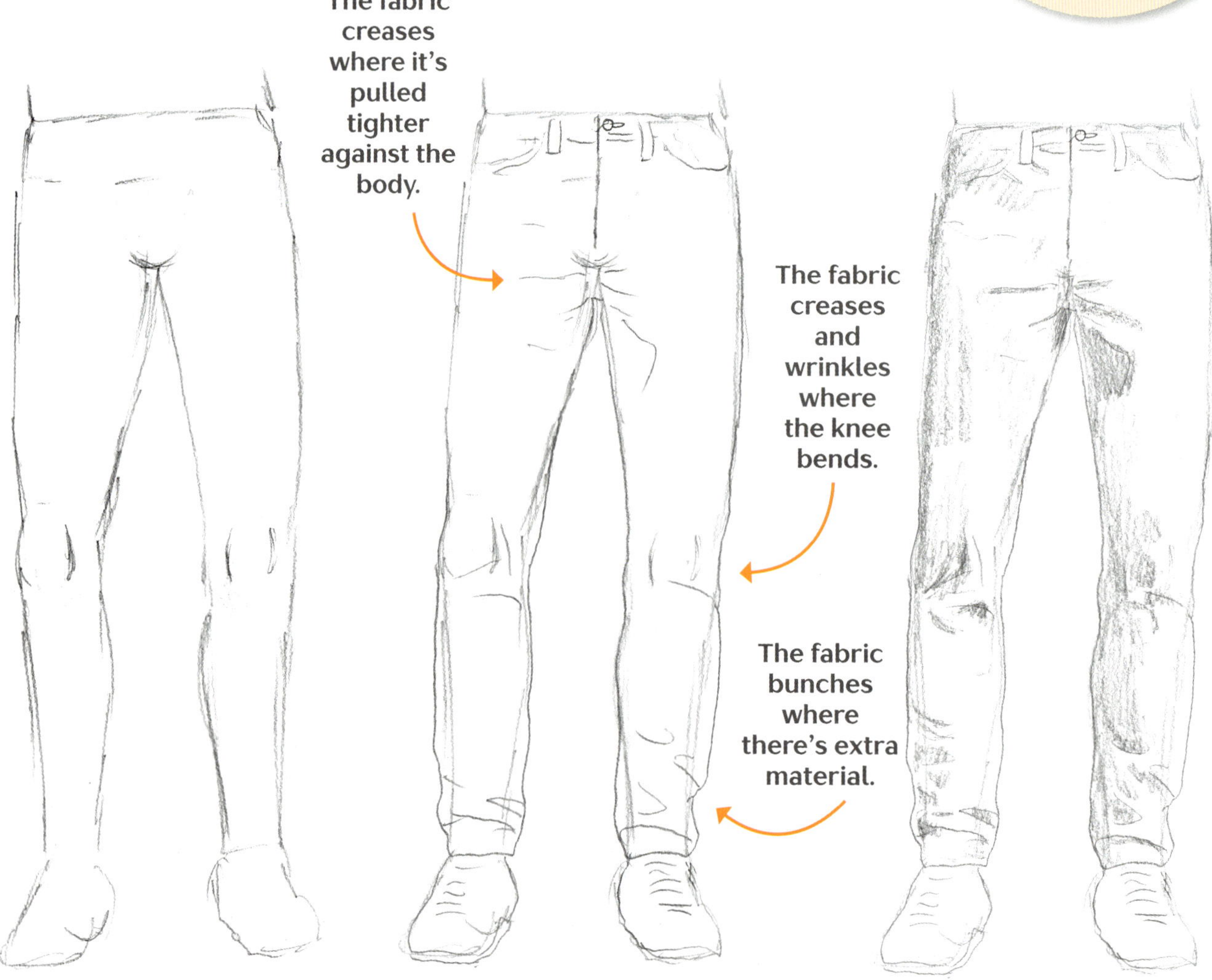

Draw the Basics
1. Draw the front view of the lower half of a body, following the steps on page 21. For guidance on drawing legs, see page 32.

Add Details
2. Draw the outline of the jeans. Here, they should extend around the leg since the style isn't skintight. Draw details like belt loops, pockets, zipper, and button closure. Draw thin lines to indicate creases in the pants and areas where the fabric has bunched and folded. These details tend to happen where the body bends, and where fabric is tighter or looser.

Add Tone
3. Erase any unneeded guidelines. Add a light layer of tone, concentrating on the creases of the pants and areas of shadow. The light source is coming from the right, so things on the left side of the drawing are darker, including the inner thigh of the leg on the right side.

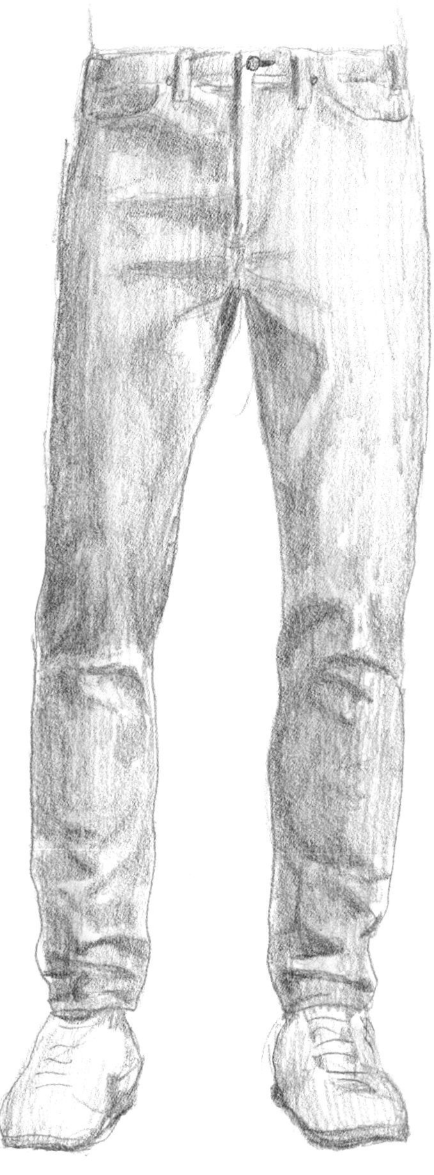 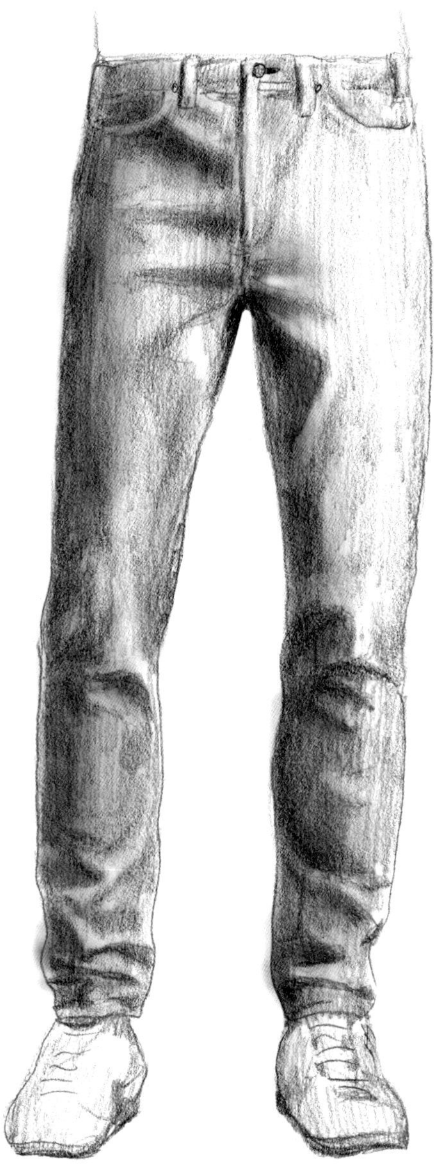

4. Blend using a blending tool, and then add another layer of tone to create a more uniform base layer. Continue to deepen shadowed areas, and use a kneaded eraser to create highlights. Further define the pockets, belt loops, and button closure.

Build Contrast

5. Add more contrast, making the shadows darker and using a kneaded eraser to further lighten the highlights.

T-SHIRT

You'll probably get a lot of practice drawing T-shirts, one of the most popular clothing items around the globe! This example features a blank shirt, but for tips on drawing clothing with lettering or designs, see page 125.

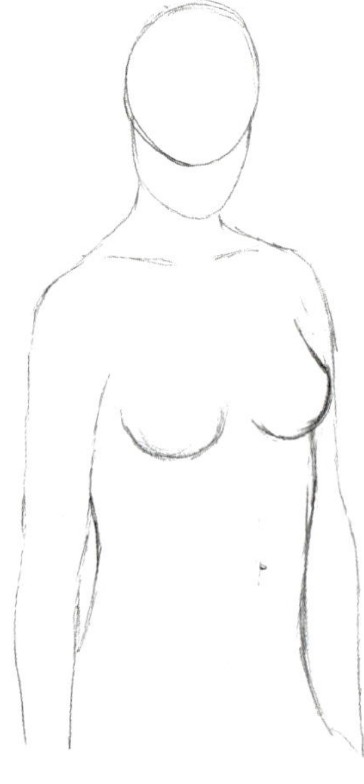

Draw the Basics

1. Draw the upper half of a body, following the steps on pages 24–25. Drawing details like breasts and collar bones before adding the outline of the shirt will help the finished product look realistic since the fabric will be drawn to accommodate the shape of the body, and you'll be able to make sure the placement of the clothing is correct.

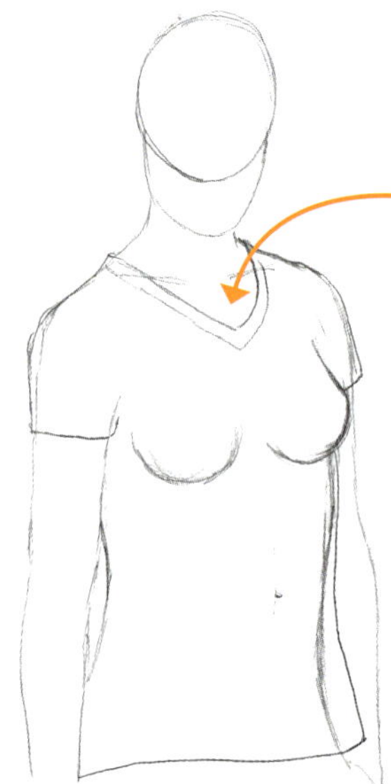

2. Draw the outline of the T-shirt around the body. The lines should follow the form of the body but extend beyond it since the shirt is loose. Draw the sleeves.

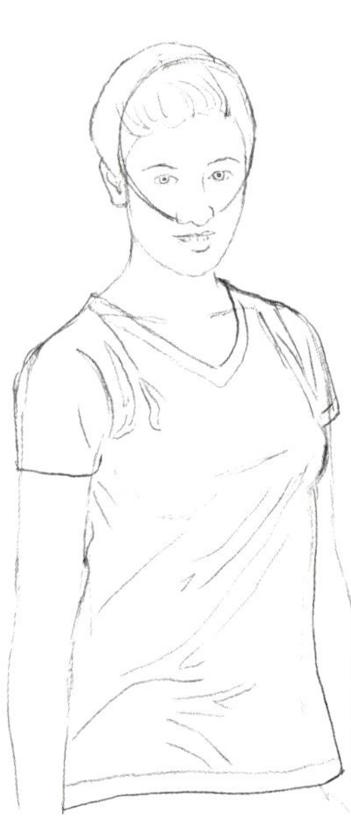

Add Details

3. Draw thin lines to indicate creases and areas where the fabric has bunched and folded. These details tend to happen where the body bends, and where fabric is tighter or looser. Here, the fabric folds around the shoulders and hips, and is pulled taut across the chest and stomach.

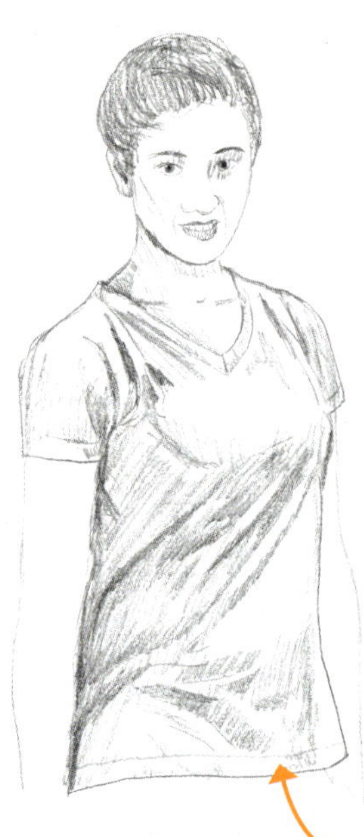

Add Tone

4. Erase any unneeded guidelines. Add a light layer of tone. Darken the areas of shadow, like the left side and the deep wrinkles in the clothing. Leave highlighted areas lighter.

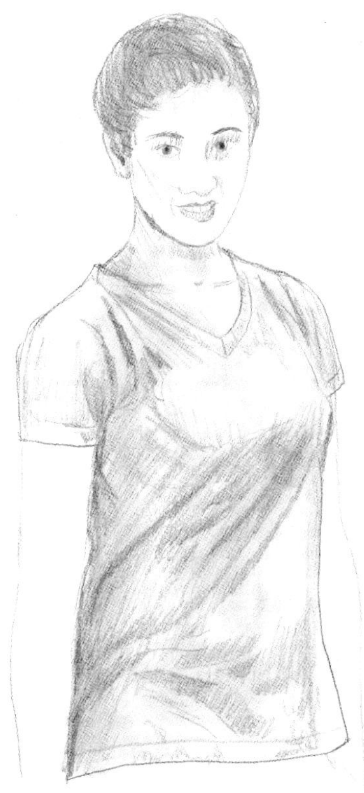

Blend and Smooth

5. Using a blending tool, soften and smooth out the tones.

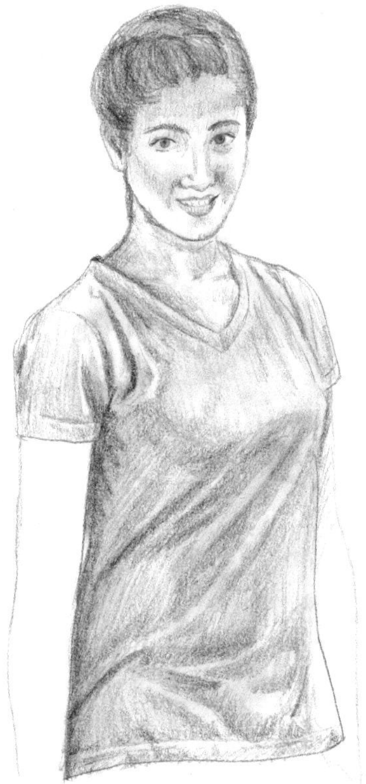

6. Add more tone to increase the contrast between the highlights and shadows. Use a kneaded eraser on the tops of the wrinkles and folds to highlight them.

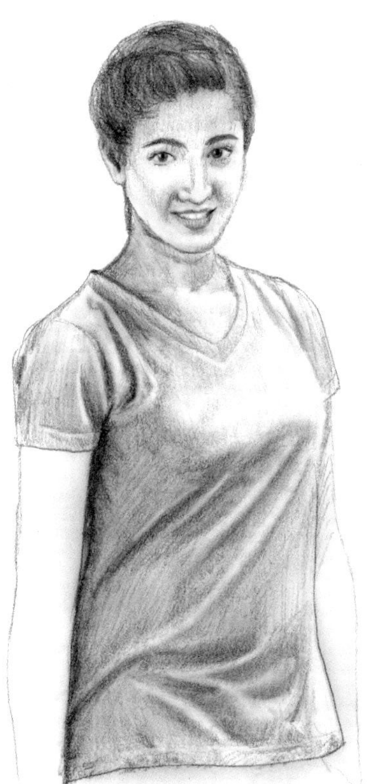

Refine & Finish

7. Continue to blend and smooth the drawing so there are no individual lines in the fabric and it looks continuous.

BUTTON-DOWN SHIRT

It might seem silly to draw a body if you're just going to cover it up, but it gives you guidelines for how to draw the shirt, which is especially helpful when drawing different body types.

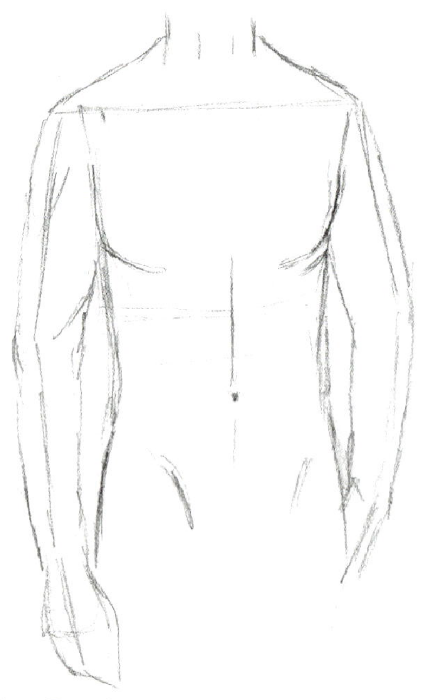

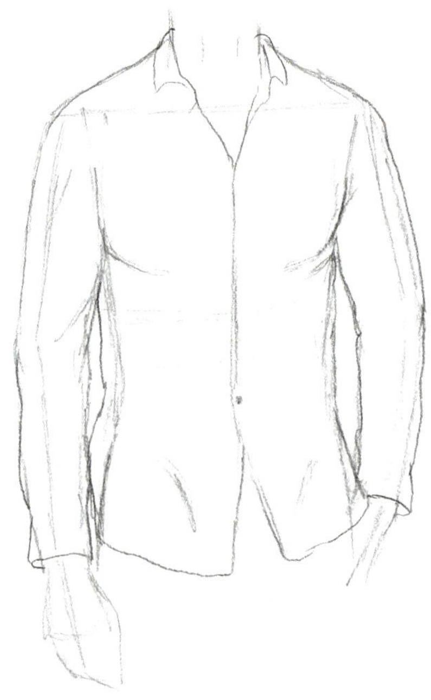

Draw the Basics

1. Draw a basic torso or body as shown on pages 28–30.

2. Draw the outline of the shirt around the body. For this drawing, it should be bigger than the shape of the body, since the shirt is not skintight. Draw the collar and the ends of the sleeves using curved lines to indicate their 3D form. Add a line down the center where the buttons will go.

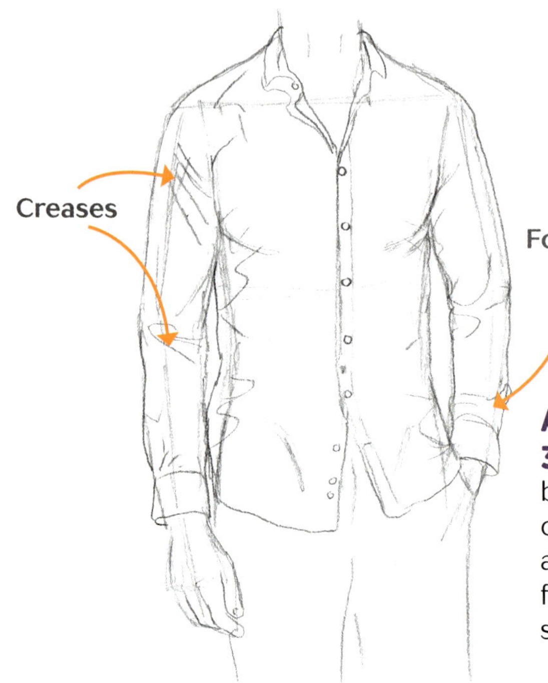

TIP
Clothing tends to bunch and fold at joints where the body bends, like the shoulders, elbows, and wrists.

Add Details

3. Add more details to the shirt, including buttons, cuffs, and seams. Using a mix of curved, wiggly, and straight lines, begin to add dimension to the shirt with creases and folds. These will help you know where to place shadows in the next step.

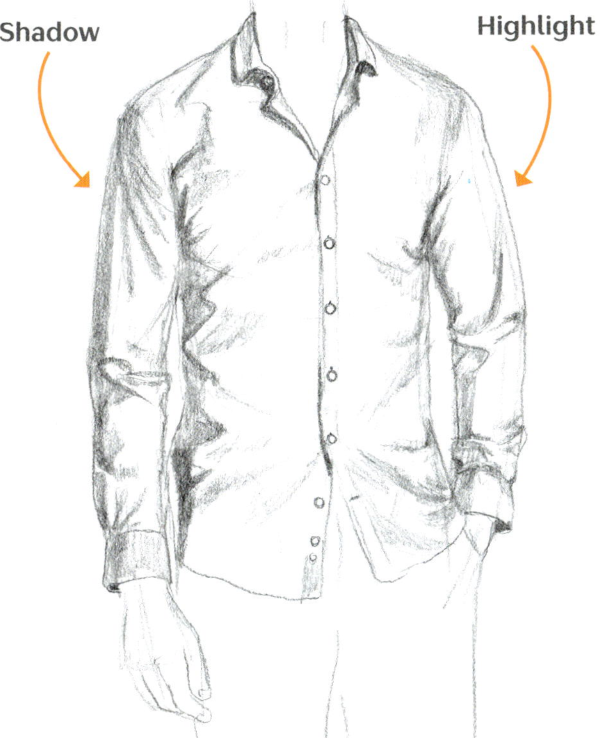

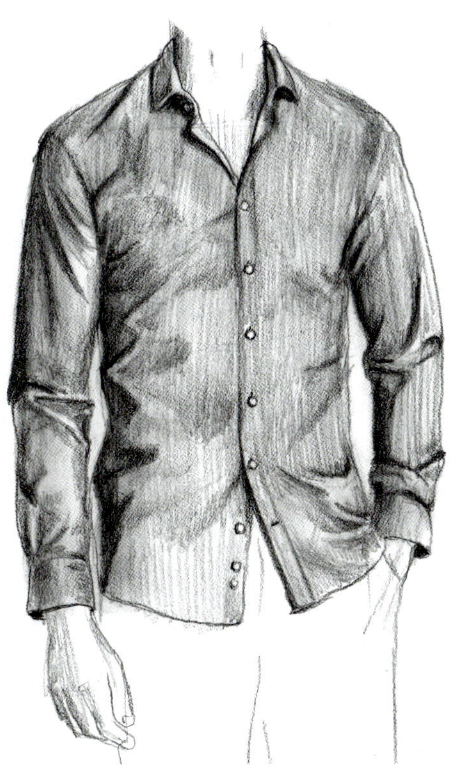

Add Tone

4. Erase any unneeded guidelines. Add a light layer of tone to the shirt, focusing on the darkest areas of shadow and the wrinkles in the clothing. The light source is coming from the right, which makes the left side of the shirt slightly darker.

Blend & Refine

5. Blend using a blending tool, and then add another layer of tone to create a more uniform base layer. Continue to deepen shadowed areas, and use a kneaded eraser to create highlights. Notice how the highlighted areas on the wrinkles and folds in the shirt make the fabric look more realistic.

SUBTLE VARIATIONS

Did you know that, traditionally, women's shirts button right over left, and men's button left over right? Keep this in mind when drawing different subjects. Structured shirts for feminine bodies usually also feature darts or seams in the chest area.

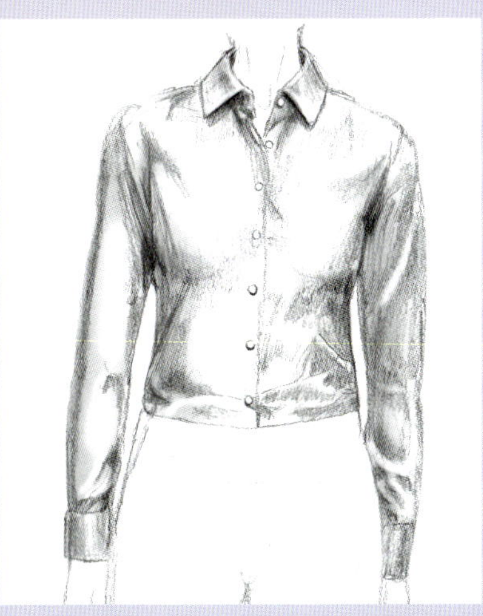

JACKET

Because this collared jacket is drawn open, think of it as if you're drawing a Button-Down Shirt (page 118) and a T-Shirt (page 116).

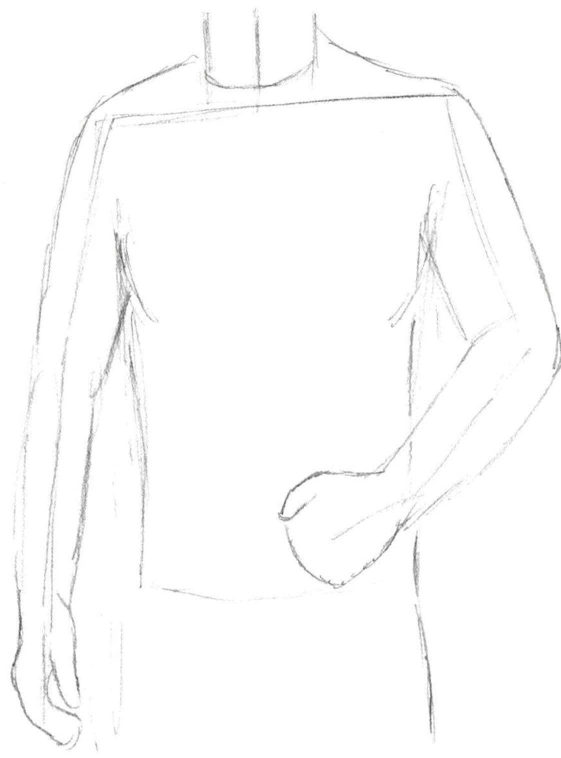

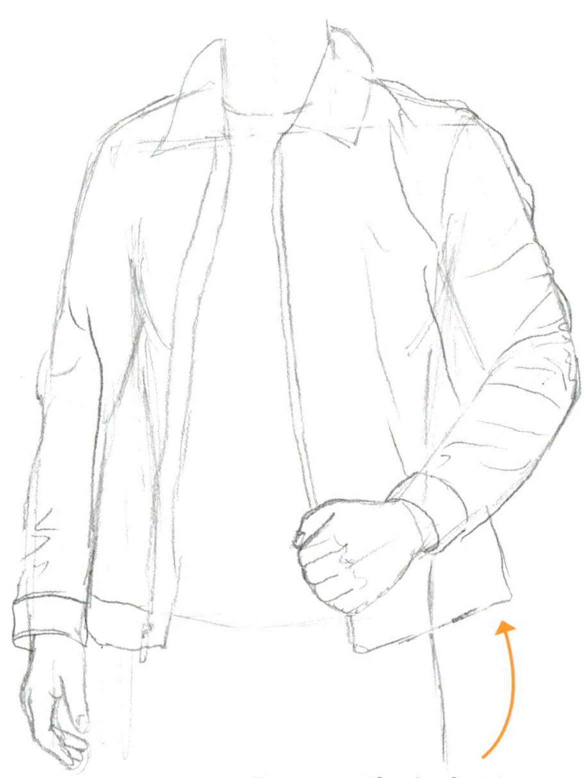

Because the jacket is worn open, the fabric extends beyond the body.

Draw the Basics

1. Draw the front view of a basic torso or body as shown on pages 28–30. In this example, one of the arms is bent, which will give the fabric a bit more texture and interest.

Add Details

2. Draw the outline of the jacket and the outline of the T-shirt underneath. Draw the collar and the ends of the sleeves using curved lines to indicate their 3D form. Add more details, including the initial sketch for the zipper, the cuffs, and seams. Begin to add dimension to the jacket, using thin lines for creases and folds. These will help you know where to place shadows in the next step.

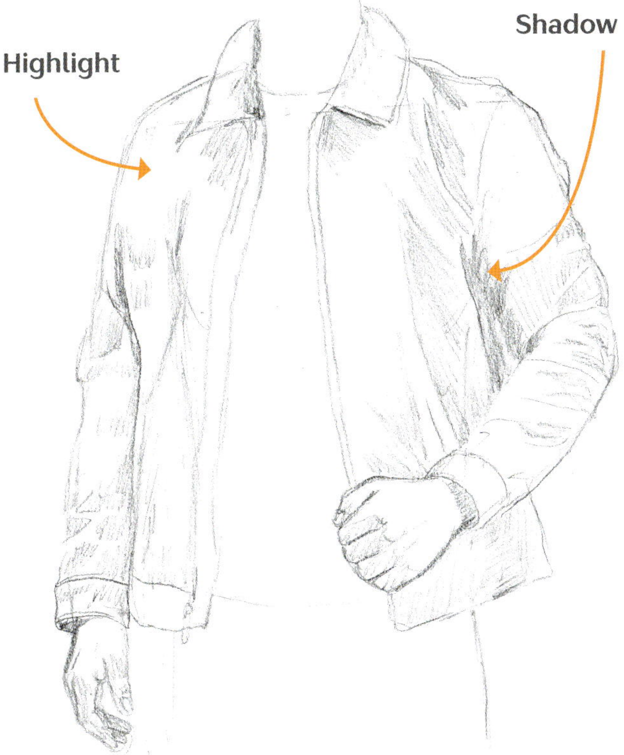

3. Erase any unneeded guidelines. Add a light layer of tone, focusing on the darkest areas of shadow, like under the arm, and the wrinkles in the clothing. Highlighted areas should be left lighter.

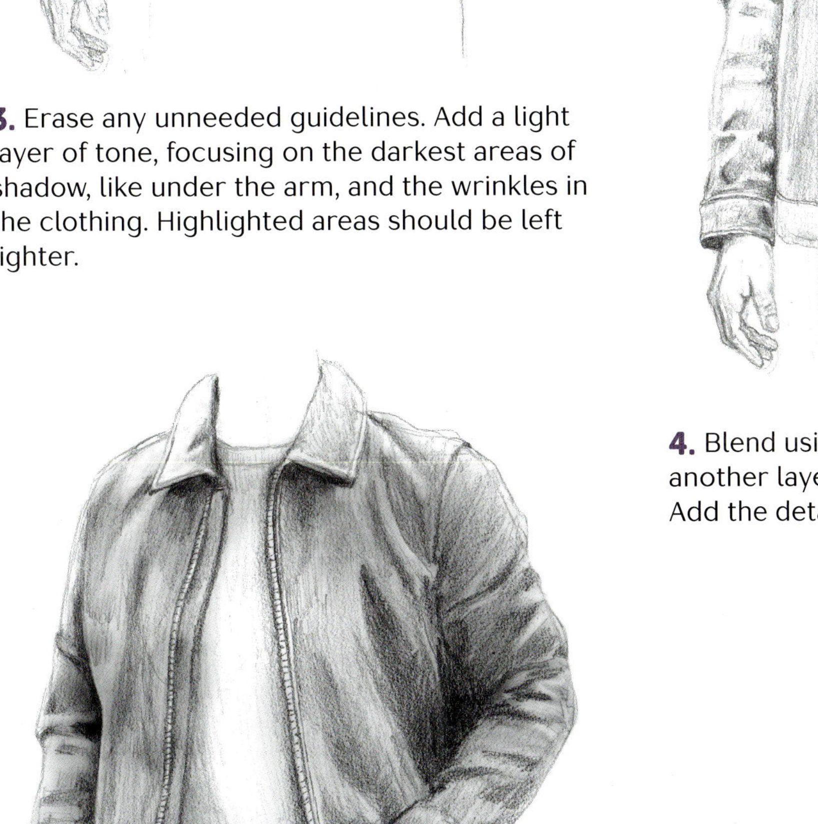

4. Blend using a blending tool, and then add another layer of tone, focusing on the midtones. Add the details to the zipper.

Refine & Finish

5. Smooth the tones, adding more as needed to deepen the shadows and create contrast. Use a kneaded eraser to create highlighted areas, and a stick eraser to make finer highlights, like those near the seams. Add even more detail to the zipper to finish the drawing.

BLOUSE

With the way the fabric of this blouse gathers and drapes, you'll get plenty of practice drawing creases, wrinkles, and folds.

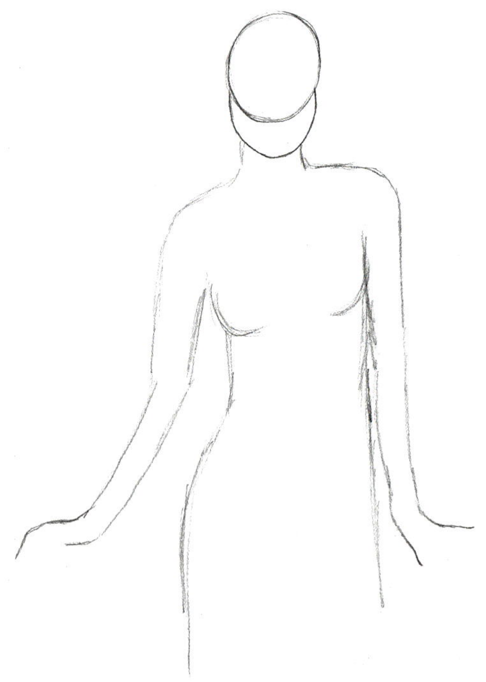

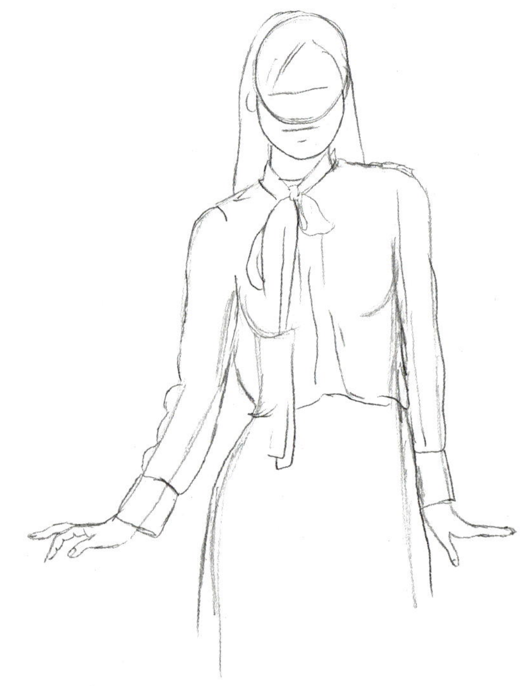

Draw the Basics

1. Draw the front view of a basic torso or body as shown on pages 24–25. In this example, both of the arms are out to the side.

2. Draw the outline of the blouse. For this drawing, it should be bigger than the shape of the body, especially in the shoulders, arms, and waist. Draw the outline of the details, including the bow tied around the neck and the cuffs at the ends of the sleeves.

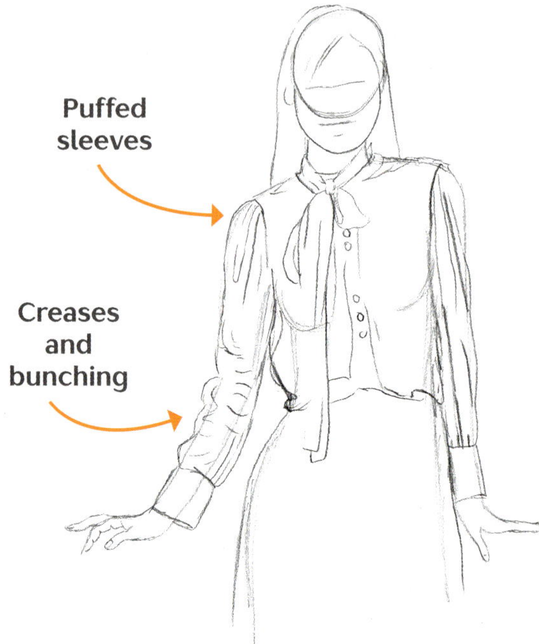

Add Details

3. Add more details to the blouse, including a row of buttons and a seam down the center. Use thin lines to add creases to the elbows, shoulders, and waist. This blouse has puffed sleeves, which cause the fabric to gather, drape, and fold.

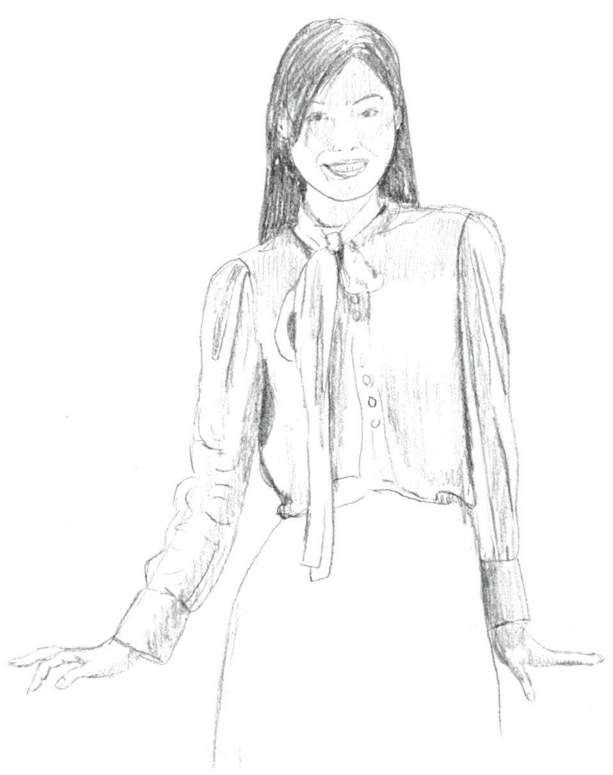

Add Tone

4. Erase any unneeded guidelines. Add a light layer of tone, focusing on the darkest areas, including the sides of the torso under the arms, the seams, and the creases where the fabric has bunched and wrinkled. The bow also has areas of shadow at the neck, inside the loops, and where its tails are casting shadows on the front of the blouse.

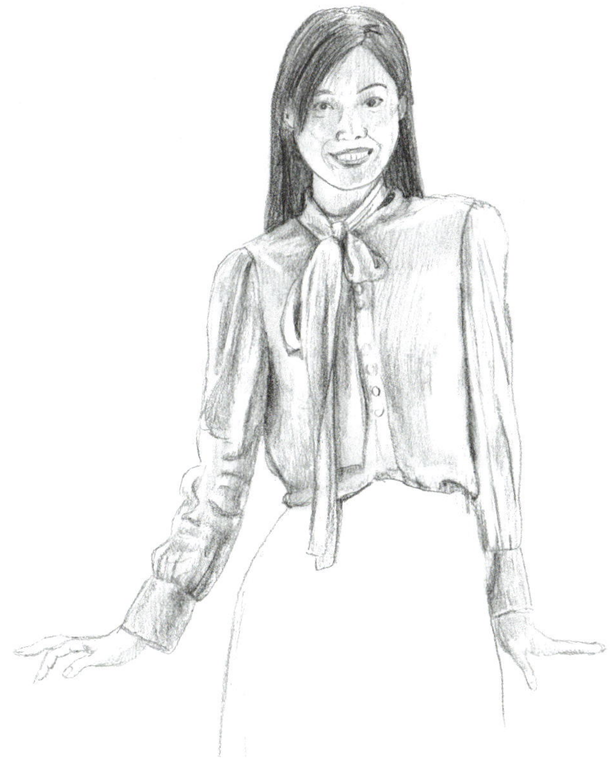

5. Blend using a blending tool. Then add more tone, focusing on midtones to even out the hues, while still keeping areas of shadow and highlight.

DIFFICULT DETAILS

When drawing difficult details, like bows, it can be helpful to practice them separately before adding them to your full drawing. Use the 15-Minute Method and break the element down to its basic shapes before adding details, tone, and shading. If you're working from a photograph, you can even try lightly tracing the element to get an idea of its basic shapes.

For example, the bow on this blouse would be made up of triangles, rectangles, and a circle.

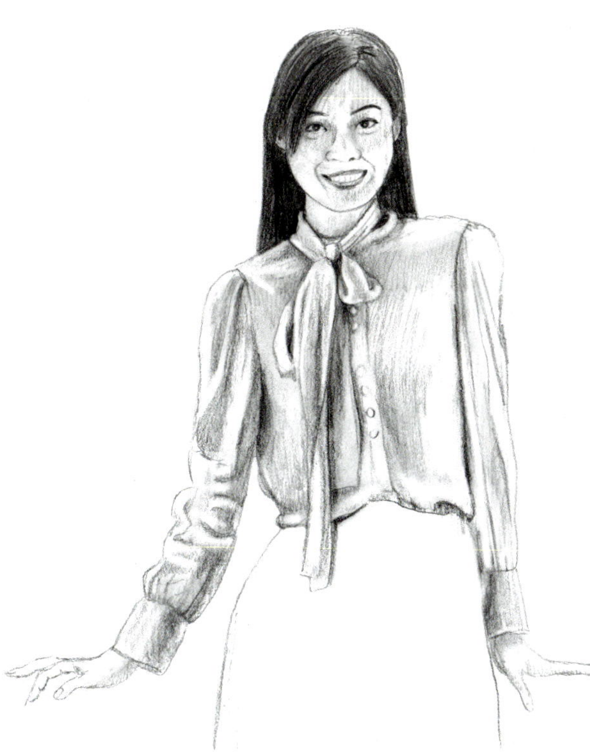

Increase Contrast

6. Refine the details. Increase the contrast by deepening the shadows and using a kneaded eraser to lighten the highlighted areas.

DRESS

I chose this dress as an example because I liked how it gave the opportunity to practice using shadows and highlights to make things look 3D.

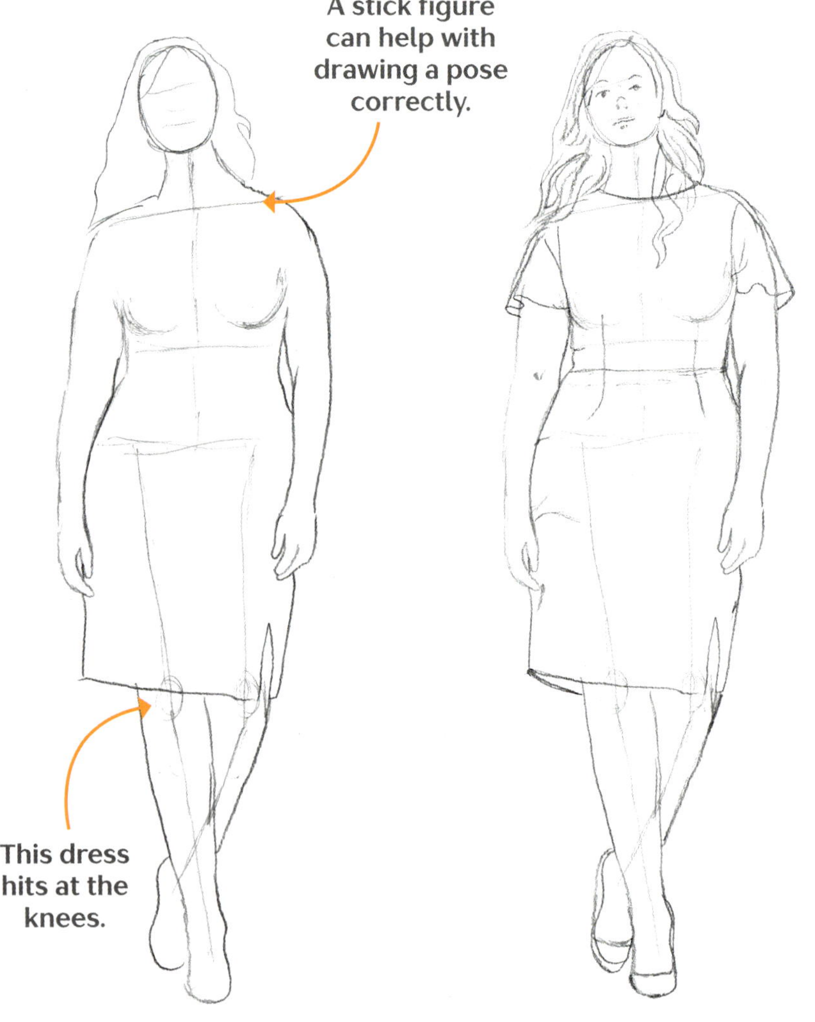

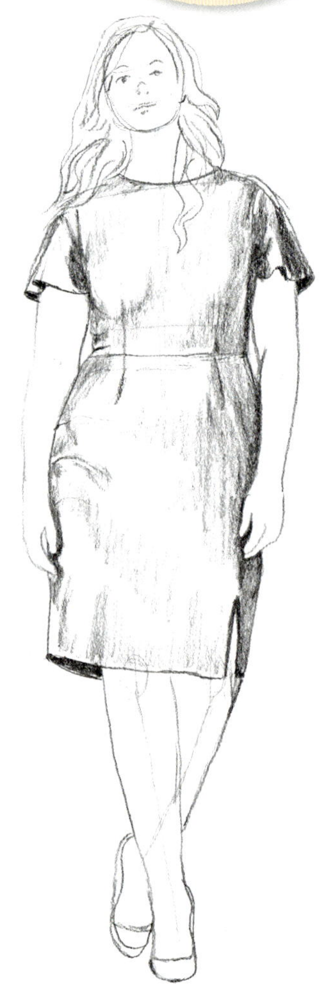

Draw the Basics

1. Draw the basic view of a body, following the steps on pages 24–25. Depending on the pose of your subject, it may be useful to start with a stick figure outline and then draw the outline of the body around it. Next, draw the outline of the skirt of the dress. This dress is form-fitting and hits at the knees.

Add Details

2. Add details to the dress, like a curved neckline and the fluttery sleeves. Draw lines for the seams at the waist and wrinkles and creases at the hips, and the additional seam at the bottom of the dress.

Add Tone

3. Erase any unneeded guidelines. Add a layer of tone to the dress. The darkest areas should have the most shadow, including under the sleeves, at the hips, and at the bottom of the dress. Highlights will happen where the dress pulls taut across the body, especially at the chest and hips.

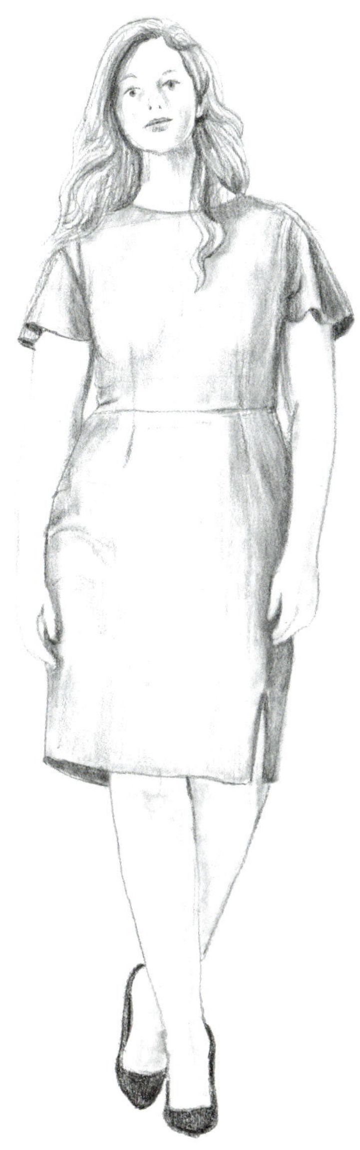

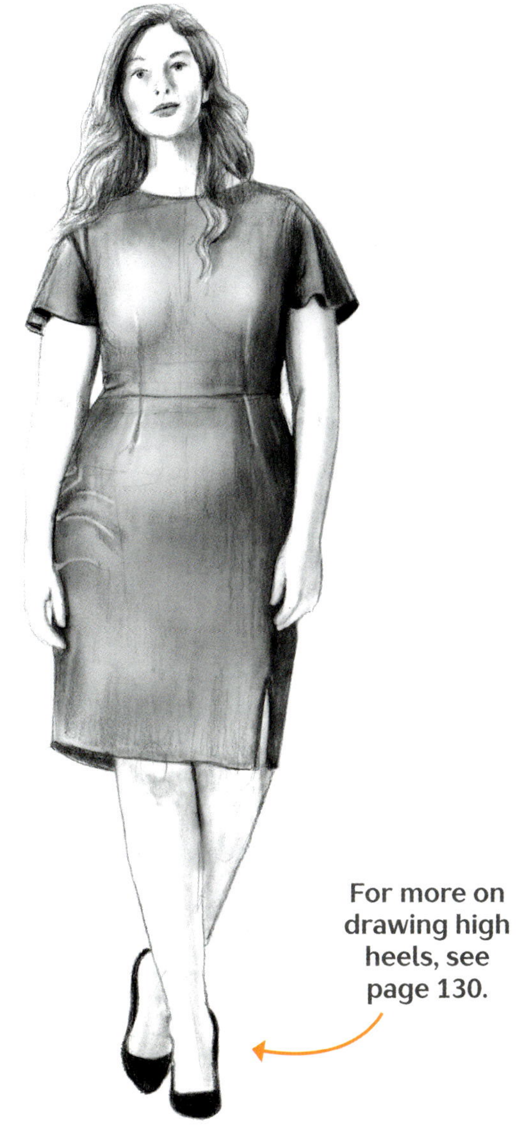

Blend

4. Blend using a blending tool. Then add more tone to even out the hues, while still keeping areas of shadow and highlight.

Refine & Finish

5. Using a mechanical pencil, add fine lines, thin shadows, and seams. Add more tone to create deeper shadows. Use a kneaded eraser to add areas of highlight and a stick eraser for fine highlights.

DRAWING DESIGNS

When drawing clothing with designs or lettering, attention to detail is key. Begin by carefully outlining the design's placement, making sure it aligns with the subject's body contours. Remember to maintain proper proportions, especially if the design wraps around the body.

Study your reference photo or even trace the design to ensure accuracy, and pay close attention to any curves or angles within the lettering or pattern, as these can greatly affect the overall appearance.

BALL CAP

Learn how to draw a ball cap from the front and from the side in these step-by-steps. To test your skills, try adding your favorite team logo.

FRONT VIEW

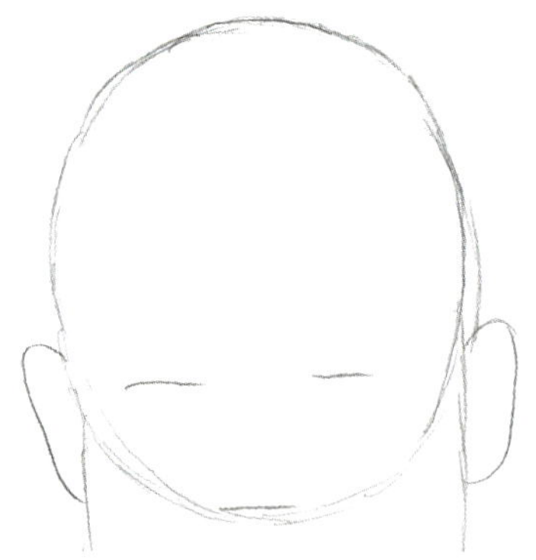

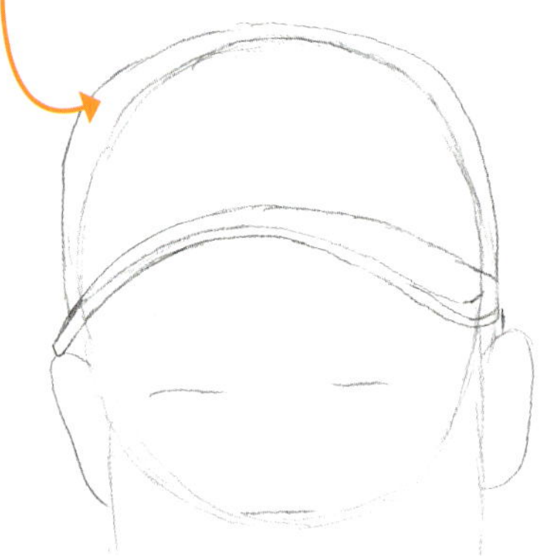

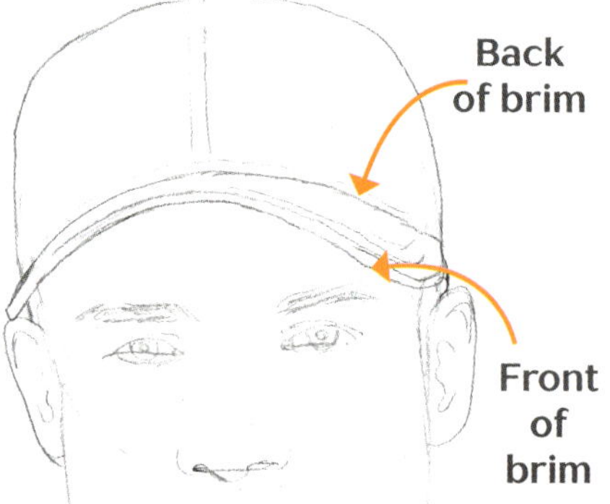

Draw the Basics

1. Draw a head following the steps on page 38. Include all necessary guidelines for the eyes and nose. Draw the ears. These will all help you make sure the cap and brim are placed correctly.

2. Draw the outline of the top of the cap around the head. It should extend down to the ears. Draw a curved line to connect the two sides where the brim attaches to the cap. Draw two curved parallel lines to form the front of the brim.

Add Details

3. Erase any unwanted guidelines. Draw the stitching details.

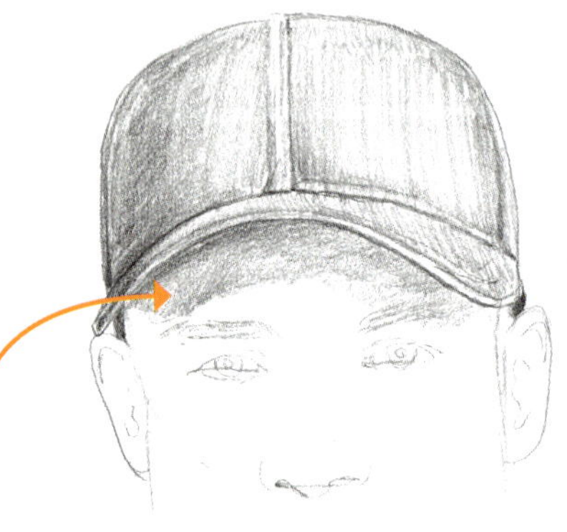

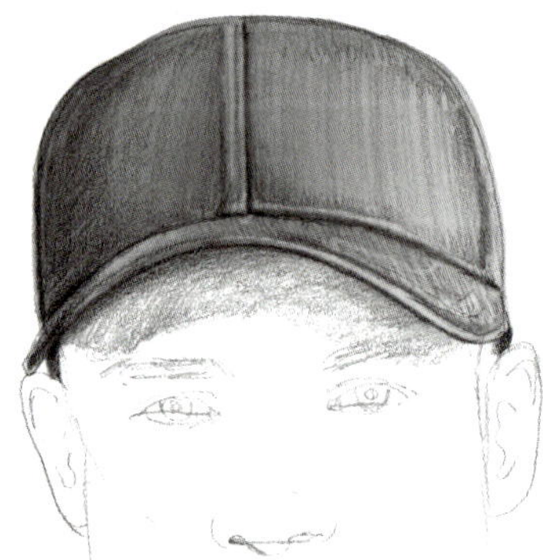

Add Tone

4. Add a light layer of tone to the cap, focusing on the seams and shadowed areas.

Blend & Define

5. Blend using a blending tool. Continue to build the tone at the seams and under the brim. Futher define the seams.

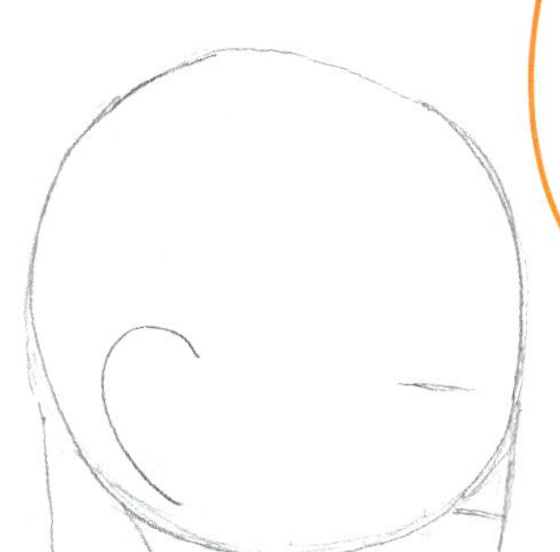

The cap bumps out a bit here, which makes it look realistic.

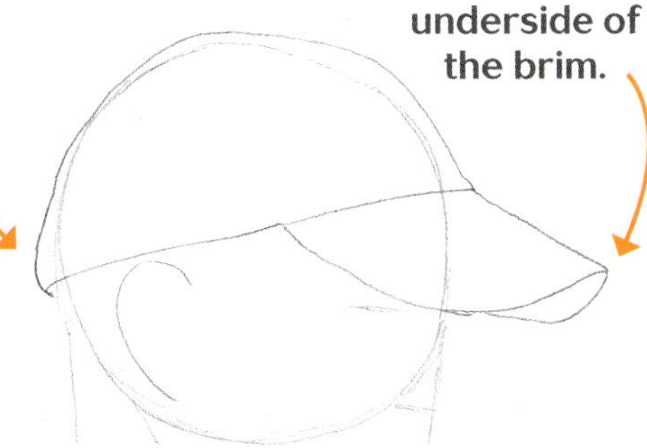

Draw another curved line for the underside of the brim.

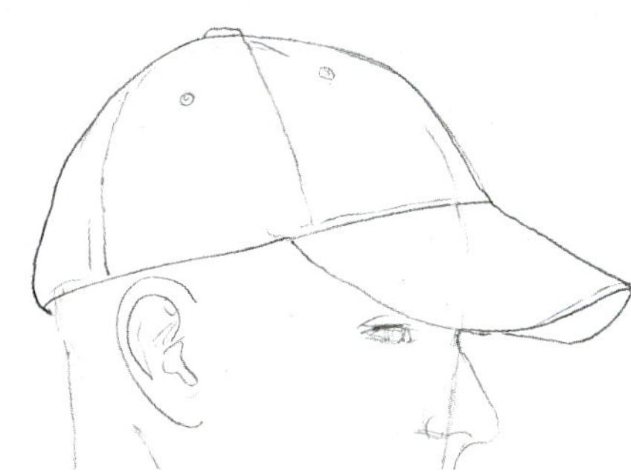

Draw the Basics

1. Draw a head in profile following the steps on page 40. Include all necessary guidelines for the eyes and nose. Draw the ear. These will all help you make sure the cap and brim are placed correctly.

2. Draw the outline of the top of the cap. It should extend a bit above the head and down to the ears. Connect the two sides. Add a line coming from the front of the cap that extends the length of the brim. Draw a curved line from the base of the cap that starts about halfway, and connect it to the end of the brim. Notice where the brim curves in relation to the eye guideline.

Add Details

3. Add any details for the seams and stitching. This cap has vertical seams, a button at the top, and some rivets.

Add more stitching details after the layer of tone.

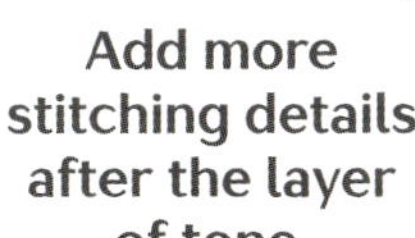

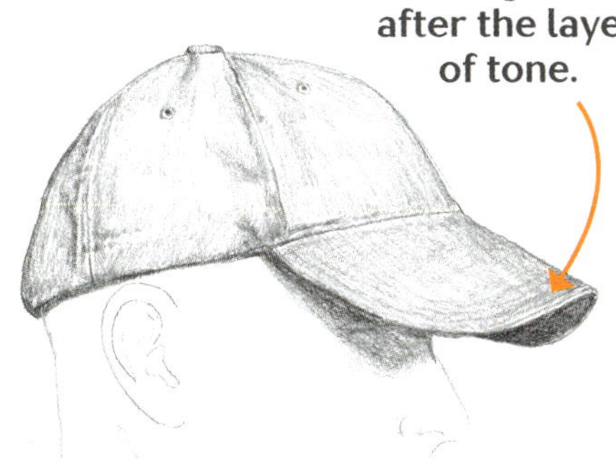

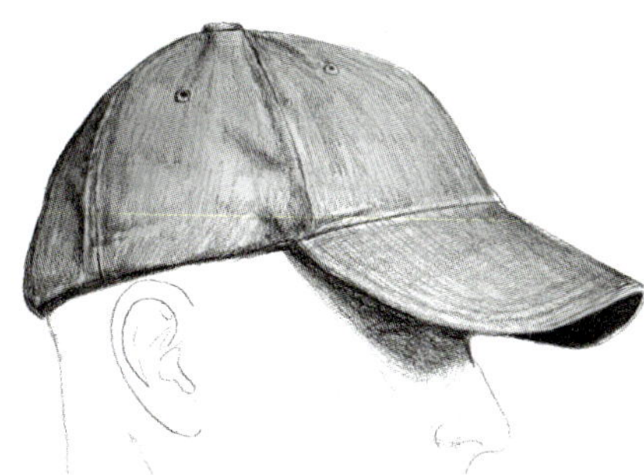

TIP
Even if the eyes are covered by shadow, you'll want to draw them, and then cover them in tone. They usually won't disappear completely in a portrait.

Add Tone

4. Add a light layer of tone, focusing on the darkest areas and any wrinkles or creases. Add more details, and use a mechanical pencil for finer lines.

Blend & Finish

5. Blend using a blending tool. Then continue to add more tone at folds, seams, and wrinkles in the fabric. Increase the shadows under the brim of the cap and on the face.

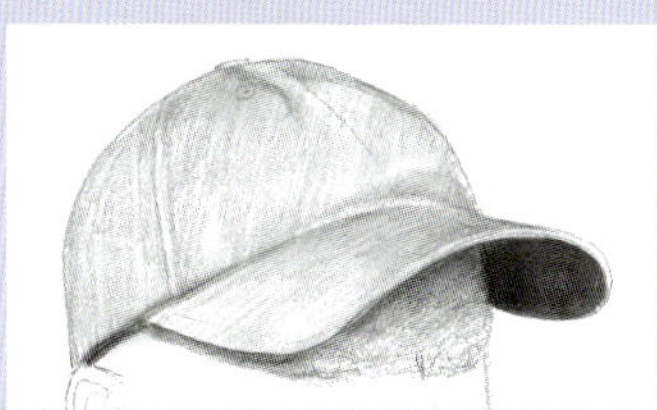

ANOTHER VIEW

When drawing a cap at a 3/4 angle, note how much of the face is covered by shadow.

SHOES

This step-by-step shows you how to draw both the front view and the side view of a shoe. It might take some time to master the crisscross laces, but practice makes perfect.

Draw the Basics

1. Draw the basic shape of the foot, using ovals for the toes and a circle for the heel. For more guidance on drawing feet, see page 33.

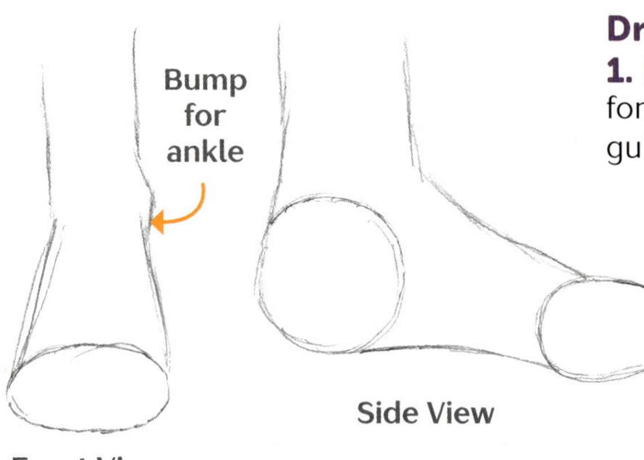

2. Draw the outline of the shoe. Note how the shoe extends around the foot in the side view, especially at the ankle.

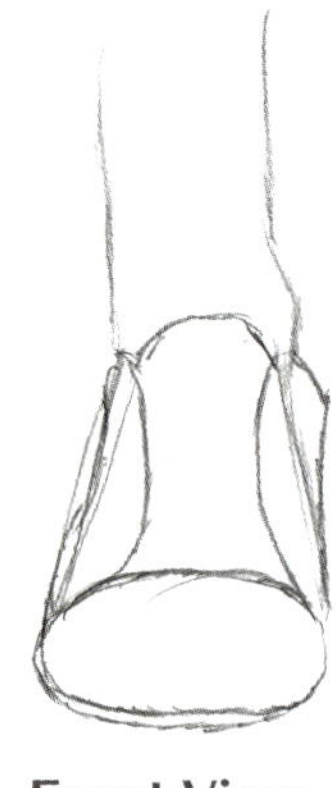
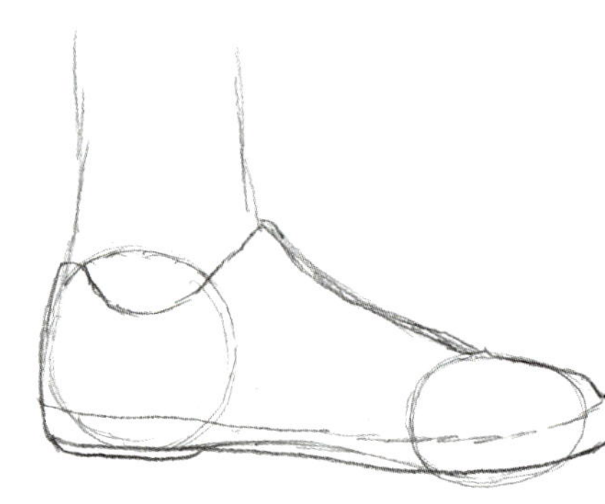

Add Details

3. Erase the guidelines no longer needed. Add details like laces, designs, and stitching. Note how the laces change when viewed from different angles.

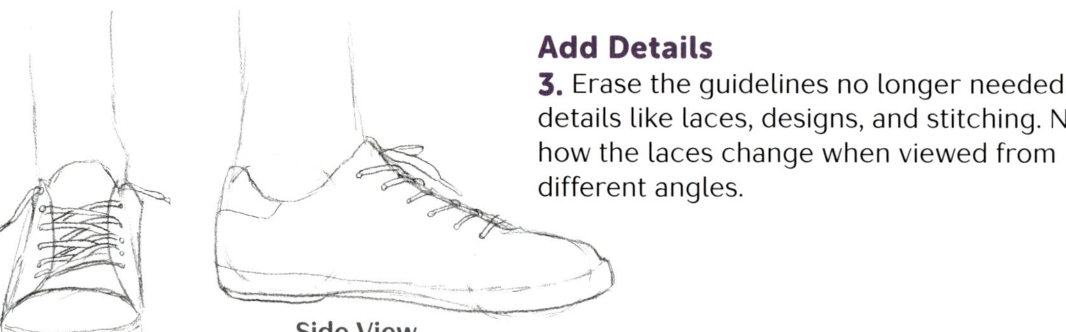

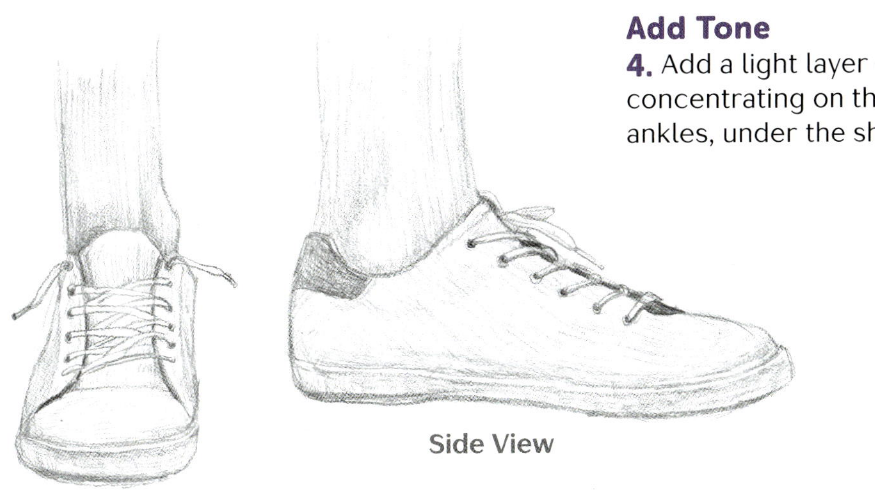

Front View

Side View

Add Tone

4. Add a light layer of tone to the sneakers, concentrating on the shadows around the ankles, under the shoes, and around the laces.

Blend & Add More Tone

5. Blend using a blending tool. Then continue to add more tone, darkening the shadows and leaving the highlighted areas lighter.

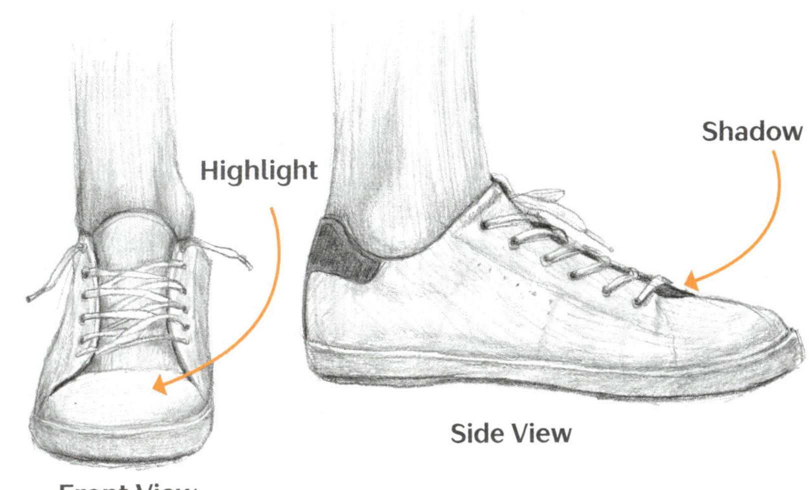

Front View

Side View

Refine & Finish

6. Smooth the tones, and continue to add more as needed to refine and finish the drawing.

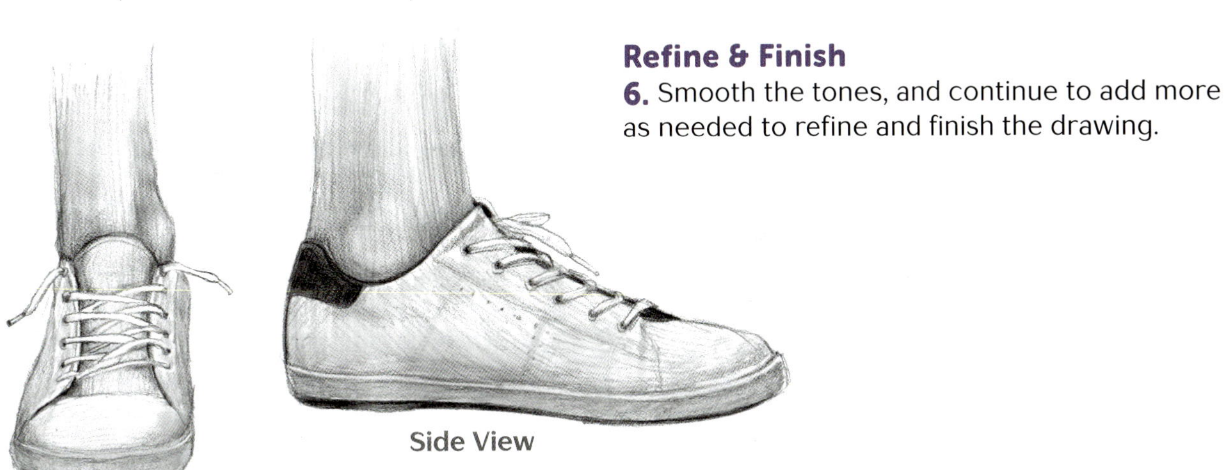

Front View

Side View

HEELS

For this demonstration, I've included the side view as well as a 3/4 view from the back. This allows the best visibility of the heels themselves since they are the defining feature of the shoe. This example also gives you practice drawing shoes where the foot is visible, which will come in handy when drawing sandals.

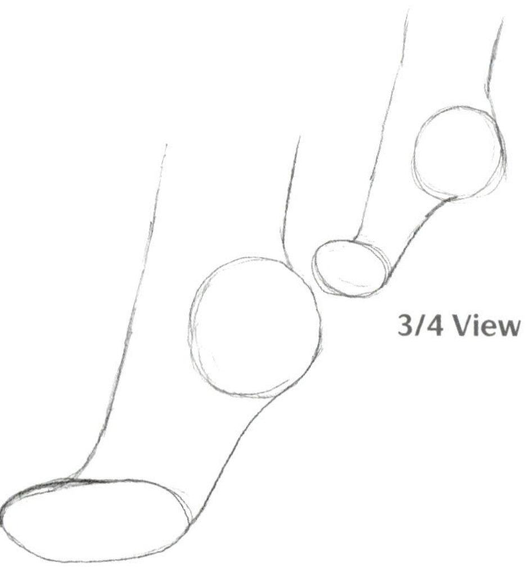

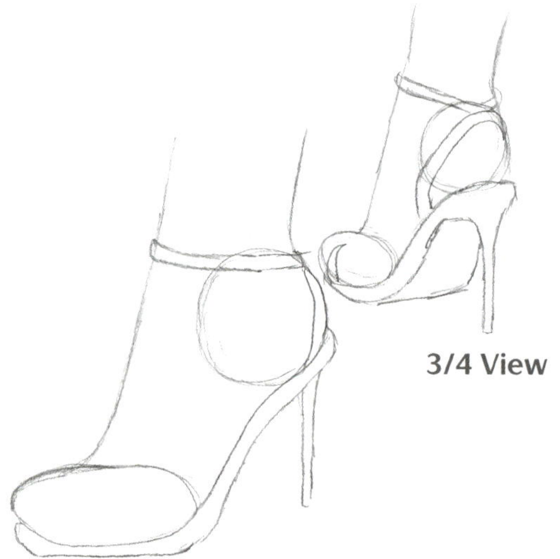

Draw the Basics

1. Draw the basic shape of the foot, using ovals for the toes and a circle for the heel. For more guidance on drawing feet, see page 33. The angle of the foot will depend on the height of the heel.

2. Draw the outline of the shoes. Notice how the heel and sole curve differently depending on the angle.

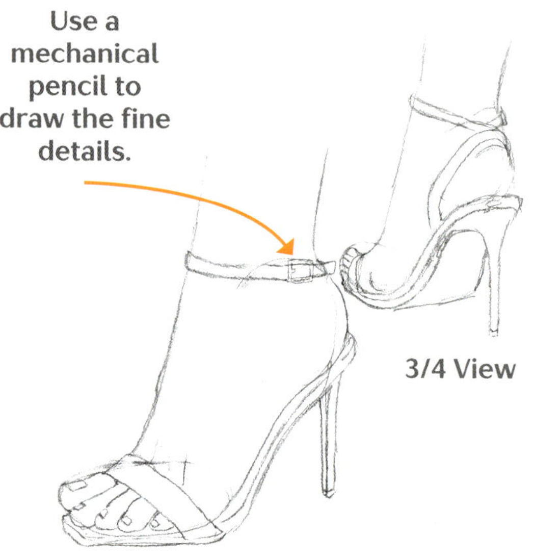

Add Details

3. Erase any guidelines no longer needed. Add details, like buckles on the ankle strap and an additional strap across the base of the toes. For this example, you'd also draw the toes at this time.

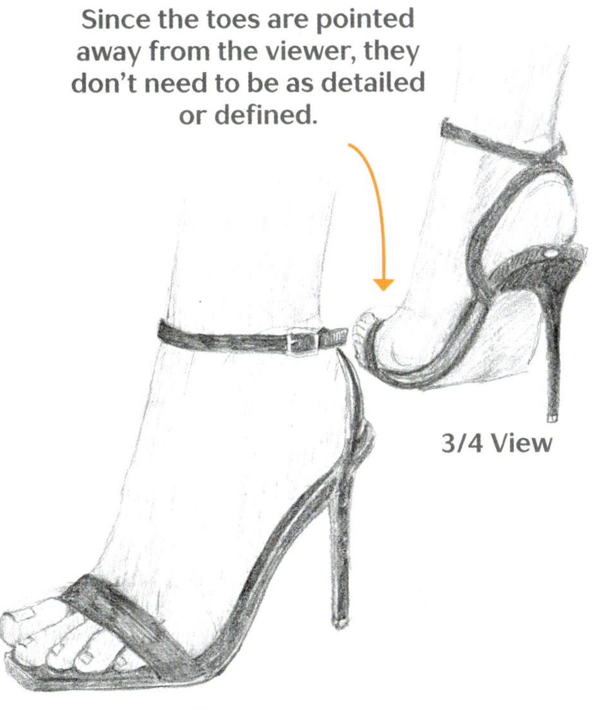

Add Tone

4. Add a light layer of tone, concentrating on the darkest areas. Leave highlighted areas light.

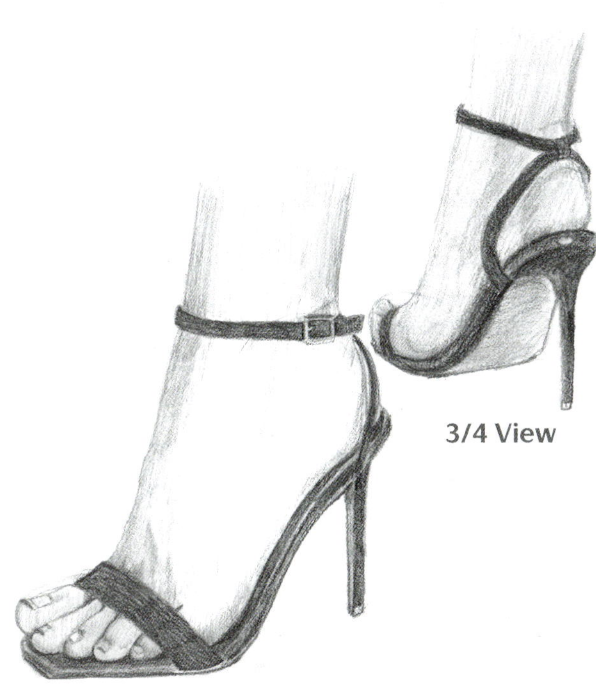

Blend

5. Blend using a blending tool. Add more tone to create more contrast between the shadowed areas and the highlights.

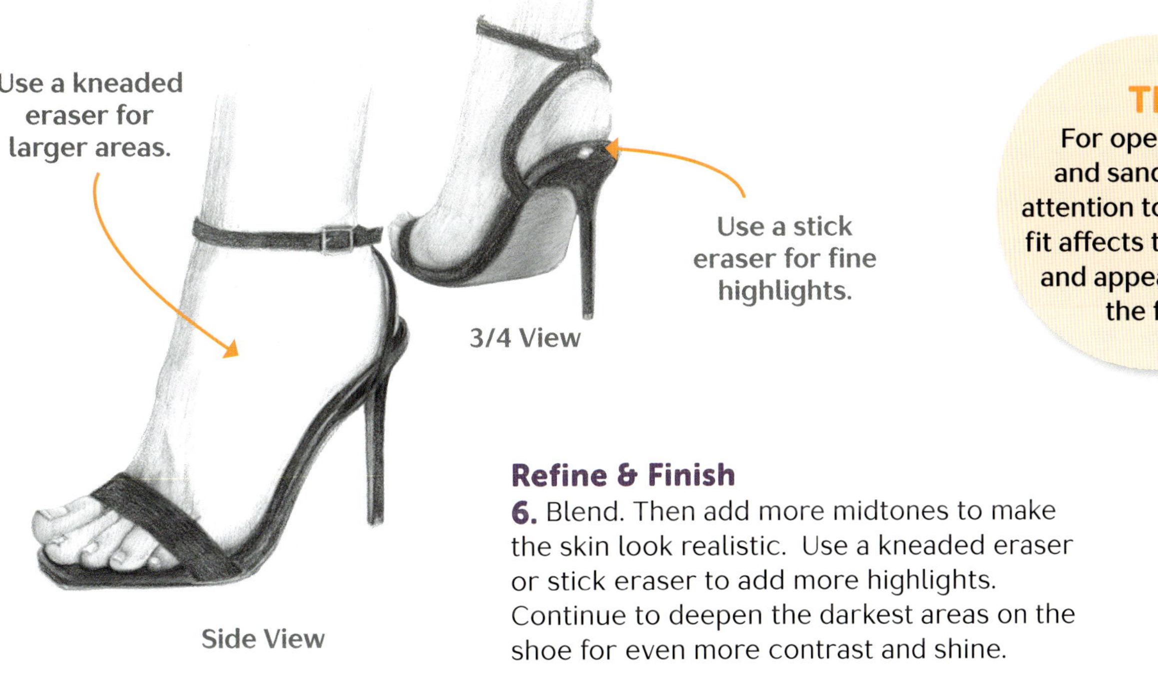

TIP
For open shoes and sandals, pay attention to how their fit affects the texture and appearance of the foot.

Refine & Finish

6. Blend. Then add more midtones to make the skin look realistic. Use a kneaded eraser or stick eraser to add more highlights. Continue to deepen the darkest areas on the shoe for even more contrast and shine.

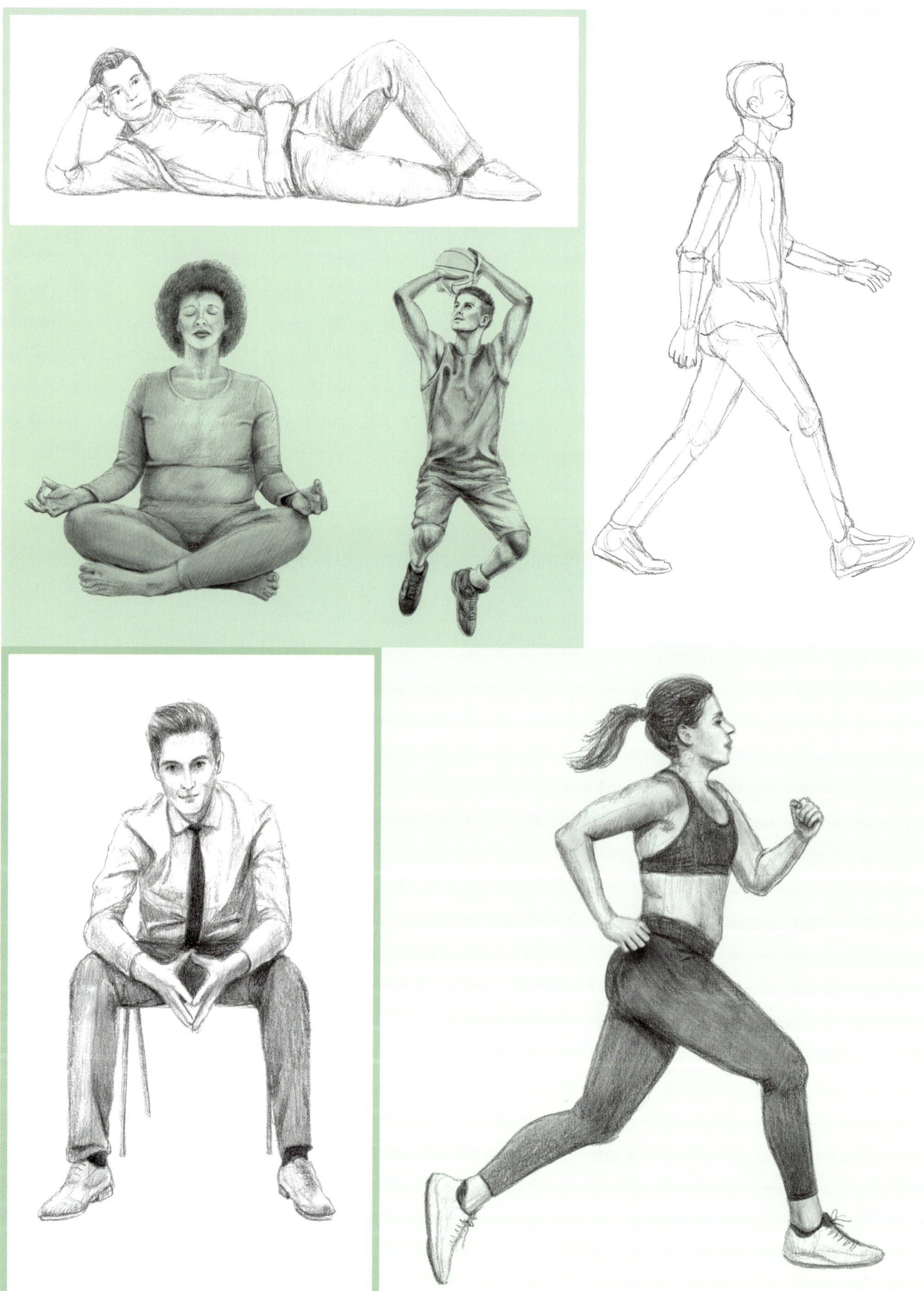

DRAWING POSITION & MOVEMENT

This chapter will take the skills you've learned so far and put them all together to create lifelike drawings of people in different poses. When it comes to drawing position and movement, it's best to start super simple! Drawing your subject with the basic shapes we've already learned and stick-figure limbs can help make even the most complicated poses much easier to visualize and understand.

For these step-by-steps, the primary focus of the instructions will be drawing the body, with the hair, facial features, and clothing being secondary. Previous tutorials that could offer useful guidance are listed, too.

LYING DOWN

If your subject is lying on something specific, sketching the outline of that item first will help you anchor your portrait and capture how the body and object affect each other.

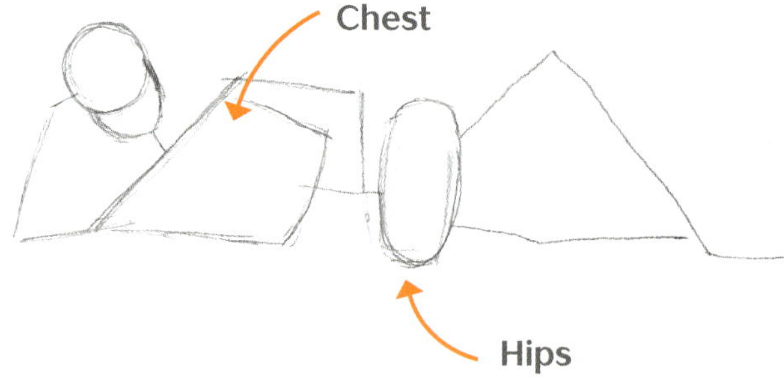

Draw the Basics

1. Draw a head and body, referring to chapters 1 and 2 for guidance as needed. Capture the pose by using lines to connect the basic shapes.

2. Add circles for the joints, including the wrist, shoulder, elbows, and knees. Use this form as a guide to draw the outline of the body. Keep in mind that things like clothing, weight, musculature, age, and the pose will affect the shape of the outline.

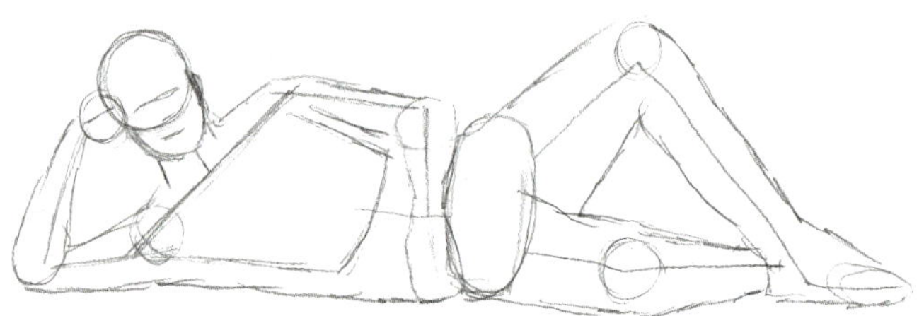

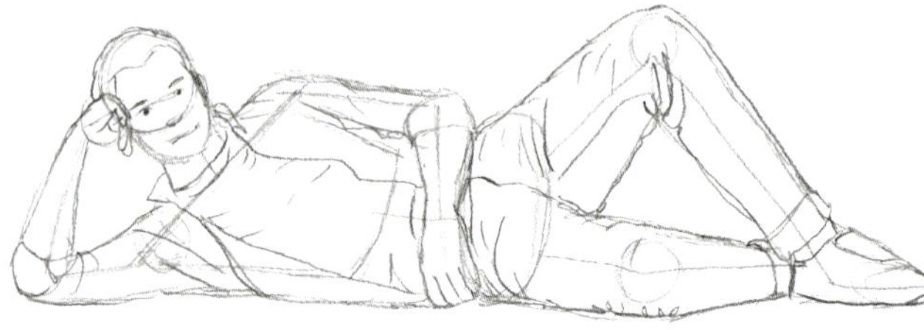

Add Details

3. Add details to the drawing, including the outline of the clothing. Begin to refine the features. Draw the lines in the clothing where the body bends, such as along the knees, shoulders, groin, and elbows.

Add Tone

4. Quickly fill in the areas with the darkest shadow using a medium tone. Continue to refine the features of your subject.

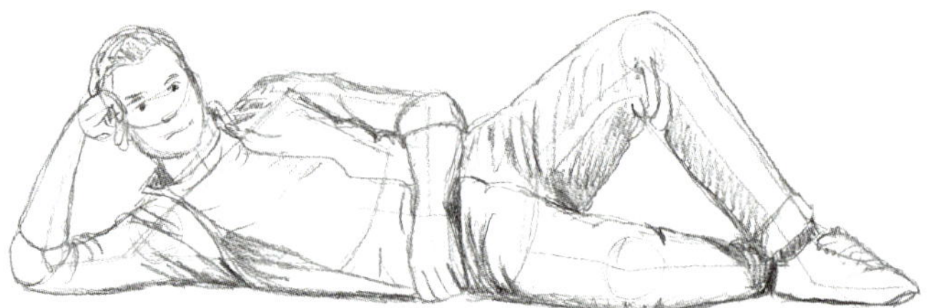

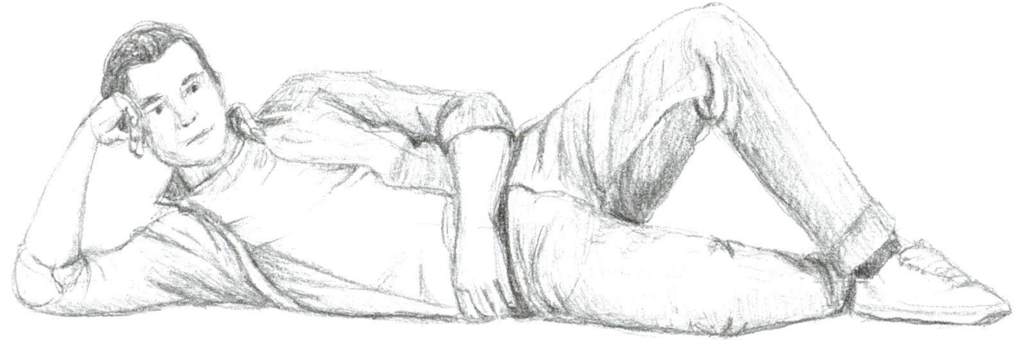

5. Erase any guidelines no longer needed. Add another layer of tone, focusing on the midtones. Deepen the tone of the darkest areas. Continue to refine the features of your subject.

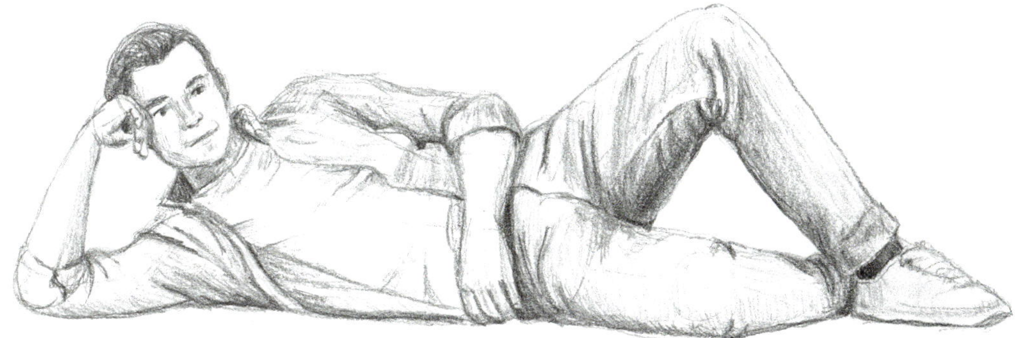

6. Blend using a blending tool. Then add another layer of tone to create smoother transitions between tones. Deepen the darkest areas. Continue to refine the features of your subject.

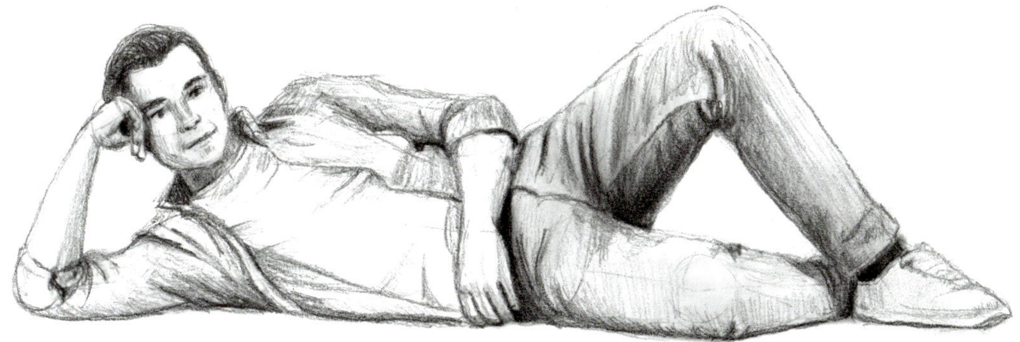

Refine & Finish

7. Blend and smooth the tones, adding more to define the contrast as needed. Use a kneaded eraser or stick eraser to clean up smudges and add highlights.

HELPFUL TUTORIALS

- **Short Hair (page 92)**
- **Bored (page 74)**
- **The Hand (page 31)**
- **Jacket (page 120)**
- **Pants (page 114)**
- **Shoes (page 128)**

WALKING

To help your drawing be more accurate, take a walk and pay attention to how your arms, legs, feet, and torso move, and make note of what happens to your clothing as you go.

Draw the Basics

1. Using basic shapes, draw a head and a body in profile, referring to chapters 1 and 2 for guidance as needed. Draw circles for the joints, including the shoulder, elbow, wrists, knees, and ankles. Capture the pose by using lines to connect the basic shapes.

2. Use this form as a guide to draw the outline of the body. Keep in mind that things like clothing, weight, musculature, age, and the pose will affect the shape of the outline.

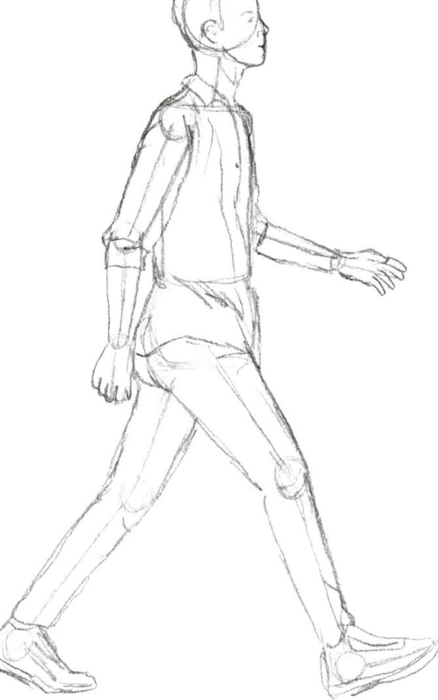

Add Details

3. Add details to the drawing, including the outline of the clothing. Draw the lines in the clothing where the body bends when walking, such as at the waist, knees, and elbows. Begin to define the features.

Highlight

Shadow

Add Tone

4. Erase any guidelines no longer needed. Add a light layer of tone to the entire drawing, leaving highlighted areas lighter. Then add more tone to darken the shadowed areas. Continue to refine the features of your subject. Because this light source is coming from the upper right, the highlights are focused around the face and shoulders.

5. Add more tone to create contrast and make the drawing feel more realistic. Continue to refine the features of your subject.

When drawing a side view of someone walking, the leg farther from the viewer will be in shadow.

Blend & Refine

6. Blend using a blending tool to smooth the tones. Add more tone to deepen shadows, and use a kneaded eraser or stick eraser to create highlights.

HELPFUL TUTORIALS

- Profile View (page 22)
- Short Hair (page 92)
- Button-Down (page 118)
- The Leg (page 32)
- Slim Pants (page 112)
- Shoes (page 128)

RUNNING

This tutorial has a lot in common with the drawing of someone walking (page 136), but the position of the limbs is more exaggerated, which gives the sense of faster motion.

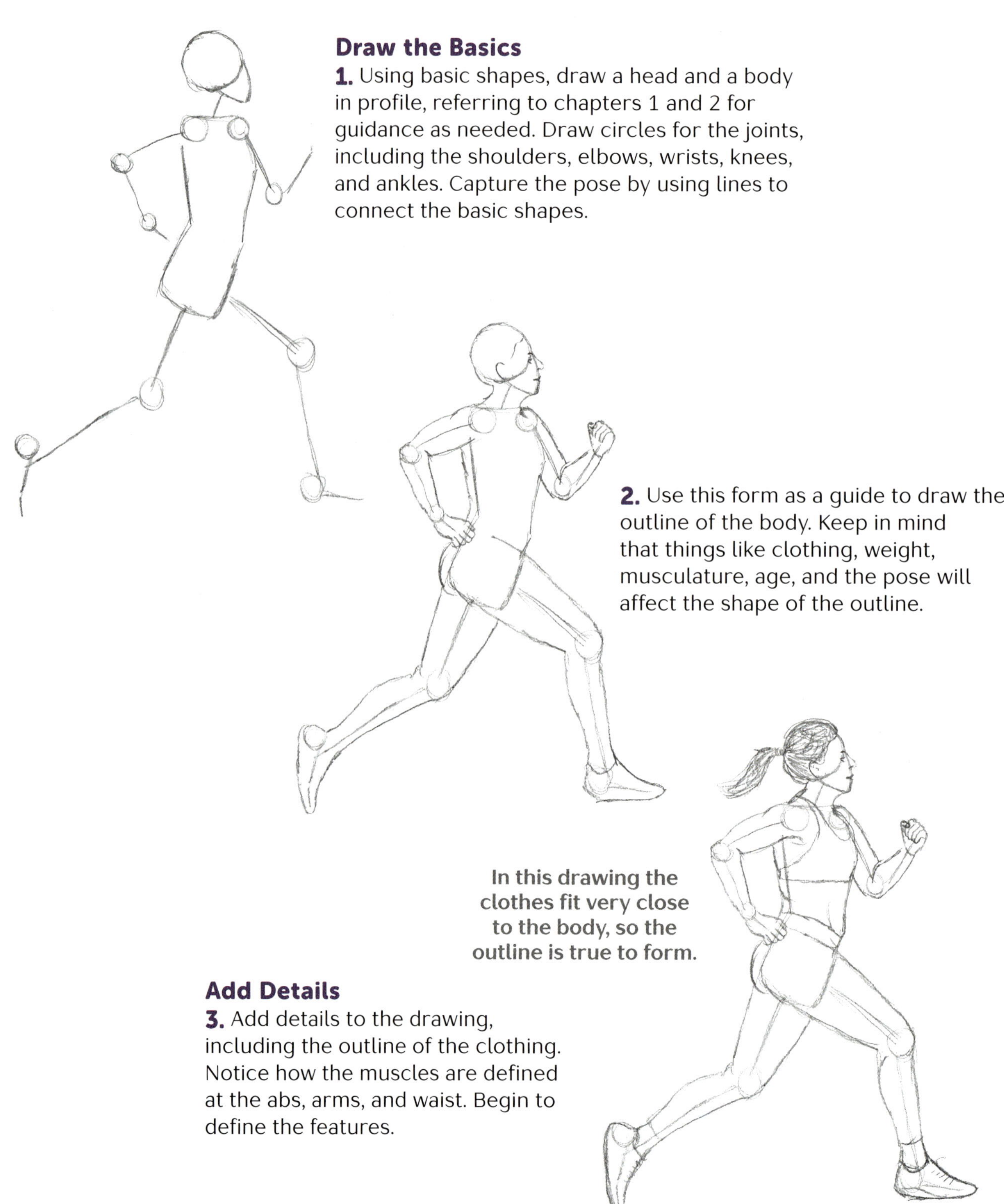

Draw the Basics

1. Using basic shapes, draw a head and a body in profile, referring to chapters 1 and 2 for guidance as needed. Draw circles for the joints, including the shoulders, elbows, wrists, knees, and ankles. Capture the pose by using lines to connect the basic shapes.

2. Use this form as a guide to draw the outline of the body. Keep in mind that things like clothing, weight, musculature, age, and the pose will affect the shape of the outline.

In this drawing the clothes fit very close to the body, so the outline is true to form.

Add Details

3. Add details to the drawing, including the outline of the clothing. Notice how the muscles are defined at the abs, arms, and waist. Begin to define the features.

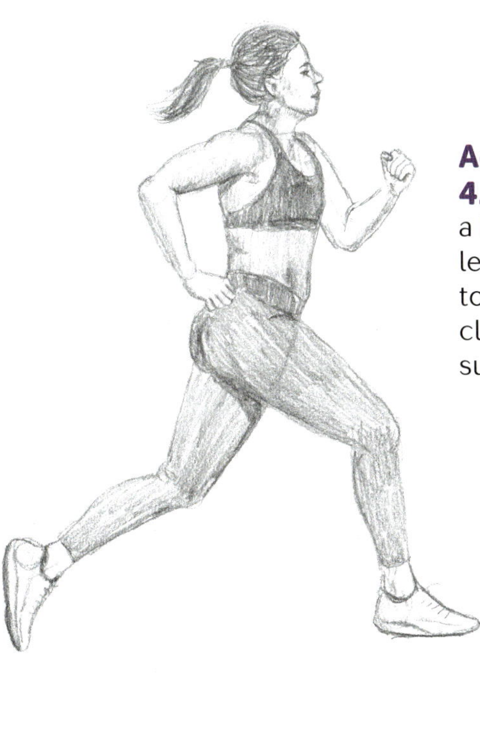

Add Tone

4. Erase any guidelines no longer needed. Add a light layer of tone to the entire drawing, leaving highlighted areas lighter. Then add more tone to darken the shadowed areas and the clothing. Continue to refine the features of your subject.

5. Add more tone to create contrast and make the drawing feel more realistic. Continue to refine the features of your subject.

Blend & Refine

6. Blend using a blending tool to smooth the tones. Add more tone to deepen shadows, and use a kneaded eraser or stick eraser to create highlights.

HELPFUL TUTORIALS

SITTING

Because this person is facing forward, you'll need to be aware of perspective and how it affects features, such as feet and forearms.

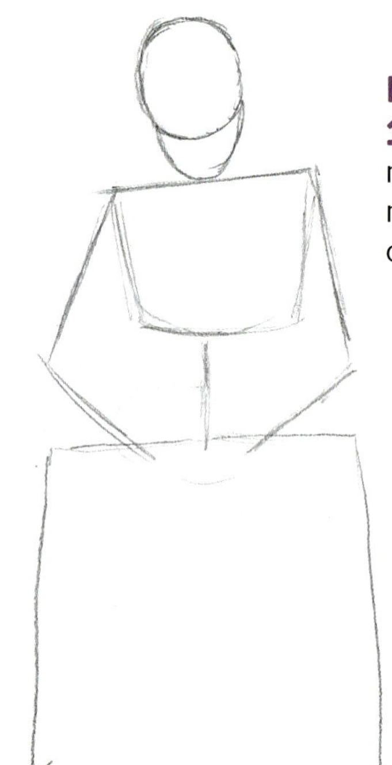

Draw the Basics

1. Using basic shapes, draw a head and a body, referring to chapters 1 and 2 for guidance as needed. Capture the pose by using lines to connect the basic shapes.

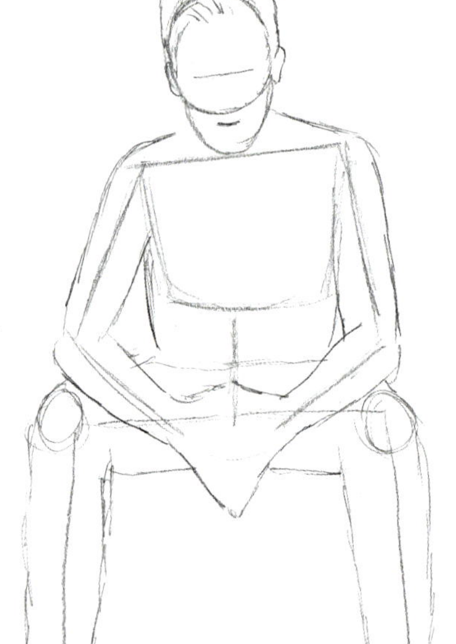

TIP
The elbows are resting on the thighs, so the body is hunched over, which hides most of the neck and narrows the shoulders.

2. Draw circles for the joints, including the shoulders, elbows, wrists, knees, and ankles. Use this form as a guide to draw the outline of the body. Keep in mind that things like clothing, weight, musculature, age, and the pose will affect the shape of the outline.

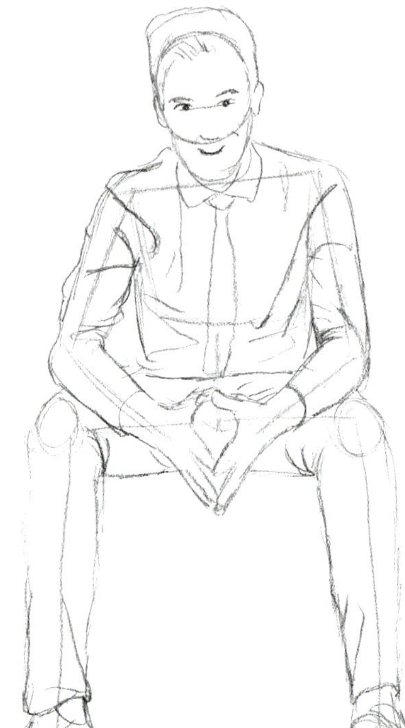

Add Details

3. Add details to the drawing, including the outline of the clothing. Draw the lines in the clothing where the body bends when sitting, such as at the waist, knees, and elbows. Begin to define the features.

Add Tone

4. Quickly fill in the darkest areas using a medium tone, and leave the highlighted areas lighter. Continue to refine the features of your subject.

The lines from the previous step can help you place the shadows.

5. Erase any guidelines no longer needed. Blend using a blending tool. Then add a light layer of tone to the entire drawing, leaving highlighted areas lighter. Then add more tone to darken the shadowed areas. Continue to refine the features of your subject.

Blend & Refine

6. Blend using a blending tool to smooth the tones. Add more tone to deepen shadows, and use a kneaded eraser or stick eraser to create highlights.

HELPFUL TUTORIALS

- Short Hair (page 92)
- Button-Down (page 118)
- The Leg (page 32)
- Pants (page 114)
- Shoes (page 128)

LEGS CROSSED

This step-by-step is great for practicing drawing highlights and shadows where clothing folds and bunches since the subject's sleeves are pushed up to the elbows.

Draw the Basics

1. Using basic shapes, draw a head and a body, referring to chapters 1 and 2 for guidance as needed. In this example, the body is a 3/4 view. Draw circles for the joints, including the shoulders, elbows, wrists, knees, and ankles. Capture the pose by using lines to connect the basic shapes.

2. Use this form as a guide to draw the outline of the body. Keep in mind that things like clothing, weight, musculature, age, and the pose will affect the shape of the outline.

The chair is drawn around the shape of the hip and thigh.

Add Details

3. Add details to the drawing, including the outline of the clothing. Draw the lines in the clothing where the body bends when sitting, such as at the waist, knees, and elbows. Begin to define the features.

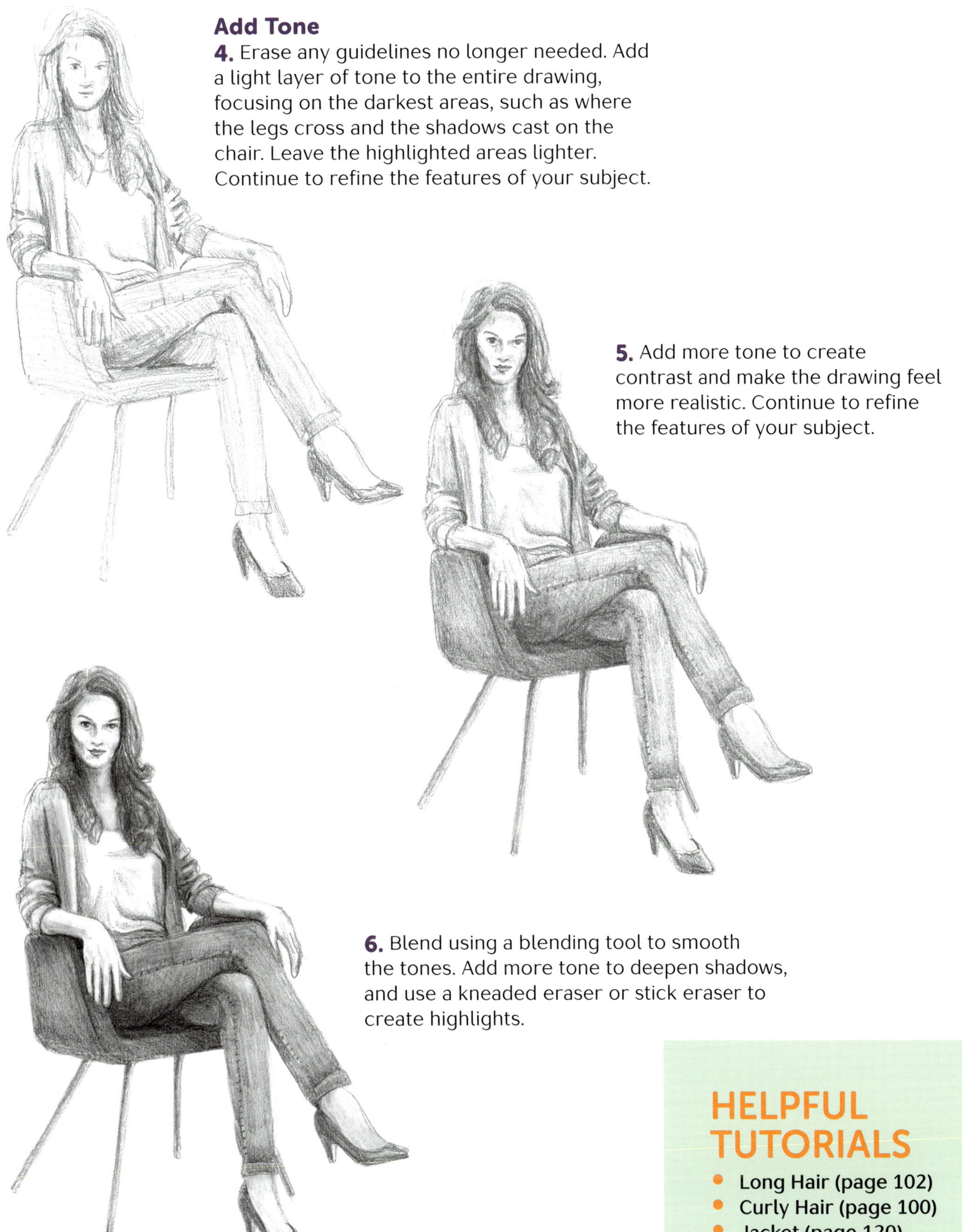

Add Tone

4. Erase any guidelines no longer needed. Add a light layer of tone to the entire drawing, focusing on the darkest areas, such as where the legs cross and the shadows cast on the chair. Leave the highlighted areas lighter. Continue to refine the features of your subject.

5. Add more tone to create contrast and make the drawing feel more realistic. Continue to refine the features of your subject.

6. Blend using a blending tool to smooth the tones. Add more tone to deepen shadows, and use a kneaded eraser or stick eraser to create highlights.

HELPFUL TUTORIALS

- Long Hair (page 102)
- Curly Hair (page 100)
- Jacket (page 120)
- T-Shirt (page 116)
- Slim Pants (page 112)
- Heels (page 130)

YOGA

This peaceful drawing is a great opportunity to practice drawing crossed limbs and foreshortening.

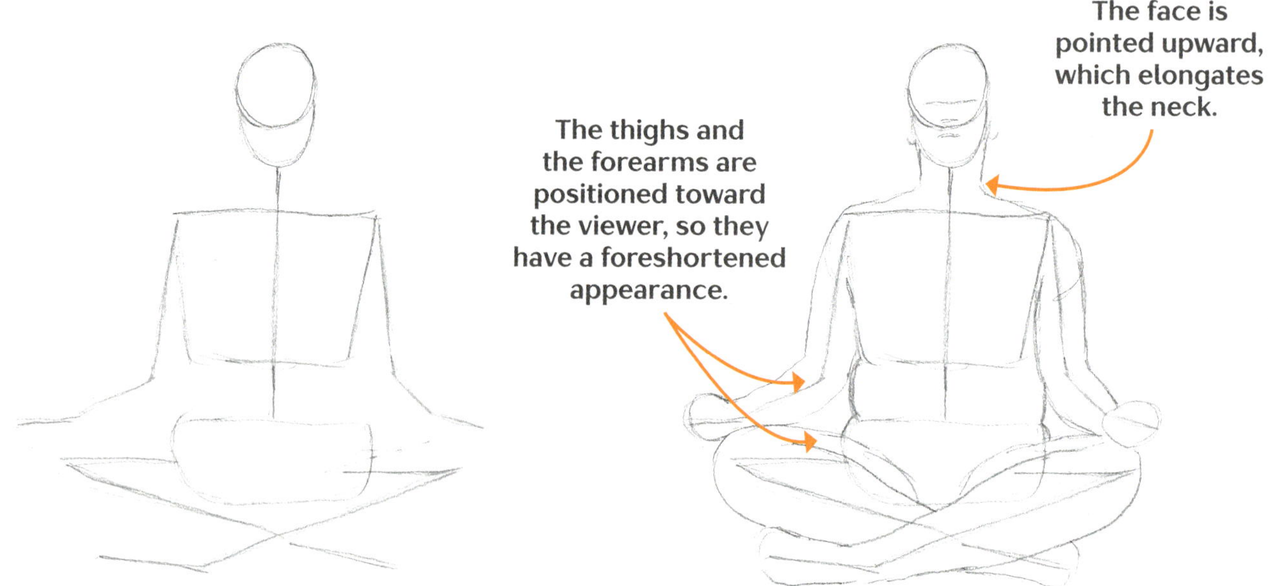
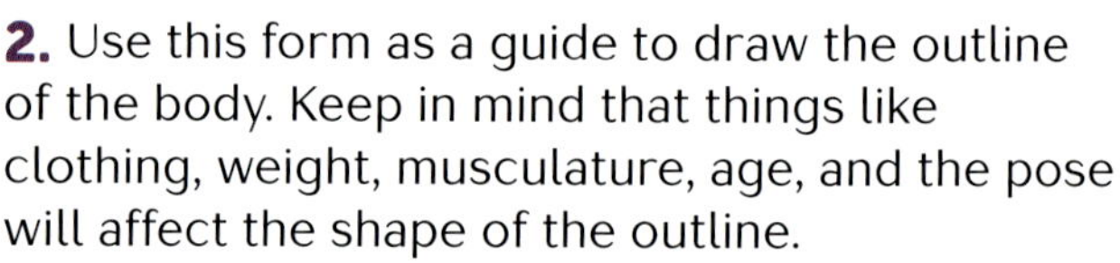

Draw the Basics

1. Using basic shapes, draw a head and a body, referring to chapters 1 and 2 for guidance. Capture the pose by using lines to connect the basic shapes.

2. Use this form as a guide to draw the outline of the body. Keep in mind that things like clothing, weight, musculature, age, and the pose will affect the shape of the outline.

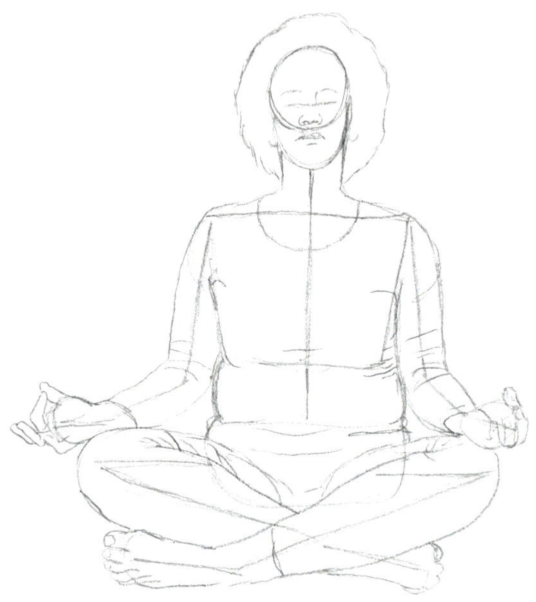

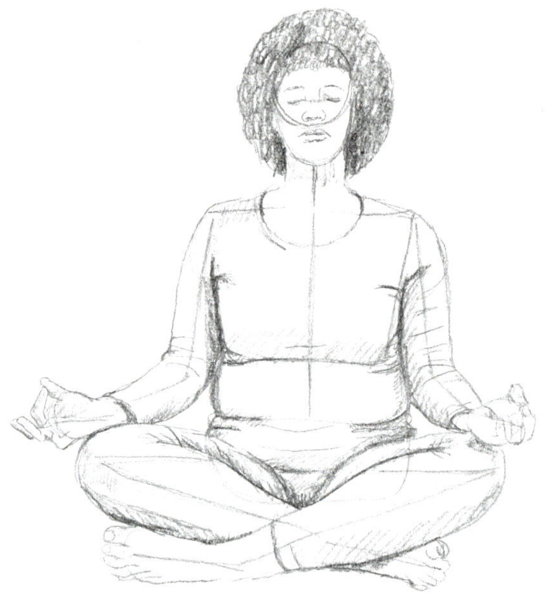

3. Add details to the drawing, including the outline of the clothing. Draw the lines in the clothing where the body bends when sitting, such as at the waist, knees, and elbows.

Add Tone

4. Add a light layer of tone to the darkest areas, leaving highlighted areas lighter. Refine the features.

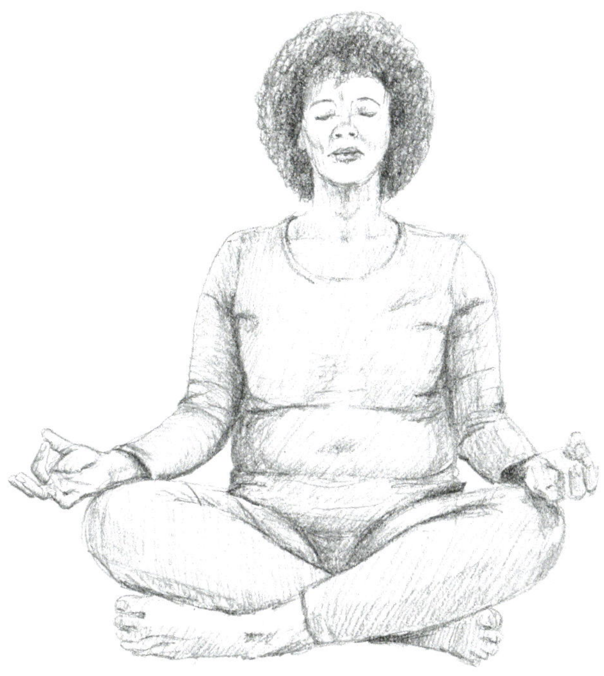

5. Erase any guidelines no longer needed. Add a light layer of tone to the entire drawing, focusing on the midtones. Then add more tone to darken the shadowed areas. Continue to refine the features of your subject.

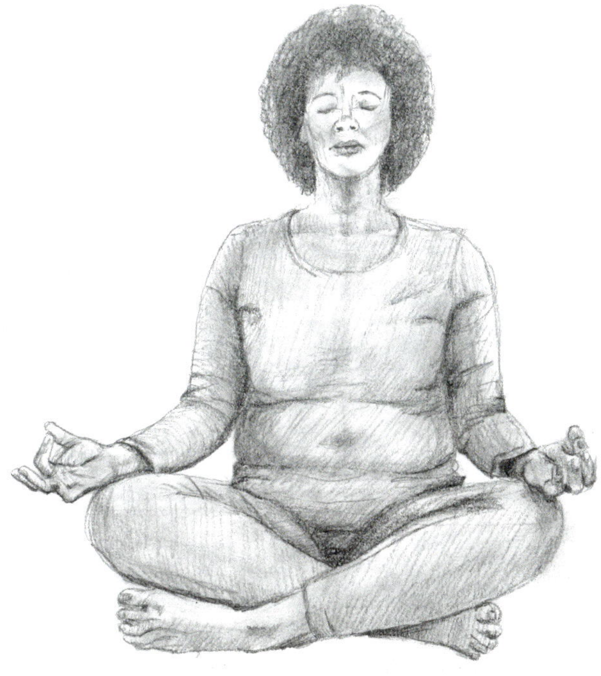

6. Blend using a blending tool. Then add another layer of tone, deepening the darkest areas, such as under the arms, where the legs touch, and at the ankles.

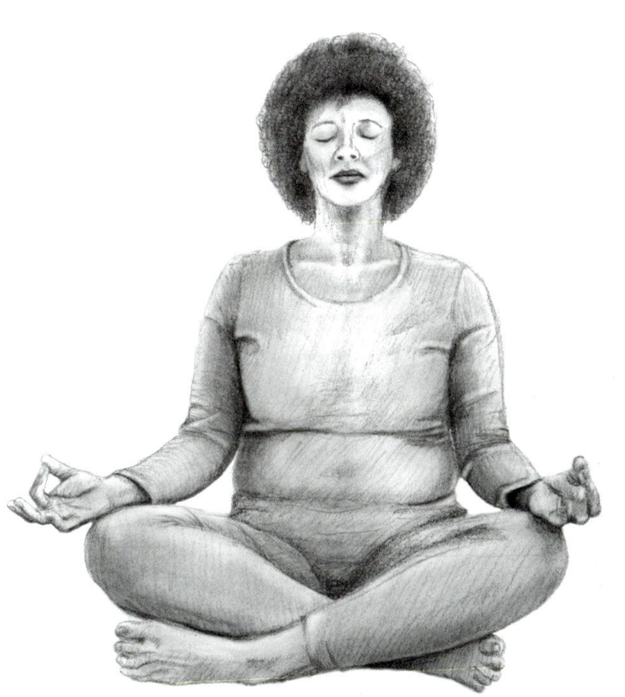

Blend & Refine

7. Blend again to smooth the tones. Add more tone to deepen shadows, and use a kneaded eraser or stick eraser to create highlights.

HELPFUL TUTORIALS

- Relaxed (page 72)
- T-Shirt (page 116)
- The Hand (page 31)
- Slim Pants (page 112)
- The Foot (page 33)

JUMPING

This tutorial requires you to draw realistic muscles, which are more defined when a person is jumping or playing a sport. With practice, your drawing is sure to be a slam dunk!

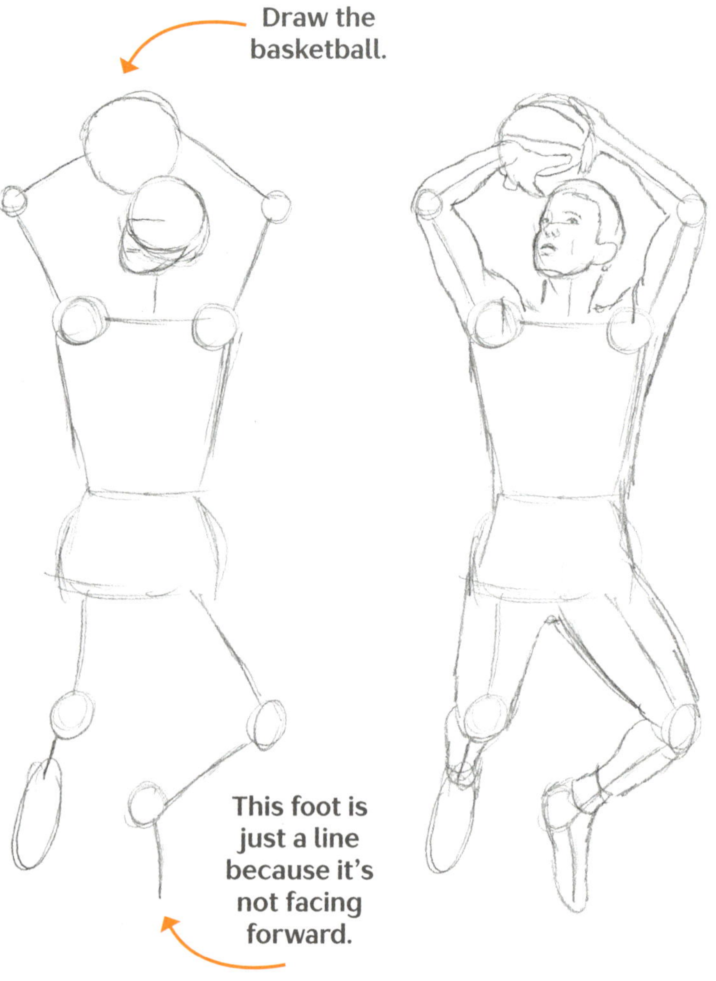

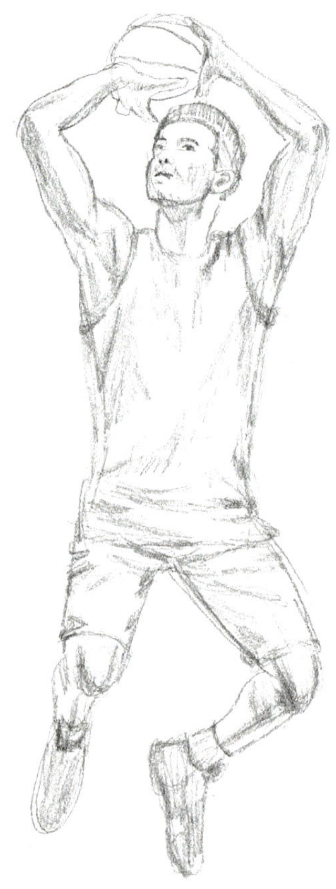

Draw the Basics

1. Using basic shapes, draw a head and a body, referring to chapters 1 and 2 for guidance as needed. In this example, the body is a 3/4 view. Draw circles for the joints, including the shoulders, elbows, wrists, knees, and ankles. Capture the pose by using lines to connect the basic shapes.

2. Use this form as a guide to draw the outline of the body. Keep in mind that things like clothing, weight, musculature, age, and the pose will affect the shape of the outline. Begin to add details to the drawing.

Add Details

3. Add details to the drawing, including the outline of the clothing. Draw the lines in the clothing where the body bends when jumping, such as at the waist, knees, and elbows. Begin to define the features. Then erase any guidelines no longer needed. Add a light layer of tone, focusing on the darkest areas and leaving highlighted areas lighter. Continue to refine the features of your subject.

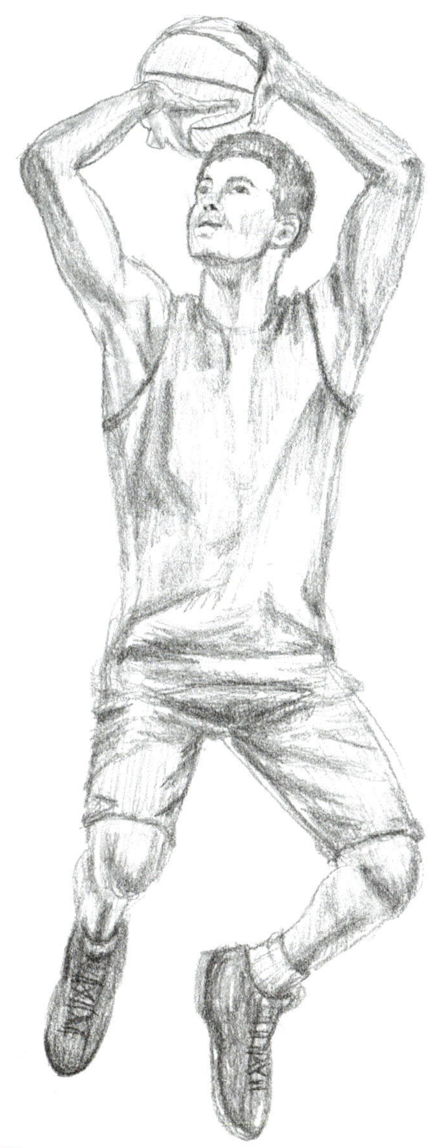

Add Tone

4. Add more tone to create contrast and to ease the transition between different tones.

HELPFUL TUTORIALS

- Short Hair (page 92)
- Concentrating (page 82)
- The Arm (page 30)
- T-Shirt (page 116)
- The Leg (page 32)
- Shoes (page 128)

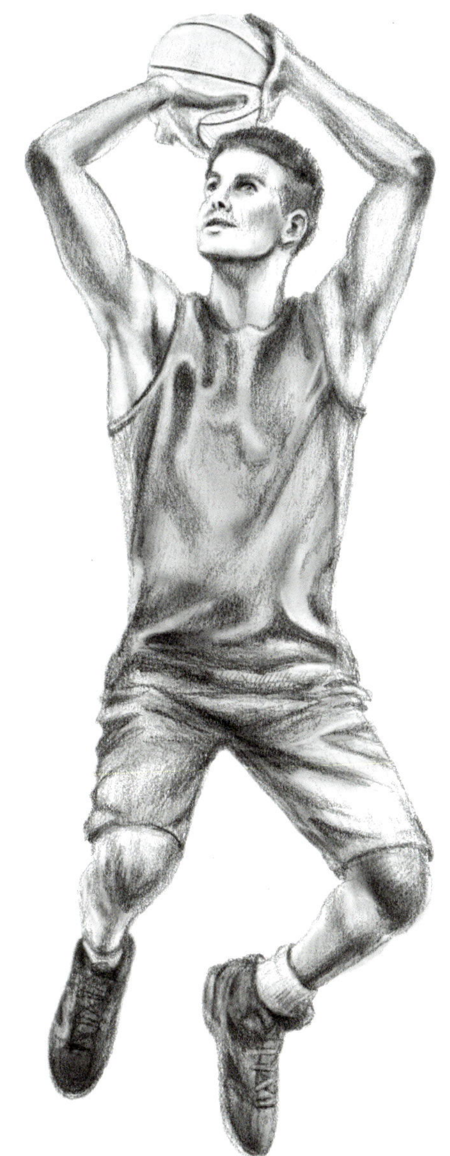

5. Blend using a blending tool to smooth the tones. Add more tone to deepen shadows, and use a kneaded eraser or stick eraser to create highlights.

DANCING

The light coming from above gives this graceful dancer a serene, angelic appearance. Pay special attention to the contrast between the highlights and the other tones of the drawing to make it feel realistic.

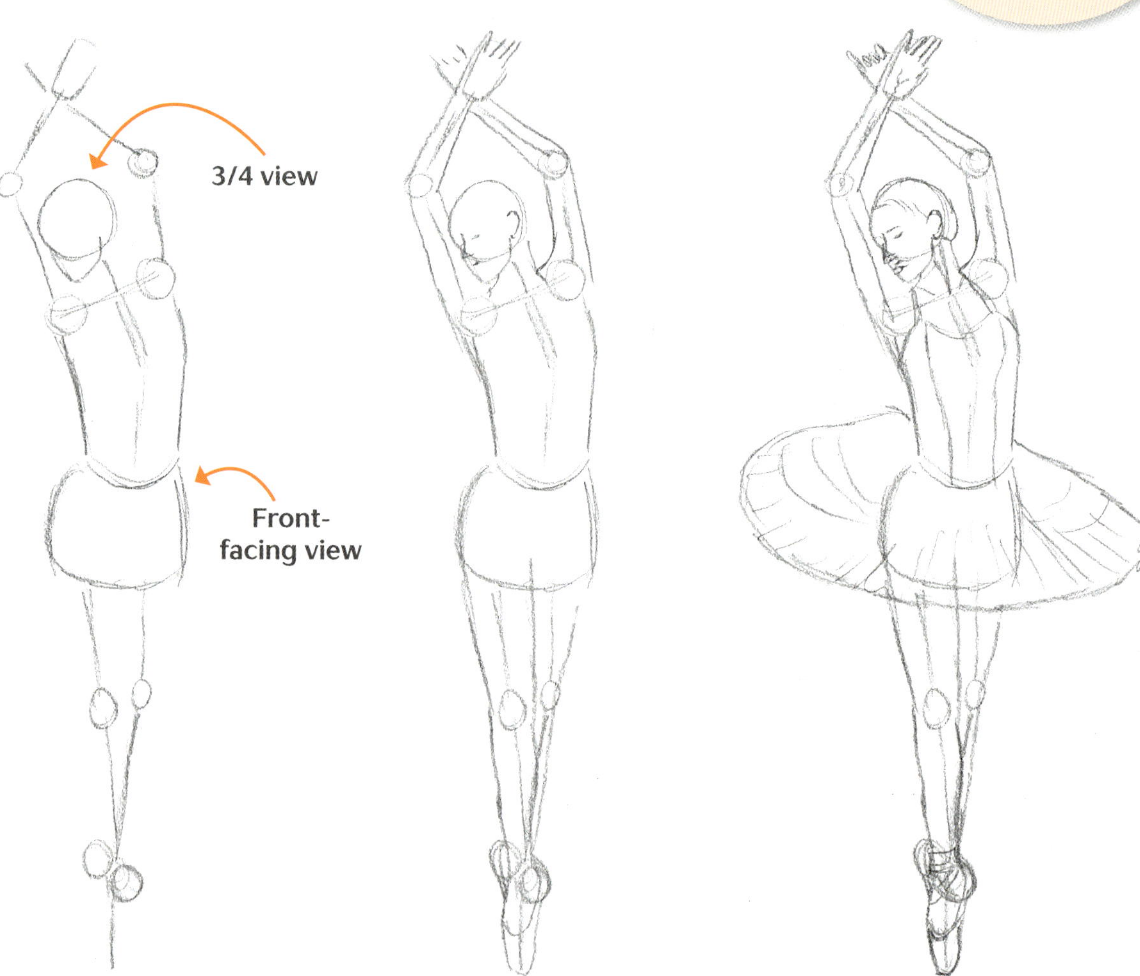

Draw the Basics

1. Using basic shapes, draw a head and a body, referring to chapters 1 and 2 for guidance as needed. In this example, the subject has a mix of different views. Draw circles for the joints, including the shoulders, elbows, wrists, knees, and ankles. Capture the pose by using lines to connect the basic shapes.

2. Use this form as a guide to draw the outline of the body. Keep in mind that things like clothing, weight, musculature, and age can affect how thick the outline appears. Begin to draw the features.

Add Details

3. Add details to the drawing, including the outline of the clothing. Draw the lines in the clothing where the body bends when moving, such as at the waist, knees, and elbows. Continue to refine the features.

HELPFUL TUTORIALS
- Updo (page 106)
- Relaxed (page 72)
- Hands (page 31)
- Dress (page 124)
- Heels (page 130)

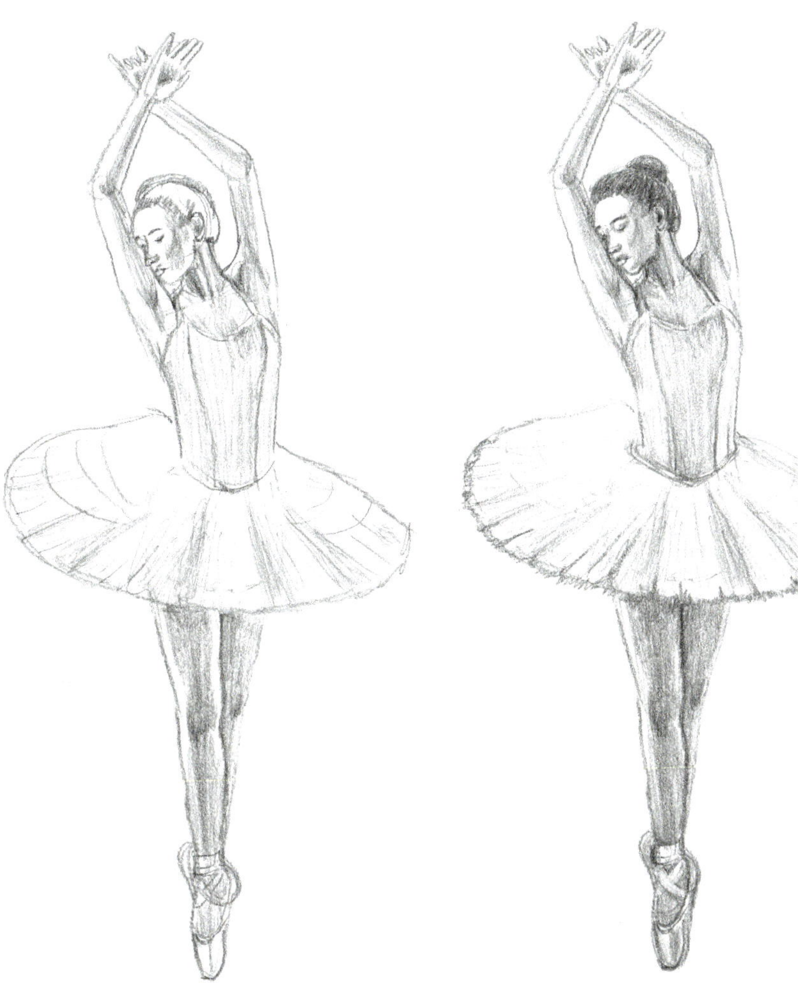

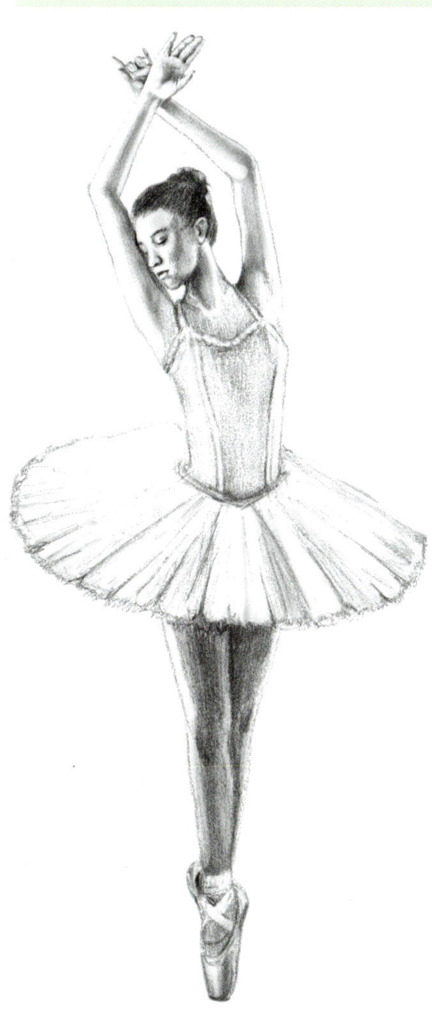

Add Tone

4. Erase any guidelines no longer needed. Add a light layer of tone to the entire drawing, leaving highlighted areas lighter. Then add more tone to darken the shadowed areas. Continue to refine the features of your subject.

5. Blend using a blending tool. Then add another layer of tone, focusing on the midtones.

Blend & Refine

6. Blend again to smooth the tones. Add more tone to create contrast and make the drawing feel more realistic. Continue to refine the features of your subject. Use a kneaded eraser or stick eraser to create highlights.

Final Note

Focusing on simple shapes and proportions when drawing a human figure can help beginners break down the complex form into manageable parts. By using basic shapes like circles, ovals, and rectangles as a foundation, artists can establish the correct proportions of the body parts. This approach can make the figure more visually appealing and realistic, even for those who are new to drawing human forms.

This book aims to provide a wide range of faces, facial features, and expressions for drawing practice. The variety ensures artists can explore different characteristics and styles. This exposure to various faces can help enhance drawing skills and creativity. We tried to incorporate diverse representations, but including every race and body type in a book can be challenging due to limitations in space and time. We want to acknowledge the importance and value of diversity and inclusion in art while recognizing the constraints that may have influenced the final choices.

Drawing People is a valuable resource for improving your artistic skills. By practicing the techniques offered, you can enhance your ability to capture the human form accurately and expressively. With practice and dedication, you can use this book on your journey towards becoming a skilled artist adept at portraying people in your artwork.

—Catherine

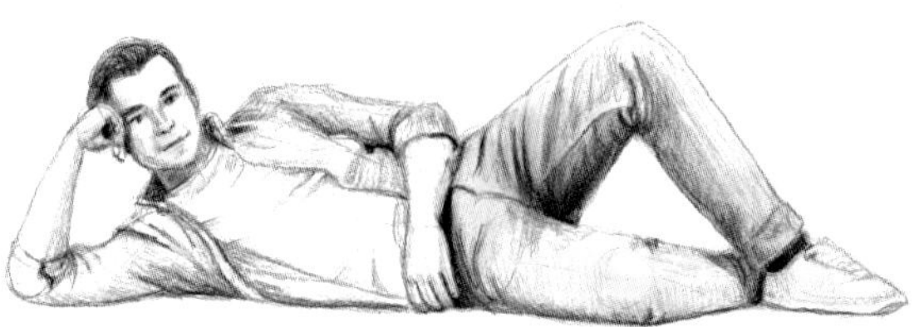

Index

faces 50–55
front view 21
hands 31
proportions 20
side view 22–23
torsos 29
midtones 10, 11
mood enhancement 73
motion 14–15, 136–141, 146–149
mouths 38, 39, 46, 79

N

neutral expression 70
noses 37, 38, 39, 41, 45

O

observation 14
occlusion shadows 11

P

pants 112–115
paper 17
pencils 17
perspective 12–13
ponytails 108–109
proportions
    bodies 20–21, 150
    faces 34–35
    heads 34

R

reference images 16
relaxed expression 72–73
ringlets 101
rule of thirds 13
running 138–139

S

sad expression 70, 84–85
scared expression 88–89
scumbling 11, 61, 95
shading 11
shadows 10, 11, 146
shirts
    blouses 122–123
    button-down 118–119
    T-shirts 116–117
shoes 128–131
short hair 92–93
shoulder-length hair 98–99
side lighting 73
sitting 140–141
slim pants 112–113
smiling 76–77
stick erasers 17
stippling 11
surprised expression 71, 80–81
symmetry 36

T

teeth 47
tone 10
torsos
    front views 28
    side views 29
tortillons 17
tracing 16
T-shirts 116–117

U

updos 106–107

V

value 10

W

walking 136–137
weight
    in arms 30
    in hands 31
    in legs and feet 33
    in torsos 29
wrinkles 63, 79

Y

yoga 144–145

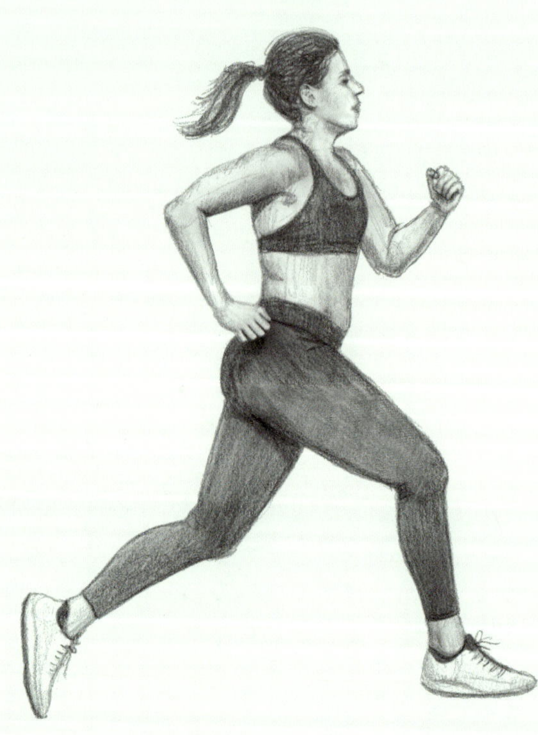